Becoming to a Woman

by Elaine Magalis

BOLTED DOORS AND BURGEONING MISSIONS

Revised and Expanded Edition with New Foreword and Program Guide

by Cheryl A. Hemmerle

Conduct Becoming to a Woman
Copyright © 1973 by Elaine Magalis

Revised and Expanded Edition with New Foreword, Afterword and Program Guide
Copyright © 2003 Women's Division

A publication of the Women's Division produced by:
General Board of Global Ministries
The United Methodist Church
475 Riverside Drive
New York, NY 10115

Printed in the United States of America.
Library of Congress Catalog Card Number: 2003114971
ISBN 1-890569-70-4
Cover Design by Hal Sadler

All biblical quotations, unless otherwise noted, are from the New Revised Standard Version (NRSV) of the Bible, copyright © 1989 by the Division of Christian Education of the National Council of the Churches of Christ in the United States of America. Used by permission.

Please address critiques and comments to:
Editor of Program Resources
General Board of Global Ministries
The United Methodist Church
475 Riverside Drive, Room 1478
New York, NY 10115

To
Alice Wäcker Magalis
and
Kate Wäcker,
my mother and grandmother

—E.M.

Table of Contents

Foreword vii

Suggestions for Individual and Group Study xi

Preface xviii

What is the Sphere of Woman? 1

Go Out into the Highways and Hedges 19

Oh Dear, I Had to Pray for Grace When I Read That 39

Grit is Needed as Well as Grace 67

They Carried Flowers Day by Day into Malodorous Abodes 101

Shall She Be Allowed to Preach? 137

Epilogue 163

Afterword: Thirty Years Later 171

Appendix
That Handful of Women 183
Conduct Becoming to a Member of United Methodist Women 192
Women's Organizations in the United Methodist Tradition 193
The Journey to United Methodist Women 194
Websites Related to the History of Women in Church and Society 197

Timeline 199

Resources 221

Endnotes..225

Bibliography 237

The Authors 241

FOREWORD

"It is for us to remember that those to whom we look in the past were in fact looking ahead." [1]

Conduct Becoming to a Woman was written over 30 years ago. That seems like another time and another place altogether for women at the dawn of the 21st century. I was only eleven years old then and just beginning to understand the differences between girls and boys in my generation. Notwithstanding, I have benefited greatly from the accomplishments of the generations of women who have gone before me. And despite an oppressive, conservative upbringing complete with traumatic and abusive experiences (not unlike many girls of every generation), I developed a strong understanding of the traditional and nontraditional roles of women. To some extent, I fell right in line with many of my foremothers who battled social and religious stereotypes of "what a woman or lady should be" by somehow finding a balance in the middle—one minute tackling a neighborhood boy in a game of football and the next minute imagining myself as his doting inferior, or at least his helpmeet and the mother of his children.

And even though so much ground has been gained in the generations since *Conduct* was first released, I hear the same messages and ideologies of past centuries coming from the mouths of today's generations of younger women, and I witness their struggles to find their own voices and their own "conduct" amid a still sexist, oppressive and male-dominated church and society. Yes, "We've come a long way," but we still have so very far to go before all people—created equal and equally blessed by God—experience that same equality in church, synagogue, mosque and country.

The Women's Division has chosen to print a revised and expanded edition of *Conduct Becoming to a Woman* for two reasons. First, Elaine Magalis' original text is an incredible account of the contributions of women in the predecessor denominations of The United Methodist Church, and its historical significance should not be lost from our libraries—and more importantly— our narrative tradition as an organization of women in mission for over 130 years. Secondly, our contributions as women organized for mission have continued to this day and will continue into the future through the efforts of younger members. It is primarily for their sakes—those young women just starting out in the organization—that this revised and expanded edition of *Conduct* is being printed. The original text from the 1973 edition is retained in its entirety. Sidebars have been added to each chapter that feature photographs and brief biographies of many of the women mentioned in the text. In addition, there is a program guide for each chapter; a new chapter entitled "Afterword: Thirty Years Later" that brings the struggles and accomplishments of women in church and society into the 21st century; an expanded timeline of women's involvement in history from the 1800s to the present; and an updated bibliography and resource list.

Since 1996, the Women's Division has made a concerted effort to enlist younger women as members and leaders in the organization. I have had the privilege of pioneering this work since its inception and have seen thousands of young women ages 12 to 25 come alongside their older sisters in the organization to work on behalf of women, children and youth around the world. Many of these young women are pioneers in their own right: organizing units among their peers, planning and conducting gatherings and providing leadership at every level of the organization. Many have already "graduated" from the ranks and moved into full time missionary work or are pursuing careers in medicine, technology, engineering and ministry, as well as choosing marriage, motherhood and other vocations.

The key difference for these young women is that they have choices. They are not confined to the traditional roles prescribed to our foremothers in the 19th and 20th centuries. Something very significant has happened to drastically change the climate in this country for women. Conduct once thought to be unbecoming to a woman is, in fact, very becoming. Girls and young women are taught that they can achieve everything and anything their male counterparts endeavor to achieve. Their place is everywhere and anywhere God calls them in church and society. And in all of these places, they can expect and demand the same rights and privileges as boys and men.

However "becoming" this 21st century reality is for girls and women in the United States (but still not entirely realized by all), our sisters in other countries and within other religious and cultural environments do not have the same rights and privileges. Therefore, our work as women organized for mission continues in much the same vein as it did when Isabella Thoburn and Clara Swain first set sail for India and when Elaine Magalis penned the original text of *Conduct*. Women must be afforded the right to govern their own lives and receive the same benefits as men, without exception. This, and nothing less, is conduct becoming to a woman.

This revised and expanded edition of *Conduct Becoming to a Woman* is fondly dedicated to all the young women who have worked with the Women's Division since 1996 to pave the way for future generations of young women organized for mission. They are the heralds of stars of our past and the lanterns into our future.

Cheryl A. Hemmerle
New York, 2003

Suggestions for Individual and Group Study

The program guide that follows each chapter of *Conduct* is based upon principles of storytelling and invites the reader to engage with others in sharing personal and collective histories as Christian women organized for mission. While the program guide is designed to be used with three to eight people, it can be adapted for use individually, with one other person or with a larger group. The book and program guide can also be adapted for use in a retreat setting of a few hours to a few days.

The program guide is designed to be used over the course of seven 90-minute sessions, reading one chapter before each session (in most cases), and using the program guide to discuss and engage the material from that chapter during the session. While the program guide has been designed with a particular focus and format, you are encouraged to adapt it for the needs, interests and concerns of your group and to make adjustments as needed to fit your time frame.

Basic Program Guide Format for Groups

The program guide follows the same basic format for each session. After the focus statement, which is the same for every session and is the foundation for study, discussion and reflection, there is an opening worship that includes some singing, a litany, scripture reading, prayer and/or reflection. In most cases, you will need to secure a song leader and/or accompanist. If this is not possible, consider inviting someone from the group to lead the singing a cappella or reading the words in unison. The songs chosen for use during worship can be found in *The United Methodist Hymnal, Global Praise 1* and *Global Praise 2*. If the tunes are unfamiliar, you are encouraged to select other songs you feel are appropriate. Consider assigning different parts of the opening worship to members of the group or inviting them to volunteer at the beginning of the group session.

After the opening worship, there are a series of questions for discussion and reflection. Depending upon the size of your group and the amount of time you allot for discussion and reflection, you may want to select particular questions or at least list them in priority order. Also, you may need to divide people into smaller groups for discussion and reflection so that everyone has an opportunity to share. You are welcome to add other questions that come to mind from your own reading and reflecting upon the text.

"A Voice from the Past" follows the questions for discussion and reflection. This is usually a quotation from one of our foremothers that is relevant to the material presented in the chapter. Use the quotation to spark discussion or reflection. You can also use any of the material found in the chapter, particularly the sidebars and extensive quotations within the text.

The program guide continues with "Rising to the Challenge" which is an opportunity for the group members to engage in some personal exploration and commitment. In most cases, "Rising to the Challenge" will include some tangible expression of commitment or call to action that builds upon the group discussion and reflection and invites the participants to continue the journey beyond the group experience.

To provide an opportunity for wrap-up and sending forth, each session ends with a closing worship that is similar in format to the opening worship. Again, adjust the music to fit the needs and comfort level of your group members and make sure to include others as readers and song leaders, etc. There is a checklist of things for each group member to accomplish and/or consider before the next group session. Be sure to highlight these before everyone leaves. Also, identify someone to lead the next group session and take care of any other logistics. Close the session with the "Sending Forth."

Basic Ground Rules for Group Study

In order to facilitate a truly cooperative group experience, you are encouraged to employ a few basic principles.

1. Honor the confidentiality of statements made in the group.
2. Share only to the level of comfort.
3. Raise all questions. There is no such thing as a "dumb question."
4. Speak no more than once (or twice) before everyone has had a chance to speak at least once.
5. Speak in "I" statements rather than in generalizations or telling someone else's story.

6. Do not interrupt another person when she is speaking.
7. Use shared leadership and group facilitation. To accomplish this, invite a different person to lead each session. The leader's role will be to call the group together and guide the discussion and reflection process for the session.
8. Everyone teaches and everyone learns.
9. An atmosphere of trust and respect for each person's experience and knowledge is critically important to the group process. We exist in community and start from our own life experiences. Because of the way many of us have been raised and the signals and incentives our society gives to women, we have some special needs when it comes to justice-oriented, faith-based educational and group processes. Many women have not had the opportunity to think big about their own lives or how the world might be different. We need to be encouraged to do so. Many also have not had the chance to develop and sharpen their critical thinking skills. We need to be challenged to do so. Rare is the opportunity for women to have the time and safe environment to uncover their deepest longings, their frustrations, fears, anger and hurts related to their own lives. Hopefully, participation in the group process will empower each woman to go deeper into herself as she learns, grows, shares and experiences her individual journey and our collective journey as women organized for mission.

Exploring Your History (Herstory)

As a part of listening to and learning from the stories of our foremothers in mission, you may also want to explore your own story. To do this, you will want to get a notebook or journal, preferably with unlined pages, and a set of fine-point, permanent markers that will not bleed through the pages. This journal will be your personal documentation of your journey— your "herstory."

The purpose of this self-exploration is to discover the great mystery of becoming, the great mystery of God's presence in your life. To discover that mystery, you will explore the many contexts of your life: personal history in your family of origin, the influences of early years as well as your present situation, your work experiences and your faith experiences, to name a few. Woven together, these contexts continue to create the person you are always in the process of becoming. Keep in mind that the goal of this exploration is self-knowledge and that you can choose whether or not to share your self-discovery with others.

In addition to or instead of keeping a journal for your personal thoughts, feelings and reflections related to reading and exploring *Conduct,* consider creating a personal timeline. To accomplish this, you will need an 8½" by 14" or 11" by 17" sheet of white paper and some colored markers or pencils. Position the paper with the longer side running horizontally (landscape). Draw a horizontal line across the entire page and about 3" from the top. Next, make a short, vertical line at the far left side of your horizontal line and enter your date of birth at the bottom of this vertical line. Then make a similar vertical line on the far right side of your horizontal line and about 1" in from the edge of the page. Enter today's date or the date of your first group meeting under this vertical line. Using the following suggestions, you can fill in your timeline with important personal history. Feel free to add other important events or experiences to your timeline that are prompted by these questions or others that arise for you as you create your personal history. As with your journal, you do not have to share any of this with your group unless you choose to do so.

STEP #1: YOUR HISTORY OF BEING FEMALE

Select one color (different from your drawn lines) to use when completing this step of your timeline. Write short notes to document or draw a symbol to represent each experience. Include dates whenever possible.

1. What were the personal social and cultural circumstances into which you were born? Draw a symbol of this on your timeline where it starts, next to your birth date.
2. What kind of circumstances were your society and country experiencing when you were born, i.e., war, depression, economic crisis, boom time, etc.? Draw a symbol of this on your timeline, showing how long the period lasted.
3. How did these social and cultural circumstances—both personal and in the larger world—influence your assumptions about the world and your place in it as you were growing up? Do you still hold any of these assumptions?
4. Did you experience any major changes in your understanding of the role of women as a child, youth, adult? If so, when? Why? Mark these points on your timeline with a symbol or picture and date. How did the change affect your view about what you thought was "normal" or "acceptable" or what you took for granted?
5. As you were growing up, what was your attitude about being a girl/woman? How has this attitude changed over time? When and why

have these changes occurred?
6. Think of key moments in your life when you received either affirmation or were devalued because of your gender. Who offered the affirmation or devalued you? What feelings did you experience? How have these experiences shaped your own concepts of what a woman is and who she is supposed to be? What influence do these experiences still have on you today?
7. Mark on the timeline when you first came to grips with what it meant to be a woman. What happened? What did you realize? Were there other events related to your understanding of being a woman? Mark these on your chart with symbols and approximate dates if you can remember them.
8. When did you first realize that there were societal, cultural and religious differences between men and women? What happened? How did you feel? Add a symbol or picture and rough date to record this. Are there other important learnings or experiences to put on your timeline related to the development of your understanding of being a woman? If so, add these to your timeline.

STEP #2: YOUR FAITH JOURNEY

Select one color (different from step one) to use when completing this step of your timeline. Write short notes to document or draw a symbol to represent each experience. Include dates whenever possible.

1. At the time of your birth, what were the spiritual or religious beliefs of your primary caregivers? Make a symbol of this to put next to your birth date and shade or otherwise mark the time period for which this held.
2. Mark on your timeline the date of your baptism. If you were confirmed into church membership, mark this date.
3. If you have gone through important evolutions in your religious identity, mark these moments or periods on your timeline, e.g., converted from one faith to another, joined The United Methodist Church or one of its predecessors, changed denominations, etc. Indicate dates and a symbol or picture with each.
4. Try to remember the first experience you had of the Holy, of something sacred, of a mystery larger than yourself, of experiencing grace. Mark this on your timeline. Add any subsequent similar moments.
5. Have you experienced any time when you lost hope or your belief in God was tested? If so, add this to your timeline. When did it happen? What

happened? How was the faith crisis resolved?
6. Think about how your understanding of God has evolved. Can you identify certain pivotal moments or characterize your beliefs into certain time periods? Try to mark this on your timeline.
7. Mark the periods of membership in different churches or congregations with dates and symbols or a short note. How has your church membership shaped your reading of the Bible or understanding of God? Your understanding of the roles of women?

STEP #3: YOUR HISTORY OF SOCIAL CONCERN AND ACTION

Select one color (different from the other two steps) to use when completing this step of your timeline. Write short notes to document or draw a symbol to represent each experience. Include dates whenever possible.

1. When did you first sense life was not always fair to you? To others? How did this happen? How did you respond? Mark this on your timeline with a date if possible and symbols.
2. Have there been other occasions in your life where you experienced or witnessed great injustice? How did you respond? Mark these on your timeline. How have these experiences changed your views?
3. How did you come to learn of United Methodist Women or its predecessor organizations? Mark the date you joined the organization and mark other dates of mergers or reorganizations within your particular predecessor organization or denomination.
4. How have you been involved in the organization, e.g., offices held, specific events or activities that are prominent in your memory?
5. What are some major issues of justice and equality that you have engaged in throughout your life? Mark these on your timeline and include a symbol or write a short note to document each experience. What do you feel you accomplished by engaging in these activities?

REFLECTING ON YOUR PERSONAL HISTORY TIMELINE

Now look over all three layers or pieces of your timeline. Do any interesting connections pop out? Do you see any patterns developing? Do you see any of the three "layers" influencing another? Are there any surprises? What insights about your life have you gained as a result of this exercise? Consider keeping the timeline and adding to it throughout your involvement in the study and beyond.

Family Tree: Genealogy

A final suggestion for exploring your own history (herstory) is to create your family tree or genealogy. To accomplish this, research your family's history and draw a chart of the different generations in your family, beginning with your own immediate family. There are many websites, computer software packages, and books available to help you explore your family history and develop a genealogy. What will make this genealogy particularly useful and relevant to your study of *Conduct* will be to concentrate on the women in your family's history. Gather information, facts, artifacts and photographs of your foremothers and reflect on their history. Use these basic questions to guide your exploration.

1. What do you know about the women in your family? Develop a narrative for each of them and tell their stories.
2. What were their lives like? Under what conditions did they live? What were their religious, cultural and social experiences?
3. What, if any, employment did they hold outside the household? Were they married? What roles did they play in the family?
4. How have these women in your family's history made an impression or had an impact on you and your life choices?

PREFACE

In the 19th century American women emerged from the confines of home and pew to join in two world-shaking movements of their day—Protestant Christian missions and woman's rights. The drama that began then is still continuing today. Unfortunately, this book can only touch lightly on the varied and exciting history of churchwomen in the United States. For reasons of space it is limited to the women of the five denominations that constitute the present day United Methodist Church—United Brethren, Evangelical, Methodist Episcopal, Methodist Episcopal, South, and Methodist Protestant—though the women of other denominations were no less fascinating and important. It is also limited to only a few of a multitude of spirited personalities, women who pressed their Christian concern into forbidden avenues and created a new world for themselves and millions who followed.

Conduct Becoming to a Woman is not meant to be a comprehensive history. Its purpose is to communicate something of the struggle of the forebears of the present day churchwoman—and perhaps to help her gain new perspective on her own life and work. If it can give her some sense of her own history (or herstory), some feeling for her beginnings, then it will have fulfilled its aim.

Some women will discover as they read this book that black women receive little notice in it, and only one, Amanda Smith, is considered in any detail. Part of the problem is that in the last century in the five denominations discussed, black people were usually recipients of mission rather than partners in mission. Black women have only gradually come to share on an equal basis with white women in the advance of the church's mission (and some will argue that equality is still a future and not a present reality).

Another reason for the black woman's absence from this book is a lack of historical data. There were black women missionaries to Liberia very early in the history of Methodist missions. But no records of their activities were kept and, often, their names were not even set down.

Though black women, of necessity, have always been more concerned with racial than sexual prejudice, women like Sojourner Truth and Harriet Tubman were as important to the women's as to the abolitionists' crusades of the 19th century. And within the black denominations, black women were far in advance of their white sisters: African Methodist Episcopal women were given ordination as early as 1868.

I would like to make one other point in passing. There will be many people who feel I have omitted some of the most important missionaries and missions leaders, organizations, places and events of churchwomen's history in the writing of this book. In many instances I can only agree with them, and apologize. Especially important has been the history of the past four or five decades—the involvement of women in the civil rights movement, the peace movement, the women's rights movement and the worldwide struggle for justice, liberation and development. It is impossible in this book to mention the individuals and groups and their particular contributions. If only there could have been another volume, or two, or three.

I want to thank a number of people for helping me in both researching and writing: Evelyn Sutton and her companion librarians at the Commission on Archives and History at Lake Junaluska, North Carolina; Esther George, the librarian at the Evangelical United Brethren Library in Dayton, Ohio; and librarian Miriam Parsell and her assistants, Sigrun Nordby and Madeline Brown at the United Mission Library in New York City. Also deserving of special mention are Mary McLanachan who took time to talk with me and search for resources she thought might be valuable, and the members of the Women's Division of the Board of Global Ministries who read and evaluated the manuscript (especially Ellen Kirby who also contributed information for the "Epilogue"). Residents of the Brooks-Howell Home in Asheville, North Carolina, also gave several hours of their time, and their stories provided some of the inspiration, if not necessarily the subject matter, for portions of the book.

I would also like to mention Ann Firor Scott's fine book, *The Southern Lady, From Pedestal to Politics, 1830–1930,* which proved an invaluable resource for the first chapter.

Finally, I want to thank Sally H. Levy, whose thorough and occasionally ruthless editing of the first draft did much toward making *Conduct Becoming to a Woman* a readable piece of writing.

Elaine Magalis
New York, 1973

WHAT IS THE SPHERE OF WOMAN?

She was a lady. Everyone from the kitchen help to the minister could testify to her unfailing serenity and shy good humor, her perfect devotion to her family and kindness to those less fortunate, her profound culture and delightful charm—and her boundless piety. She moved down the street with the grace of a queen, corseted and petticoated in the latest fashion. Yet her bearing was modest and simple. Small children glowed when she smiled at them, and gentlemen bowed reverently and competed for the privilege of helping her into her carriage.

She ran her household efficiently. Distinguished visitors to her home found warm hospitality, succulent meals and refined conversation. After dinner, gathered about the piano in the growing dusk, they were enchanted by the melodies her slender hands created and by the caroling of her dulcet voice. They marveled at her exquisite needlework on armchairs and tables. And they noted happily the tender respect she showed her husband, her deference to his opinions, the adoring look on her face when he spoke.

The whole family attended religious services, and her husband contributed liberally to the church. Her children, young ladies and gentlemen all of them, watched their mother worshipfully as she bowed her head, her Bible and hymnbook resting in her lap. To her gloved fingertips she was the consummate lady, exemplifying in herself the chastity, purity and piety of her sex.

This was the woman 19th century America admired. Young girls were brought up to emulate her and young men to cherish and protect her—for she needed protection, this fragile treasure of Christian civilization. She was delicate and wan and had to be guarded from too much sunlight, muddy roadways and the hard vulgarities of the masculine world. But properly cared for, this frail bearer of purity and piety was the supposed bastion of society, the guarantor of the family and of the moral strength and civility of the race. As one Methodist minister admonished in a book of advice to young girls:

Anna Howard Shaw
Methodist Episcopal Church

Born in Newcastle-on-Tyne, England, on February 14, 1847, Anna Howard Shaw came to the United States in 1851. Cut off from all school privileges, she took advantage of every book and paper that fell in her way. At fifteen, she began to teach and continued for five years. Soon after becoming a Methodist at age 24, her ability to speak was recognized, and in 1873 the district conference of the Methodist Church in her locality voted unanimously to grant her a preacher's license. It was renewed annually for eight years. She graduated with honors in 1878 from the theological department of Boston University. During her pastorate in East Dennis, Massachusetts, she applied to the New England Methodist Episcopal Conference for ordination. Although she performed better on her examination than any candidate that year, her ordination was refused on account of her sex. The case was appealed to the General Conference in Cincinnati in 1880, where the refusal was confirmed. Determined, she applied for ordination to the Methodist Protestant Church and received it on October 12, 1880, becoming the first woman ordained in that denomination. She supplemented her theological course with one in medicine from Boston University and is believed to be the first woman to hold the double distinction of Reverend and Doctor.

—General Commission on Archives and History, The United Methodist Church

What is the sphere of woman? Home. The social circle. What is her mission? To mold characters—to fashion herself and others after the model character of Christ. What are her chief instruments for the accomplishment of her great work? The affections. Love is the wand by which she is to work moral transformations within her fairy circle. Gentleness, sweetness, loveliness, and purity are the elements of her power. Her place is not on life's great battlefields. Man belongs there. It is for him to go forth armed for its conflicts and struggles, to do fierce battle with the hosts of evil that throng our earth and trample upon its blessings. But woman must abide in the peaceful sanctuaries of home and walk in the noiseless vales of private life. There she must dwell, beside the secret springs of public virtue. There she must smile upon the father, the brother, the husband, when, returning like warriors from the fight, exhausted and covered with the dust of strife, they need to be refreshed by the sweet waters drawn "from affection's spring" and cheered to renewed struggles by the music of her voice. There she must rear the Christian patriot and statesman, the self-denying philanthropist and the obedient citizen. There, in a word, she must form the character of the world, and determine the destiny of her race. How awful is her mission! What dread responsibility attaches to her work! Surely she is not degraded by filling such a sphere. Nor would she be elevated, if, forsaking it, she should go forth into the highways of society, and jostle with her brothers for the offices and honors of public life. Fame she might occasionally gain, but it would be at the price of her womanly influence.[1]

The image of the lady imposed itself in varying degrees on the townswoman and small farmer's wife of the Northeast, on the mistress of the southern plantation, and even on the pioneering woman of the inelegant and boisterous West. The only alternative in the mythology of the time was that of the tainted "fallen woman." Black slaves and Indian squaws could not aspire to the status of the lady; they were barely women, barely human.

In fact, however, most women didn't have the leisure or the opportunity to live up to the ideal set before them—they worked too hard. They were in every way more worldly and more preoccupied, more haggard, tougher, and just plain sweatier than the fabled lady. On the farms they worked 15 and more hours a day, spinning, weaving and sewing, manufacturing soap and the family crockery, milking and butchering and canning for the long bitter winters. They risked their lives over and over again in childbirth, and they mourned as most of their children died. In the first half of the 19th century four out of five children were not expected to live beyond their fifth year. Hours were spent by the sickbed, and the sensibilities, said to be so refined in the true lady, saw to it that bed pans were emptied and bloody sheets washed. It was enough to survive: "forming the character of the world and determining the destiny of the race" were incidental to the real job of living from day to day.

It was worse for the woman who moved from a settled town or rural community to homestead in the West. She left every security she had ever known to make the jolting trip on buckboard and horse through dark, inhospitable forests and over endless plains of stifling brown dust. The new "home" might be 30 or 40 miles from the nearest neighbors, and the neighbors a bewildering assemblage of what looked to her like homicidal savages. All her efforts to maintain the self-denying composure expected of a Christian lady, could and frequently did, crumble in the face of brutalizing work, poverty, loneliness and fear. Anna Howard Shaw, one of the pioneers in the woman's suffrage movement, recalled that her mother had seen her family through economic deprivation and even shipwreck, but when she saw the crude, windowless hut her husband had built for her in the Michigan wilderness, her nerve was shattered.

What is the Sphere of Woman?

"Many women have done excellently, but you surpass them all." Charm is deceitful, and beauty is vain, but a woman who fears the Lord is to be praised. Give her a share in the fruit of her hands, and let her works praise her in the city gates.

—Proverbs 31:29–31

It was late in the afternoon when we drove up to the opening that was its front entrance, and I shall never forget the look my mother turned upon the place. Without a word she crossed its threshold, and standing very still, looked slowly around her. Then something within her seemed to give way, and she sank upon the ground. She could not realize even then, I think, that this was really the place father had prepared for us, that here he expected us to live. When she finally took it in she buried her face in her hands, and in that way she sat for hours without moving or speaking. For the first time in her life she had forgotten us; and we, for our part, dared not speak to her. We stood around her in a frightened group, talking to one another in whispers. ...[2]

At the beginning of the 19th century a woman who didn't marry could only expect to be a maiden aunt or perhaps a dressmaker. If she were exceptional she might write a book. By 1850 women were employed in the mills of the Northeast and in the one-room schoolhouses of rural America. But since they were paid as little as a half or a third of a man's salary, they still had to depend on a male relative. They were also expected to live in circumstances where their fabled virtue would be carefully protected. Chaperoned boardinghouses were provided for factory workers; teachers lived at home or were boarded with respectable families while they waited hopefully for marriage and the fulfillment of their God-given role in society.

Perhaps some were not all that eager. Their jobs had provided at least a meager independence, while in most states the married woman could hold no property of her own and had no legal right to any money she earned. Her children were her husband's by law, and, in the unlikely event of a separation, he retained custody. Unless the gentleman was financially well-off, marriage meant a life of continued hard work and unquestioning obedience—even if her Lord and Master should turn out to be a wife-beater, an adulterer or a drunkard. (After all, a lady's virtue was supposed to reform where even angels had failed.) One probably apocryphal story has it that a fond lover declared to his bride, "We shall be one, darling, and I will be that one."[3]

Even wealthy southern women, the most "ladylike" of American women, sometimes resented their financial helplessness. One belle and lady of leisure had inherited a part of her father's estate after her marriage. It went to pay her husband's debts.

> Why feel like a beggar, utterly humiliated and degraded when I am forced to say I need money? I cannot tell, but I do; ... this thing grows worse as one grows older. Money ought not to be asked for, or given to a man's wife as a gift. Something must be due her, and that she should have, and no growling and grumbling nor warnings against waste and extravagance, nor hints as to the need of economy, nor amazement that the last supply has given out already. What a proud woman suffers under all this, who can tell?[4]

Though many southern women were poor and had about as much chance to be ladylike as their northern and western sisters, the myth of the lady was nowhere more dominant than in the South. The wealthy and near-wealthy struggled painfully to live it. "We owe it to our husbands, children and friends to represent as nearly as possible the ideal they hold so dear," wrote one Louisiana woman.[5]

The southern belle was raised to be slightly light-headed: a lady's powers of reasoning were supposed to be diminutive. She was also expected to be physically delicate and innocent of worldly things, and for these reasons to need masculine protection. This she was to gain with the charms and grace poets praised and ministers extolled. Her husband, in exchange for shielding her from the vulgarities of the world, would theoretically benefit from her naturally religious nature and her moral perfection. She was to give him children and run his household, to care for him with unstinting devotion, never raising her voice, always modest, cheerful and sympathetic.

Wives, be subject to your husbands as you are to the Lord. For the husband is the head of the wife just as Christ is the head of the church, the body of which he is the Savior. Just as the church is subject to Christ, so also wives ought to be, in everything, to their husbands. Husbands, love your wives, just as Christ loved the church and gave himself up for her, in order to make her holy by cleansing her with the washing of water by the word, so as to present the church to himself in splendor, without a spot or wrinkle or anything of the kind — yes, so that she may be holy and without blemish. In the same way, husbands should love their wives as they do their own bodies. He who loves his wife loves himself. For no one ever hates his own body, but he nourishes and tenderly cares for it just as Christ does for the church, because we are members of his body. For this reason a man will leave his father and mother and be joined to his wife, and the two will become one flesh. This is a great mystery, and I am applying it to Christ and the church. Each of you, however, should love his wife as himself, and a wife should respect her husband.

—Ephesians 5:22–33

But neither inferiority nor angelic virtue could survive the realities of life on the plantation. The planter's wife worked at least as hard as the northern farmer's wife even though she did less with her own hands. Single-handedly she ran a huge establishment with dozens and sometimes hundreds of slaves; she was an administrator, human relations expert and specialist in a multitude of industries and crafts. She managed a small garment industry to clothe herself and her family, as well as her charges, sometimes doing as much of the spinning, weaving, cutting and sewing as the workers she directed. Gardening, butchering, the producing of yeast, lard and soap, and janitorial duties crowded her days. She trained slaves, supervised them, and saw to their needs; she mediated quarrels and dispensed justice. She had to have some knowledge of medicine and midwifery; epidemics were frequent, pregnancies were even more frequent, and someone was always sick. In addition to all this she was often the bookkeeper for the plantation, and, when her husband was away, she saw to the planting, harvesting and sale of crops.

Like her northern sister, the southern woman was continually bearing children. No romanticization of motherhood relieved her of the fear and suffering associated with endless pregnancies and the illnesses and deaths that attended them. Despite the physical and mental stress she bore with a popularly approved but dearly obtained angelic mien, the southern lady continued to believe along with her husband that she was fragile, irrational and dependent.

Nevertheless there was resentment, and it found its way into diaries and letters. The plantation mistress spent her days chiding, cajoling, sympathizing and demanding, trying to govern a motley crew of black men, women and children she could neither understand nor completely trust. When they were obsequious she was bewildered; when they were hostile she was frightened; in either case she was anxious and irritated. Sometimes she felt as if she was in bondage to her own slaves. In addition, she suffered the nighttime visits of her husband to the female slave quarters. As a lady schooled in silent compliance, she could only acquiesce even while dreading the results of these adulteries: the mulatto babies she would soon have to midwife, and the venereal disease her husband casually risked before coming back to her bedroom.

Not all southern women viewed their slaves with antagonism. Close friendships developed, especially between black and white women, and many planters' wives came to resent the enslavement of people for whom they had genuine feeling. Whether out of antagonism or love, most southern women were secretly abolitionists, and a few openly so.

In the South and the North in the first years of the nineteenth century, education was thought to be unnecessary and dangerous for women. It might seriously undermine their femininity and inspire unwholesome ambitions. But in the 1820s in the North and a decade later in the South, the inadequacy of women's education was seriously debated and female seminaries began to appear. Their primary function was to cultivate more of the same mythical ladies, not to stimulate minds. The educated woman would make a more efficient manager of household affairs, a mother worthy of the respect of her sons and a more amiable companion to her husband.

> Shall the beautiful half of creation be just like a collection of pictures and statues, pleasing to the eye but having no graces of mind to match these external graces ... [and] as soon as she opens her mouth shall enchantment vanish by the utterance of coarse and vulgar ideas, and of low, ungrammatical language? [6]

Before the Civil War a significant number of women in the South and a multitude of northern women had been educated to the point of frustration: they wanted more and better schooling for themselves and their daughters. Paradoxically, their limited education had not bred "ladies," but discontented women with "unnatural" ambitions. It was more difficult than ever to be the perfect ladies that men, society and God demanded. Ambition, they knew,

Boston Female Society for Missionary Purposes

In 1800, a Baptist "invalid" named Mary Webb founded the Boston Female Society for Missionary Purposes, a group of Congregational and Baptist women whose purpose was to encourage current efforts to spread the gospel throughout the world. Webb's group gave money both to American home mission organizations and to the British work in India. Following the Boston example, women across New England supported missions by founding "Mite Societies." Once the American Board was founded, women began to channel their money through it. Although the Boston Society neither became a national organization nor sent its own missionaries, it was the earliest women's nondenominational foreign missions organization of which there is record, and it was a remarkable though short-lived ecumenical accomplishment for its time, thanks to the efforts of Mary Webb.

came from pride and vanity—and humility was the appropriate virtue for gentlewomen.

The woman others thought a paragon of virtue often felt herself to be in danger of losing her own soul. "Mr. B (her husband) says we must try to live holier. O that I could. Spent some time today reading, weeping and praying."[7] "Help me O Lord for I am poor and weak, help me for I am desolate, in Thee alone have I hope."[8] "As for myself I find my heart so full of sinful feelings that I am ready to say 'I am chief of sinners.'"[9] "Lord I feel that my heart is a cage of unclean beasts."[10] "I see so much of sin, so many things to correct that I almost despair of being a perfect Christian."[11] Diaries were full of mention of sins too awful to record and references to cold hearts. Women continually prayed for composure, patience and contentment with their lot.

Though men filled diaries, letters and revival confessions with the same sentiments, Christian humility and submission to God's will for them were compatible with aggressive behavior and ambition. A woman was permitted no worldly aspirations for herself—only for others. Religion contributed liberally to keeping women within the bounds of their "God-ordained sphere." As if biblical admonitions to "keep silent in the churches" and "obey their husbands" weren't enough, the ladies were advised that the very weaknesses that made them inferior to and dependent on men also guaranteed them a place next to the angels. To try to advance beyond those weaknesses was to sin against nature and God. Abject humility and service to others was the Christian way, and the ladies should be perfect Christians. Nevertheless, when women took their first timid steps into "man's world," it was in the name of Christianity.

Despite the exaggerated power of the myth of the lady in the South, it was in the North that women first had the time and leisure to cultivate the myth in themselves. The wives of bankers, mill owners and distinguished ministers in the large cities and prosperous towns of the Northeast found themselves freed of hard physical labor and with time to spare. In cities like Boston they were subject to influences and peoples from abroad, while southern women, if occasionally idle, lived in a comparatively closed, provincial world. Of course, the prosperous lady of the North never stepped out of her sphere—far from it. She merely chose to use her newly acquired leisure in the way most profitable to her soul. If she served her family and neighbor before, now her realm of service expanded. She deepened her religious commitment, and, instead of further enslaving her, it began to free her.

In 1800 the Boston Female Society for Missionary Purposes was organized by Miss Mary Webb. Though she was crippled and went about Boston in her green baize chair, Mary Webb was capable, energetic and brave. Just as brave was another woman, Mrs. Hannah Stillman, a minister's wife, who founded that same year the Boston Female Asylum for orphan girls when "prompted to step beyond what was then considered to be the limit of female duty."[12] Through the next several years female societies sprang up throughout New England and beyond. Especially popular were the Cent Societies with membership dues of a cent a week, 52 cents a year.

Limited in what they could do by reason of their sex, women concentrated on praying for the salvation of the heathen and raising funds for male societies to administer and disburse. Though most men finally approved, particularly when they saw the sums the ladies could deliver, they were quick to warn them that propriety demanded they stay within certain bounds. Some women, made anxious by their confusion as to what those bounds should be, questioned the editor of a religious journal "whether it be right for females to meet together for prayer" or whether "some apostolic prohibition" forbade it; he assured them that there was no problem.[13] However, some gentlemen evidently entertained suspicions of this new phenomenon. Many years later a Methodist leader remarked that he always attended women's prayer meetings: "You can never tell what these women might take to praying if left alone."[14]

Because women had little access to money, what they gave often came by dispensation from husbands and fathers. Even the sacrifice of a new winter bonnet sometimes required male approval. They were granted a little more liberty with the egg or butter money they earned; then again, at their society meetings they industriously spun, wove and sewed articles for sale.

Within the first two decades of the 19th century women in the Northeast had established their right to raise funds, pray together and educate themselves and their children about missions. Without knowing it, and certainly without the knowledge of the gentlemen who looked on fondly, they had taken the first step towards emancipating themselves from the constricted world of "the lady."

PROGRAM GUIDE

WORSHIP CENTER

Prepare a worship table or designate a space to assemble a candelabrum with five candles, matches and an opened Bible. If you do not have a five-candle candelabrum, consider using five votive or taper candles in glass holders. The candles will be lit during the opening worship at the appropriate time.

FOCUS STATEMENT

This is a story of Protestant Christian mission and women's involvement. It is the story of the struggle for women's rights in church and society. "If it can give [you] some sense of [your] own history (or herstory), some feeling for [your] beginnings, then it will have fulfilled its aim."[15] We are here to communicate the struggle of our foremothers in the Methodist tradition and to gain a new perspective on their life and work. As we read, study, discuss, reflect, pray and worship, may we come to appreciate the course they have charted for our future as women organized for mission and accept our role to continue the story and the journey toward women's full and equal participation as partners in God's mission.

OPENING WORSHIP: "The Ceremony of Lights"[16]

CALL TO COMMUNITY FOR STUDY AND REFLECTION:

The leader, standing or sitting behind the candles, reads the focus statement (see above) and then continues with the opening worship.

Leader: *Lighting the Christ candle.* Let your light shine before others, so that they may see your good works and give glory to God in heaven *(Matthew 5:16, adapted from NRSV).*

HYMN: "I Want to Walk as a Child of the Light" *(The United Methodist Hymnal, #206, verse one)*

Leader: Jesus says, "You are the light of the world." *Lighting the first candle.* Behold, I kindle the light of our spiritual growth so that we may know God.

All: **May we keep its flame shining brightly in our hearts.**

Leader: *Lighting the second candle.* Behold, I kindle the light of our social action so that we may experience freedom as whole persons through Jesus Christ.

All: **May we keep its flame shining brightly in our hearts.**

Leader: *Lighting the third candle.* Behold, I kindle the light of our membership nurture and outreach so that we may develop a creative, supportive fellowship.

All: **May we keep its flame shining brightly in our hearts.**

Leader: *Lighting the fourth candle.* Behold, I kindle the light of our mission education and interpretation so that we may expand concepts of mission through participation in the global ministries of the church.

All: **May we keep its flame shining brightly in our hearts.**

Prayer: *Read by the leader or another member of the group.* O Lord, open my eyes that I may see the needs of others; open my ears that I may hear their cries; open my heart so that they need not be without succour. Let me not be afraid to defend the weak because of the anger of the strong, nor afraid to defend the poor because of the anger of the rich. Show me where love and hope and faith are needed, and use me to bring them to those places. And so open my eyes and my ears that I may this coming day be able to do some work of peace for thee. Amen.[17]

QUESTIONS FOR DISCUSSION AND REFLECTION

Together, reflect on these questions. List examples from the first chapter of Conduct: *"What is the Sphere of Woman."*

1. What was the conduct or behavior that was acceptable or expected of a woman in the 19th century?
2. What duties or roles could a woman in the 19th century hope to perform? What rights and/or privileges could she expect to attain?

3. Who determined these standards? Where did they come from?
4. What were the rewards or benefits for women who abided by these standards?
5. What were the consequences for women who chose to challenge or disregard these standards?

Select several scripture passages from the list below to read and discuss or assign one or more passages to smaller groups of two or three people each and ask the smaller groups to discuss the passages using the following questions.

- Proverbs 31:10–31, (especially verses 29–31), "Ode to a Capable Wife"
- Matthew 9:20–22, "The Woman with the Hemorrhage" (see also, Mark 5:25–34 and Luke 8:43–48)
- Matthew 15:21–28, "The Canaanite Woman's Faith" (see also, Mark 7:24–30)
- Matthew 26:6–13, "The Anointing at Bethany" (see also, Mark 14:3–9)
- Mark 12:41–44, "The Widow's Offering" (see also, Luke 21:1–4)
- Luke 7:36–50, "A Sinful Woman Forgiven"
- Luke 13:10–17, "Jesus Heals a Crippled Woman" or "The Bent-Over Woman"
- John 4:7–30, "Jesus and the Woman of Samaria"
- John 8:3–11, "The Woman Caught in Adultery"
- I Corinthians 11:2–16, "Head Coverings"
- Ephesians 5:21–33, "The Christian Household"
- I Timothy 2:8–15 and 3:11, "Instructions for Women" (see also, I Corinthians 14:34–36)
- I Peter 3:1–7, "Wives and Husbands"

1. How does this scripture passage support or challenge "conduct becoming to a woman" as presented in the book's first chapter, "What is the Sphere of Woman?"
2. How would you define "conduct becoming to a woman" and "the sphere of woman" in today's society and church? What forms the basis for your definitions?

Invite the smaller groups to report briefly or allow time for the larger group to share comments on the passages you selected and the questions for discussion and reflection.

A VOICE FROM THE PAST

Share this quote with the group and invite brief reflections.

At a [woman's suffrage rally] held in San Francisco, Rabbi Vorsanger, who was not in favour of suffrage for women, advanced the heartening theory that in a thousand years more they might possibly be ready for it. After a thousand years of education for women, of physically developed women, of uncorseted women, he said, we might have the ideal woman, and could then begin to talk about freedom for her. When the rabbi sat down there was a shout from the audience for me to answer him, but all I said was that the ideal woman would be rather lonely, as it would certainly take another thousand years to develop an ideal man capable of being a mate for her.

— Anna Howard Shaw,
in her autobiography, *The Story of a Pioneer* (1915)

RISING TO THE CHALLENGE

Assign readers for the following reflection.

Leader: How many times have you heard: "It's just like a woman … "? Think of it this way:

Reader 1: It's just like a woman to pour out extravagant blessings on one whom she loves—without counting the cost! *The woman who anointed Jesus, Matthew 26:6–13 and Mark 14:3–9.*

Leader: How are you, like our foremothers, pouring out extravagant blessings without counting the cost?

Allow time for personal reflection and sharing.

Reader 2: It's just like a woman to let her old self unfold—unashamedly showing her transformed self to onlookers! *The Bent-Over Woman, Luke 13:10–17.*

Leader: How are you, like our foremothers, allowing yourself to unfold and be transformed?

Allow time for personal reflection and sharing.

Reader 3: It's just like a woman to have faith in a dream that everyone says is unreachable and impossible—and then to create a commotion when it happens! *The Woman with the Hemorrhage, Matthew 9:20-22, Mark 5:25–34 and Luke 8:43–48.*

Leader: How do you, like our foremothers, have faith in a dream that seems unreachable or impossible?

Allow time for personal reflection and sharing.

Reader 4: It's just like a woman to stand in front of her accusers—hoping her silence will give voice to their guilt! *The Woman Caught in Adultery, John 8:3–11.*

Leader: How are you, like our foremothers, speaking out—verbally or silently—for injustice?

Allow time for personal reflection and sharing.

Reader 5: It's just like a woman to talk back to an authority figure who thinks he has all the right answers—knowing he seems to have missed the point she wanted to make! *The Canaanite Woman, Matthew 15:21–28 and Mark 7:24–30.*

Leader: How are you, like our foremothers, holding your ground in the face of opposition?

Allow time for personal reflection and sharing.

Reader 6: It's just like a woman to enjoy the attention of a stranger—having no regard for the rules and taboos of polite society! *The Samaritan Woman, John 4:7–30.*

Leader: How are you, like our foremothers, challenging the "rules" and "taboos" of polite society?

Allow time for personal reflection and sharing.

Leader: It's just like a woman—isn't it? It's just like God![18]

SONG: "Woman in the Night" *(The United Methodist Hymnal, #274)*

Leader: "Do not fear, for I have redeemed you; I have called you by name, you are mine" (Isaiah 43:1b). A name means that a person has a beginning and a history of relationships. Take a few moments to recall what you know about your name. From where did it come? How did you get your name? What particular nationality or culture does it reflect? What does your name mean? Who chose your name for you?

Allow time for people to share briefly whatever they want with the group about their names.

Leader: To call each other by name is a special privilege. To choose the name by which you want to be called is an empowering experience. To be called by name means that you are recognized as someone by someone else. As a name is called give that person your undivided attention. Let your blessings wrap that person in a mantle of love and peace. Do not hurry. Take time to be present and to hear the name as it is called.

One at a time, each person says:
  I am (the name she wants to be called).
  I am a child of God!

After each person speaks her name, all respond by saying:
  You are (repeat the person's name as it was given).
  You are a child of God!

After all have spoken.

Leader: Think of those women in your life, named and unnamed, who have been an example to you. What gifts have they given you? What did you learn from them? What would you want to tell them now?

When the group is ready, break the silence and share one or two thoughts that came to you as you remembered.

CLOSING WORSHIP

SCRIPTURE: Proverbs 31:29–31

Leader: *Standing behind the lighted candles.* What is the sphere of woman—in the 19th and 20th centuries and today? How do we, as women, see ourselves? Whose eyes are we looking through? Whose ears are we listening with? Whose shoulders are we standing on? What work do we engage in today that exemplifies "conduct becoming to a woman?" Four lighted candles burn as symbols of our PURPOSE as women organized for mission for over 130 years. They surround the Christ candle—the source of all light and life—which is freely given to everyone and everything. It is the light of Christ that illuminates our way and guides us in our lives as women in church and society.

HYMN: "I Want to Walk as a Child of the Light" *(The United Methodist Hymnal,* #206, verse two)

Leader: May God bless the members of this unit of United Methodist Women.

All: **May God bless all members and units of United Methodist Women.**

Leader: In the name of Christ, our Friend and our Savior. Amen.

All: **Amen. Amen.**

HYMN: "Be Thou My Vision" *(The United Methodist Hymnal,* #451, verse one)

PREPARING FOR THE NEXT SESSION

Before the group is dismissed, the leader should highlight the following opportunities for study and reflection beyond the session. Remember to select a leader and make any assignments, as needed, in preparation for the next group session.

1. Continue to reflect on the questions from chapter one, "What is the Sphere

of Woman?" and make additional notes in your journal.
2. Read the next chapter, "Go Out into the Highways and Hedges," in preparation for the next session.
3. Review the questions for discussion and reflection in the program guide that follows chapter two, "Go Out into the Highways and Hedges." Begin to make notes on your thoughts and feelings related to the material in this chapter.
4. Consider exploring your own history (herstory) by creating a personal timeline. See "Suggestions for Individual and Group Study" on page xi for details.

SENDING FORTH

Leader: In the name of Love, go! Give voice to the silence. See one another. Hear one another. Care for one another. Love one another. It's that simple. It's that hard. Go!

As the group disperses—sharing signs of God's peace, if desired—the leader extinguishes the candles.

GO OUT INTO THE HIGHWAYS AND HEDGES

For Christians it was an age of grand dreams for a world civilized by the Christian faith. The command, "Go ye into all the world," had gripped them. With the exuberant confidence that led others to conquer wilderness, nations and markets, they set out to convert souls and cultures. After generations during which missions were unfashionable, churchmen were once again stirred to action by the specter of half the world smothered in a darkness so palpable to them that it almost seemed as if St. Paul's "spirits of the air" were literally wrestling godless lands to their pitch-black, smouldering breasts. The Christian imagination burned with a vision of naked, wild-eyed people flaying their bodies before grotesque idols of brass and stone.

Women openly wept at the stories they heard of their unbaptized sisters. The derisive comment of the Chinese gentleman, that the custom of binding women's feet, maiming and crippling them, "was originated to keep the sex from their innate low propensity to gad and gossip," enraged churchwomen.[1] The viciousness of his words could only be explained by Satan's dominance and Christ's absence. They heard with horror that Chinese girls were drowned at birth, that Indian widows immolated themselves on their husband's pyres rather than live on as hated outcasts. If some American women felt that they were unjustly restricted, how much worse was it for the [Asian] women who were veiled and locked away from all but their female relatives—unseen, untaught, sold into marriage to old men when they were still children. Christian men had reason to want the world saved for Christ, but women had even more reason: the liberation of their own sex.

In the first American party of missionaries to set sail for [Asia] were two young wives, Ann Judson and Harriet Newall. The story of their lives was to find its way into homes in every part of the country: girls grew up with it— daydreaming tales of womanly valor and playing "missionary" instead of "house." Although Ann and Harriet were only "assistant missionaries" to their husbands, they were heroines to generations of American women.

Ann Judson

Ann Hasseltine Judson was one of two missionary wives sent to India in 1812 by the American Board of Commissioners for Foreign Missions, the first American foreign mission-sending agency. She and Harriet Newell were the first to be set apart as "assistant missionaries" by Reverend Jonathan Allen to "teach these women, to whom your husbands can have but little, or no, access. Go then, and do all in your power, to enlighten their minds, and bring them to the knowledge of the truth. Go, and if possible, raise their character to the dignity of rational beings, and to the rank of Christians in a Christian land. Teach them to realize, that they are not an inferior race of creatures; but stand upon a par with men. Teach them that they have immortal souls; and are no longer to burn themselves, in the same fire, with bodies of their departed husbands. Go, bring them from their cloisters into the assemblies of the saints. Teach them to accept of Christ as Savior, and to enjoy the privileges of the children of God." Unrestricted by precedent and unhampered by the expectations of other missionaries, Ann Judson's early accomplishments as a missionary wife were phenomenal. In addition to childbirth and care and running a household in a foreign country, she did evangelistic work, ran a small school, and was a pioneer Bible translator into two languages.

—Excerpts from *American Women in Mission* by Dana L. Robert, 2, 7

Harriet was only 18 and Ann 22 when they left their homes for what they and their families believed to be forever. In 1812 a sea voyage was a dangerous affair. The rocky, weary, four-month journey to an unknown land of hostile strangers with bizarre habits caused neighbors to question the good sense of the young women's parents. But no one questioned the fruits of their sacrifice, certainly not the American women who read the young missionaries' letters and the diaries published after their deaths. Women laughed when the high-spirited Ann started skipping rope for exercise aboard ship, and they probed their own souls when Ann and the shy, gentle Harriet pondered biblical passages and prayed passionately for greater faith.

Less than a year after leaving her home, Harriet Newall died. At 19 she became the country's first missionary martyr. Three decades later a historian wrote of her:

> The tidings of her death made a deep and powerful impression. ... Perhaps no early missionary, even by a long life of faithful labors, has accomplished more for the heathen, than she accomplished by consecrating herself to their cause, and dying for them before the mission had found a resting place.[2]

Ann and her husband, Adoniram, went on to Burma. There the young woman learned to cook Burmese food and wear practical but appropriately modest Burmese dress. As soon as she was able to learn the language she created a child's catechism and taught every woman and child she could entice into the confines of the mission house. She made friends and cultivated the viceroy's wife, but the Burmese couldn't understand why they should adopt a foreign religion: the white people had one faith, the Burmese another—wouldn't both ultimately lead their disciples to the same salvation? After the first nine years the Judsons could report only 18 converts.

Certainly their slow progress could not be attributed to a lack of support in America. Ann's letters home were read avidly in parlors and quoted liberally in sermons. Women prayed fervently for her success. When her infant son died, they wept with her. Even men were impressed with Ann Judson and waited anxiously for news when, for two years, she struggled to rescue her husband from Burmese dungeons during the war between Burma and Great Britain. Harassed, hungry and pregnant, she bribed and cajoled viceroys and jailers. Her second baby was born and Adoniram, his legs still in shackles, was permitted to go from door to door begging for milk for the wailing child while Ann lay near death with smallpox. When Ann Judson finally died at the age of 37 she was eulogized in pulpits and newspapers and mourned by women of every denomination.

Though Ann Judson was to remain the ideal missionary wife throughout the 19th century, others found their way into the prayers of churchwomen. Local missionary societies frequently sprang up in villages and towns on the departure of a new missionary wife. Letters were exchanged, quilts and coverlets made, bundles of clothing collected, and school tablets and Bibles posted, should the "assistant missionary" succeed in securing any young scholars. While the official mission boards took little notice of her activities, the women's society sustained a close, personal relationship with her. If she returned, or died, the society usually deteriorated. The societies had no say in how their funds were spent, and with no vital connection between their efforts and the missionary's struggles in the field, enthusiasm gave way to apathy. Many societies were short-lived.

Most women, including women missionaries, could not help but think of their own role in missions as incidental. Ann Judson was exceptional, but even for her, the first task was not to bring in converts. The missionary wife's principal vocation was to care for her husband, to comfort and inspire him and bear his children; while the women at home were expected to devote some time to prayer, and to occasionally sacrifice a new dress or bonnet. If they chose to do more, they could expect to meet with mixed reactions. It was not always thought "ladylike" to collect money and conduct business meetings. It

Ann Wilkins   Mary Mason

New York Female Missionary Society
Methodist Episcopal Church

At the time that American Methodists organized their denominational mission board in 1819, Methodist women in New York City founded their own auxiliary that helped to outfit and to support the single women who went out before mid-century. The New York Female Missionary Society of the Methodist Episcopal Church was thus the main supporter of Ann Wilkins, pioneer missionary in Liberia, the Methodists' first foreign mission field. By 1861, however, the deaths of the founding generation as well as opposition from local pastors who resented the women's collection of funds killed the organization. As Mrs L. H. Daggett noted: "In the earlier years of its existence there were no local interests in the churches. The whole city was a circuit. In time, each church assumed the care of itself, as it were, having its own missionary and benevolent societies. As the Female Missionary Society was composed of managers from each church, getting their subscriptions mainly from their individual churches, they found it impossible to keep them up, as they were diverted through another channel."

—Daggett, *Historical Sketches*, 80. On the formation, work and decline of the New York Female Missionary Society, see Susan Eltscher Warrick, "She Diligently Followed Every Good Work: Mary Mason and the New York Female Missionary Society," *Methodist History* 24 (July 1996): 214–229

seems to have occurred to no one that women could have any part in sending out missionaries and setting up missions programs.

An 1825 editorial in a Jonesboro, Tennessee, newspaper, extolling the $40.25 contribution of a local women's society, illustrates the popular attitude towards woman's place in missions:

The lovely and retiring modesty of the female sex, together with their delicate structure, forbids that they shall ever rival the hardy sons of Levi in the gross service of the altar. The Kind Author of our being never designed them to "go out into the highways and hedges" in search of lost sinners, to cross the everlasting mountains and traverse the weary waste in order to proclaim "glad tidings of good things to all people!" And yet they may be abundantly useful; yea they are greatly so. They not only welcome weary pilgrims to their friendly mansions and hospitable cottages, but they warm, clothe and feed them with the best they have.[3]

Nearly 20 years later the report of a local Virginia women's society commented, "Before Christ's ascension we hear the command: 'Go ye into all the world and preach the Gospel to every creature.' Happily for our sex this command was not given to us."[4]

Not all women agreed with this interpretation of the gospel. As early as 1815 an American widow was sent out by the Baptists as a missionary to

Burma. She was properly chaperoned by a married couple, of course. Almost immediately after reaching the field she married, much to the relief of all concerned—including Adoniram Judson who feared the polygamous Burmese would think her someone's second wife.

Widows seemed to have a greater degree of independence than other single women, possibly because they were thought to have benefited from their experiences with male authority. Nevertheless, the other single women who followed were not all widows. Most of them were unmarried teachers who went to foreign posts or to domestic stations where they ministered to the American Indian. They were frequently unnamed in the reports of mission boards, probably out of embarrassment at sending ladies out to do such rude work.

The Methodist Episcopal Board of Missions sent its first single woman to foreign soil in 1834. Miss Sophronia Farrington went with two married couples to the Methodists' new field in Liberia. Within eight weeks, two of the party died, and shortly after, the other pair returned home in broken health. Miss Farrington refused to leave: "I have laid my life on the altar in leaving America, and I am willing that it should remain there."[5] By early 1835, after more than 20 attacks of "African fever," she was so weak she had no choice but to let herself be removed.

A year later when the 30-year-old widow, Ann Wilkins, volunteered to go to Liberia, nine missionaries had been sent out, six had died, and three had returned home in a state of collapse. At a camp meeting at Sing Sing, New York, one of those fortunate enough to have returned preached a missionary sermon. When the meeting closed, a note from Ann Wilkins was discovered in the collection plate: "A sister who has little money at her command and gives that cheerfully is willing to give her life as a female teacher, if she is wanted."[6] She was wanted, and for the next 20 years, the New York Female Missionary Society collected funds for her support, prayed for her, wrote to her, and lived out their ambitions for African souls through her.

The New York society had been in existence for nearly two decades when it assumed responsibility for Ann Wilkins' support. It was founded in 1819 when dignitaries of the Methodist Episcopal Church, who had just organized their first denominational missionary society, voted "that females attached to the Methodist congregations be invited to form a society auxiliary to this."[7] Undoubtedly they had their eyes on the substantial collections of "Mite Societies" (the Methodist version of Cent Societies). Though auxiliaries were begun in Boston, Philadelphia and other cities and towns, the New York women were unusual. Their organization persisted for more than 40 years because of one woman, Mrs. Mary Mason. From the age of 28 until her death she was its president. When she died the society died. Mary Mason and Ann Wilkins carried on a lengthy correspondence and finally became intimate friends. In their friendship they epitomized the sisterly feeling that was to become the great strength of women missionaries and mission societies in later years. Wrote Mrs. Mason to Ann Wilkins:

> Sometimes I visit you in imagination and see you surrounded by the poor, little benighted African girls, listening with eager attention to the words of instruction from your lips, watching your every action in mute astonishment; and sometimes you see the tear start from the fixed eye or a sigh is heard from the penitent heart and your heart rejoices and you are inspired with fresh courage. Then again, you look for fruit, but where you expected to gather grapes, you find only thistles. The oppressive climate throws a languor over your physical powers and, your mental faculties sympathizing with your languid body, you are ready to cry out, "Who is sufficient for these things?" Oh, my dear sister, in such times of oppression look to Jesus and, in the language of the Apostle, say rather, "I can do all things through Christ, which strengtheneth me."... You may always look to our Female Mission Board as to a family of sisters, who are ever ready to sympathize with you in all your afflictions and, as far as in their power, to lighten your burdens and to assist you in your labor of love.[8]

Life Member Certificate

Ladies' China Missionary Society
Methodist Episcopal Church

Organized by Methodist women in Baltimore, Maryland, in 1848, the Ladies' China Missionary Society raised money to support single women in mission to China. The Society women contributed money to the parent boards, despite receiving the "cold shoulder" from the clergy. Nevertheless, in 1858, the Ladies' China Missionary Society paid for three single women, appointed by the parent board, to go as teachers to Foochow, China. Two of these women, sisters Sarah and Beulah Woolston, ran a school for lower-class and abandoned girls. The course of study included literacy with the goal of reading the entire Bible, writing and composition, geography, history, arithmetic, astronomy and useful and ornamental needlework. In 1869, the Ladies' China Missionary Society merged with the newly formed Woman's Foreign Missionary Society and the Woolston sisters were adopted as its official missionaries.

There is only one picture of Ann Wilkins still in existence and it portrays her as square-jawed and heavy-browed with a rather large nose and thin, unsmiling lips. However, she was famous for her piety and sweetness. Her letters were filled with professions of love for her African charges and God, with gratitude for the prayers of her sisters in mission and pleas that they offer ever more fervent prayers. At first she instructed boys and girls at an already established manual training school but, to the great joy of the women at home, she soon started her own school for girls.

There, in that hot, humid country, she was propelled up and down the steaming river by canoe, sitting stiffly so as not to upset the craft, a parasol shading her from the burning sun. In a whitewashed house of her own design, set in a clearing in the lush, tangled green of the forest, she lived like a godly American lady, wearing long, dark dresses and observing all the proprieties. She wrote that sometimes she lay awake at night, frightened by the rumors and sounds of tribal wars. For most of her time in Africa she lived alone except for the company of native children.

Ann Wilkins wrote to Mary Mason about the progress of her pupils, but especially about "little Mary Mason." Years later her eulogists speculated that she gave her children the names of renowned Methodists so that she could surround herself with good, strong "familiars." "Little Mary" was "an extraordinary child for any country or color." Besides her work in reading, writing and sewing, she became a faithful Christian. When Ann Wilkins was sick (she had "attacks of fever at intervals of two, three and at one time of five months"), the child cared for her, "ready to hear the lowest whisper, and attend with cheerfulness to my requests." She "would listen with deep attention to religious instruction, that I used to give any of the children who came near me when I had strength to talk."[9]

Ann Wilkins was furloughed three times because of illness; after the third time she couldn't return to Liberia. She died in 1857 at the age of 51. Four years later the New York Female Society was disbanded. A long time after, Methodist women were moved by the story of a party of Liberian and British surveyors who came upon a tribe in the West African interior that refused to have anything to do with Mohammedan missionaries. As children, some of them had attended Ann Wilkins' school. They were still waiting for her God to come to them.

As the first half of the 19th century ran its course, women grew increasingly impatient with their sharply curtailed role in missions. Occasionally they were able to do something about it. In Baltimore in 1848, a Mrs. Davidson heard an address by a returned missionary to China and later com-

Clementina Butler   Lois Parker

Woman's Foreign Missionary Society
Methodist Episcopal Church

The idea for the Woman's Foreign Missionary Society emerged from the needs of missionary wives in India, Mrs. Lois Parker and Mrs. Clementina Butler, both of whom advocated sending single women to do evangelistic work among the segregated classes of Indian women. In 1869, the Butlers greeted the Parkers who arrived in Boston on furlough. After a service at the Tremont Street Church, Mrs. Butler, Mrs. Parker and Mrs. Flanders, a parishioner, met to discuss whether Methodist women could be organized along the lines recently proposed by the Congregationalist women. A meeting of the Methodist women in the Boston area was called, and despite a terrible storm, eight women founded the organization. Within two months, the Methodist women of the Boston area had adopted a constitution, established *The Heathen Woman's Friend,* negotiated with the Methodist Board of Mission, and appointed two missionaries to India, one of whom was the first woman medical missionary (Clara Swain). The first actual work undertaken by the Society was the adoption of a Bible woman in India.

plained to him that "There is no avenue for women's work in the Methodist Episcopal Church." He replied. "Create one." She did, and for the next 10 years the Ladies' China Missionary Society of Baltimore contributed $500 a year to the Methodist missions board. In 1858 another China missionary urged that "China needs an army of women ready to lay down their lives, if need be, for their own sex." No army was sent, but the board did permit the women to raise the money for a girls' school and for the support of two missionary sisters, Sarah and Beulah Woolston, to take charge of it.[10]

Still, for most women there was "no avenue for women's work." In 1861, at the outset of the Civil War, Mrs. E. C. Dowdell of Atlanta wrote to a bishop of southern Methodism arguing that women should be "put to work" in the church. They were ably and passionately working in the war effort. If they were so energetic in their patriotism, surely they could be as avid in the cause of religion. Conscious of male fears of women becoming "unwomanly," she continued:

> I shrink from the thought of women being made conspicuous save for the cause of Christ. They should come forward, not as leaders, not with many words, but as humble helpmeets, boldly taking their stand on the Lord's side, though they may encounter thereby the sneers of the world and of many so-called Christians, who have read or heard quoted portions of St. Paul's

writing about "learning in silence," "usurping authority," etc., and who never have read or heard of "those women that labored in the gospel."[11]

The "lady," gingerly stepping across the threshold of her home and into the world, had to bear the sharp scrutiny of man's proprietary gaze: did she speak too sharply, did she interject an unasked-for opinion into a conversation—was she betraying her femininity? Of course, no one could question the high motives of the women who collected money for soldiers or for missionaries, door to door, or at quilting parties, fairs and church suppers. The nurses, following the northern and southern armies to the front lines, or the occasional teacher crossing the sea as a missionary, gradually won the grudging praise of some of the most conservative gentlemen. But Dr. Mary Walker, who insisted on being an army surgeon and wearing trousers while she stitched up bodies and applied bandages, was quite another matter. She was an example of how a proper lady, in pressing her compassionate and appropriate concern for the needy too far, could be judged an aberration to womankind. Few women could conceive of so far forgetting themselves. However original, they were extremely circumspect in whatever they did. They were ladies, and they would behave like ladies.

Nevertheless, they also intended to pursue their duty as they saw it. As one woman wrote:

> The prevailing condition of the heathen world moves our compassion, and the degrading state of our own sex among them awakens anew our sympathies. If we would see the great end of missionary labor accomplished we must use extraordinary efforts, for such alone are productive of extraordinary results.[12]

Mrs. Clementina Butler was thoroughly persuaded that only the "extraordinary efforts" of American women would save the women of India. The prestigious wife of the founder of American Methodism's mission to India, she had already helped persuade Congregational women to form a denominational society in 1868. Her stories were calculated to move restless churchwomen to tears and to action.

A hardworking, energetic woman, she had struggled to open a school for girls in her first month as a missionary wife. No one would come, not to the mission house or to a rented room in the bazaar. One woman, told of her purpose, clutched her children to her and fled. When Mr. Butler asked an Indian gentleman to help, he exclaimed, "You're going to teach women to

Clara Swain
Woman's Foreign
Missionary Society
Methodist Episcopal Church

When Clara Swain left the United States in 1870 to become the world's first qualified woman medical missionary, travel was arduous at best. Writing of her journey to India, Dr. Swain said: "The latter part of our voyage was very rough and I was too sick to write, and I have five sick ones to look after besides myself ... I cannot bear to think of sea, it treated me so badly." Circumstances did not brighten when she landed in Bombay, India. Her luggage was a week late; and when she attempted to leave Bombay in a horse-drawn conveyance for Bareilly, the horse lay down and refused to go, despite all coaxing. Once arrived in Bareilly, Dr. Swain immediately went to work, treating 1,300 patients in the first year and training seventeen medical students. By 1874, she had built the Women's Hospital and Medical School, the first of all in Asia and still operating today as Clara Swain Hospital. Clara Swain used her skills as a doctor to gain an entrance for the good news that Christ had come to free India's women of sin and raise their status. She attempted to teach the love of Christ to women so spiritually ignorant that they even worshiped her sewing machine! Her missionary adventures included a brush with death in a flood and a close call while riding an elephant in another of her arduous journeys through India.

read? You will teach the cows next!"[13]

Mrs. Butler was not reluctant to tell of the ghastly joke played on her by a suave Indian man who invited her to teach English to the women in his house. Overjoyed, she and a companion went and taught their eager students, managing at the same time to include a few words of the gospel message. That same evening she learned to her horror that she had been in the city's most notorious whorehouse, teaching prostitutes anxious to improve their traffic with English soldiers.

The Sepoy Rebellion interrupted Mrs. Butler's efforts, but in its aftermath she found her first pupil, an orphan: Mr. Butler had appeared suddenly one day with the child in his arms—"a dirty little waif, half-starved, pock-marked, blind in one eye."[14] War and famine soon brought them another frightened victim, a girl found buried up to her neck and left to die. In the next several years the mission's inmates multiplied, and the orphanage flourished.

It was not only that tradition strictly forbade schooling to Indian women, Mrs. Butler explained to her heartsick listeners. The women were literally imprisoned, removed from all contact with any man but their husbands and infant sons, and from any woman not of their own caste. If anyone was to reach them, it would *not* be the male missionary.

Mrs. Butler found an ally in Mrs. Lois Parker, a missionary wife who came to Boston from India on a health furlough. Mrs. Parker had succeeded in opening a school on the mission house verandah, teaching her few students to write on the sanded floor. Other missionaries' wives followed suit. But it wasn't enough: the field needed full-time women workers, and Mrs. Parker had returned to America determined to find them.

The two missionaries and Mrs. Flanders, a sympathetic and influential Boston churchwoman, sent out to women in the Boston area notices of a meeting to be held on March 23, 1869. When the day arrived, a torrential rain drenched the city. The sexton of the church, thinking it unlikely that the ladies would venture out, locked the door. Eight women, out of the hundreds invited, huddled in the doorway until he appeared with the key. A little disheartened, they gathered in a small corner room, listened to Mrs. Parker, and then examined the constitution of the Congregational women's society that Mrs. Butler had thought to bring along. Inspired, they proceeded to organize the Woman's Foreign Missionary Society of the Methodist Episcopal Church.

The following week another meeting was called, and again it rained. This time 26 women came. They nominated officers, set dues of a dollar a year, "that membership might be within the means of every woman in the church," and adopted their own constitution. The document described the aim of the society succinctly: "For the purpose of engaging and uniting the efforts of the women of the Church in sending out and supporting female missionaries, native Christian teachers and Bible women in foreign lands. ..."[15]

Even before this second meeting the women were aware that what they were planning was not what the male officialdom of the church had in mind for them. Dr. Durbin of the General Missionary Society of the church had written them "counseling mature deliberation in view of the great gravity of the subject" and advising them to raise funds for mission work in India, and perhaps China, leaving the administration of the work to the Board of the General Society.[16] But the women had pledged themselves to meet the needs of women in foreign lands—something the men had not yet been able to do after 40 years. They wanted their organization to be in partnership with the men's, not subordinated to it. Dr. Durbin called a conference to resolve the difficulty.

On that fateful day, the men made their arguments. One protested that the money the ladies collected would be subtracted from contributions to the General Society; a bishop added that "it generally took three-fourths of the funds to pay the expenses of a lady's organization." Dr. Durbin asked what he presumed to be a rhetorical question:

"Could you ladies make the necessary arrangements for Miss A to go to India,

Isabella Thoburn
Woman's Foreign
Missionary Society
Methodist Episcopal Church

Isabella Thoburn, born at St. Clairsville, Ohio, ninth of ten children and sister of Bishop James M. Thoburn, became the first missionary of the Woman's Foreign Missionary Society. Miss Thoburn arrived in India on January 7, 1870, went to Lucknow and opened her school on April 18 of the same year, with six girls enrolled. When nine acres of desirable property were offered for sale that spring, she bought the property and, in addition to the school, established on it the headquarters of women's work in Lucknow. Out of that little school came the first Christian college for women in Asia. During her thirty years in India, the school grew to become the Isabella Thoburn College and continues today to pioneer in education for women. Isabella was later to have a part in the founding of the Elizabeth Gamble Deaconess Home and Training School in Cincinnati, Ohio. In her service abroad, she edited *The Woman's Friend,* a semi-monthly paper published in Hindi, and wrote a biography of Phoebe Rowe, an Indian woman whose evangelistic work was supported by the WFMS. She died in Lucknow, India, of Asiatic cholera at the age of sixty-one, and was buried there.

—Excerpt from *They Went Out Not Knowing,* 4

obtain bills of exchange, take care of her own voyage, provide a home when she arrives? No. Your work is to forward the money for Miss A to New York. We will credit it to your Society, keep you informed of her needs, take care of her in sickness and health. I think this to be the purpose of your constitution.[17]

The women persisted gently, giving respectful attention to all the gentlemen said. But though they made compromises, they won their point—they would not be a mere auxiliary to the General Missionary Society. They consented to "work in harmony with it, seeking its counsel and approval in all their work," and rather than taking collections in church meetings and assemblies, they would raise their funds in a way that could not interfere with the General Society's efforts.[18]

On May 26 the Woman's Foreign Missionary Society held its first annual meeting. Because it was a public meeting in mixed company, the women did the ladylike thing and "kept silent" as usual. The dignified divines in their long-frocked coats addressed the assembly and congratulated the women. Dr. Butler and Dr. Parker spoke while Mrs. Butler and Mrs. Parker sat demurely by. But afterwards the assembled women met by themselves to transact the real business.

The first item on their agenda was to send Miss Isabella Thoburn as a missionary to India. Some at the gathering were horrified—they could not possibly raise so much money so soon. But one woman stood up and squelched all opposition with a heartfelt:

> Shall we lose Miss Thoburn because we have not the needed money on hand to send her? No! Rather let us walk the streets of Boston in calico dresses, if need be, and save the expense of more costly apparel! I move the appointment of Miss Thoburn![19]

It is not recorded that any of the women "walked the streets in calico," but in September 1869, only six months after that first March meeting in the rain, they sent out two missionaries—Isabella Thoburn, a teacher, and Clara Swain, a doctor.

Program Guide

WORSHIP CENTER

Create a worship table or designate a space to display one white pillar candle surrounded by three other candles (green, red and purple) and an opened Bible. You will also need matches and a white taper candle to use when lighting the other candles. If you plan to share a "token" of membership during the closing worship, decide what you will share and secure enough to give to each person in the group. Display these in a basket and place them on the worship table.

FOCUS STATEMENT

This is a story of Protestant Christian mission and women's involvement. It is the story of the struggle for women's rights in church and society. "If it can give [you] some sense of [your] own history (or herstory), some feeling for [your] beginnings, then it will have fulfilled its aim."[20] We are here to communicate the struggle of our foremothers in the Methodist tradition and to gain a new perspective on their life and work. As we read, study, discuss, reflect, pray and worship, may we come to appreciate the course they have charted for our future as women organized for mission and accept our role to continue the story and the journey toward women's full and equal participation as partners in God's mission.

OPENING WORSHIP: "Three Candles"[21]

CALL TO COMMUNITY FOR STUDY AND REFLECTION:
As the leader reads the focus statement (see above), one member of the group lights the white pillar candle on the worship table. Another member then reads the scripture.

SCRIPTURE: I Timothy 1:3-7

Leader: The candles on our worship table represent, by color, the work of fulfilling our PURPOSE as members of United Methodist Women. They will be lighted now as we reaffirm our membership in United Methodist Women and recommit ourselves to fulfilling our common PURPOSE as women organized for mission.

Reader 1: Three candles stand awaiting light from my own hand. The first is green, hue of God's out-of-doors. It challenges us to pray for missions here and far away. And so I light a tiny flame, and pray for missions in God's name.

Reader 1 takes the unlit, white taper candle from the worship table, lights it from the white pillar candle, and lights the green taper candle. She then extinguishes the white taper candle and puts it back on the worship table.

All: **Stir into flame, O God, your gifts within us.**

Reader 2: The organization of United Methodist Women seeks to be a community of women, a community that is worldwide. As members, we seek to know God and experience freedom as whole persons through Jesus Christ. We want this freedom for ourselves and for women, children and youth around the world. We support the ministries of the church with our prayers so that all may know God and God's love for all humankind.

Leader: The green candle is lighted as we commit ourselves to fulfill the PURPOSE of United Methodist Women through prayer.

Reader 3: Three candles stand awaiting light from my own hand. The second is red as rays of setting sun; the color of the blood Christ shed for me. For me he died; for others must I live, since Christ has set me free. And so this candle burns for all humanity.

Reader 3 takes the unlit, white taper candle from the worship table and lights it from the white pillar candle. She then lights the red taper candle and extinguishes the white taper candle, placing it back on the worship table.

All: **Stir into flame, O God, your gifts within us.**

Reader 4: Our personality encompasses all of life: eating, sleeping, time with friends and family, our private moments, time at church and the things we do for others. Each member of United Methodist Women gives her time, her talents, creativity and energies to fulfill the PURPOSE. Together, our individual personalities unite to create a caring community and supportive bonds with one another. It is this community which we form that makes mission possible.

Leader: The red candle is lighted to symbolize our commitment to fulfill the PURPOSE of United Methodist Women through our individual, unique personalities, by who we are and what we do so that all may experience a creative, supportive fellowship.

Reader 5: Three candles stand awaiting light from my own hand. The third is purple, like the royal robes of kings. It is a symbol of material things. I give it light and bring unto God my silver and my gold, that all the wondrous story may be told.

Reader 5 takes the unlit, white taper candle from the worship table, lights it from the white pillar candle, and lights the purple taper candle. She then extinguishes the white taper candle and puts it back on the worship table.

All: **Stir into flame, O God, your gifts within us.**

Reader 6: In 1869, members of the Woman's Foreign Missionary Society of the Methodist Episcopal Church, our earliest missionary society, were eager to send Isabella Thoburn, an educator, and Clara Swain, a doctor, to India as missionaries to women and girls. They had no money so they declared their willingness to "walk the streets of Boston in calico" (rather than purchase more expensive fabrics) if that was the only way to get the needed money. They were determined to fulfill their purpose as women organized for mission by sacrificing their possessions. As members of United Methodist Women, we continue to use creative ways to raise money for mission. We give freely and sacrificially of that which God has given to us.

Leader: The purple candle is lighted to symbolize our commitment to fulfill the PURPOSE of United Methodist Women by freely offering our possessions, so that we may expand concepts of mission through participation in the global ministries of the church.

SONG: "Many Gifts, One Spirit" *(The United Methodist Hymnal,* #114)

QUESTIONS FOR DISCUSSION AND REFLECTION

Together, reflect on these questions. List examples from the second chapter of Conduct, *"Go Out into the Highways and Hedges" and make any obvious connections with the previous chapter.*

1. How were our foremothers in mission of the 19th century able to live out Jesus' command: "Go ye into all the world" (Matthew 28:18–20)?
2. What barriers, obstacles or challenges did they experience as they endeavored to be faithful to Jesus' command? Who or what created these barriers and challenges?
3. What situations, circumstances or "causes" motivated the women to press on in spite of barriers, obstacles or challenges?

VOICES FROM THE PAST
Use the skit, "That Handful of Women," found on page 183 in the Appendix.

RISING TO THE CHALLENGE

Leader: Women organized for mission from eight predecessor organizations and six denominations have given tirelessly of themselves through prayer, personality and possessions in response to God's call. Together, we have shared billions of dollars in financial and material resources to aid women, children and youth in the United States and more than 100 countries worldwide. Today, we accept God's call to continue this legacy of women organized for mission and join together in fulfilling the PURPOSE of United Methodist Women. Let us reaffirm our commitment as members of United Methodist Women. Will you, as a member of the organization of United Methodist Women, faithfully fulfill the PURPOSE?

All: **With God's help, I will.**

Leader: In your daily life, will you make it your intention to know God?

All: **With God's help, I will.**

Leader: For yourself and for others, will you make it your intention to experience freedom as whole persons through Jesus Christ?

All: **With God's help, I will.**

Leader: Whenever we gather as members of United Methodist Women, will you make it your intention to develop a creative, supportive fellowship?

All: **With God's help, I will.**

Leader: Through every opportunity available to you, will you make it your intention to expand concepts of mission through participation in the global ministries of the church?

All: **With God's help, I will.**

Everyone may stand as she is able and form a circle, joining hands.

Leader: You have proclaimed your intentions to fulfill faithfully the PURPOSE of United Methodist Women. Your pledge is an outgrowth of your commitment to Jesus Christ and a renewal of your desire to follow his teachings to love and to serve others. Let us pledge our support to each other as sisters to walk together along this journey. May God who has created us, Jesus Christ who has redeemed us, and the Holy Spirit who sustains and empowers us, bless us as we journey toward fulfilling God's mission through the organization of United Methodist Women. Amen.

At this point, the leader may share with each member a token or symbol of reaffirmation to fulfill the PURPOSE of United Methodist Women. Suggestions would be a membership card or membership pin or other tangible item of your choosing. As the token or symbol is shared with each member, the leader may say something like, "My sister(s), do not be afraid to attempt big things for God. Be faithful and keep at it!"[22] After you have shared the token or symbol with each member, encourage everyone to share signs of God's peace with each other as they return to their seats.

CLOSING WORSHIP

SCRIPTURE: Matthew 28:19–20

Leader: Together, let us recite the PURPOSE of United Methodist Women.

All: **The organized unit of United Methodist Women shall be a community of women whose PURPOSE is to know God, and to experience freedom as whole persons through Jesus Christ; to develop a creative, supportive fellowship; and to expand concepts of mission through participation in the global ministries of the church.**

Leader: Let us pray. Ever-living God, we pray for this, your community of women organized for mission. We ask that every member may be freed to serve you in truth and grace. We remember all women who have recognized that to be a person of faith is to respond in action.

All: **We give you thanks, O God.**

Leader: We remember all women who have faced the unknown in faith and met fear with courage. We give thanks for all women who dare to step forward and lead; for all women who have challenged the stereotypes of society and risked standing alone.

All: **We give you thanks, O God.**

Leader: We remember women who have struggled to reform our history, who have sought in their time to minister to the needs of the hurt, the disadvantaged and the alienated in our world.

All: **We give you thanks, O God.**

Leader: We remember our foremothers in the faith and in this organization, purposeful women like Ann Wilkins, Lizzie Hoffman, Ann Judson, and Minerva Strawman Spreng, who labored in the struggle before us.

All: **We give you thanks, O God.**

Leader: Make us worthy to inherit their valor and vision. Challenge us so that we do not wither and perish by holding to the familiar when it has lost its savor. As your daughters, may we be brought nearer to a new vision of your love, through the grace of our Lord Jesus Christ and the power of the Holy Spirit.[23]

All: Amen.

SONG: "Guide My Feet" *(Global Praise 1, #68)*

PREPARING FOR THE NEXT SESSION

Before the group is dismissed, the leader should highlight the following opportunities for study and reflection beyond the session. Remember to select a leader and make any assignments, as needed, in preparation for the next group session.

1. Continue to reflect on the questions from chapter two, "Go Out into the Highways and Hedges," and make additional notes in your journal.
2. Read the next chapter, "Oh Dear, I Had to Pray for Grace When I Read That," in preparation for the next session.
3. Review the questions for discussion and reflection in the program guide that follows chapter three, "Oh Dear, I Had to Pray for Grace When I Read That." Begin to make notes on your thoughts and feelings related to the material in this chapter.
4. Continue to explore your own history (herstory) by working on your personal timeline. See "Suggestions for Individual and Group Study" on page xi for details.

SENDING FORTH

Leader: Finally, sisters, whatever is true, whatever is noble, whatever is right, whatever is pure, whatever is lovely, whatever is admirable—if anything is excellent or praiseworthy—think on such things. Whatever you have learned or received or heard or seen from our foremothers—put it into practice. And the God of peace will be with you.
—Adapted from *Philippians 4:8–9*

As the group disperses, the leader extinguishes the candles.

OH DEAR, I HAD TO PRAY FOR GRACE WHEN I READ THAT

"Rivals! Rivals!" cried the Parent Board; "we cannot allow our fields thus intruded upon; if they want to work let them gather for our garner; no need of two barns for what can be put into one!".... Many good brethren, not clearly understanding the attitude of the Society, seemed to fear that underneath this independent movement there might be lurking something of a "Woman's Rights" spirit, and that by giving aid to the Society they might be encouraging a mild form of that theory.[1]

A leader of the Methodist Protestant Woman's Foreign Missionary Society, writing these words in 1896, gives the "good brethren" no credit for what was generally accurate insight: the spirit of "Woman's Rights" not only "lurked" in the women's societies—it was a robust and lively presence. If many women denied it, fearing any association with the popularly reported version of the suffragette: a ranting virago (an overbearing woman) venting her spleen on the public stage, they nevertheless fought lustily for a voice in the councils of the church. There were always parsons, prelates and ecclesiastical bureaucrats to circumvent and mollify. But opposition only refined women's tactics and strengthened their resolve. In the 1870s, women's societies multiplied, and their ranks swelled.

Despite the traditional domesticity of genteel southern women, enthusiasts for missions in Nashville and Baltimore were dreaming of an independent society even before the Civil War. By 1872 they were organizing, and two years later word of their efforts reached the Board of Missions of the Methodist Episcopal Church, South. The gentlemen responded graciously, but they either misunderstood or ignored the women's intentions. "This Board recommends the formation of Woman's Missionary Societies throughout our

Minerva Strawman Spreng
Woman's Missionary Society
Evangelical Association

At age twenty, Minerva Strawman was invited to a missionary tea given by the Woman's Missionary Society of the United Brethren Church. Delighted with what she saw and heard, she asked her father, a minister and member of the Board of Missions of the Evangelical Association, if the women in their church could have such a society. She was advised that a petition would have to be presented to the Association's Board of Missions for approval. One was written and signed by fifty women and presented to the Board in 1880. It was approved, and Miss Strawman immediately organized the first Woman's Society in the Evangelical Assocation. Minerva Strawman Spreng was elected third vice-president of the Woman's Missionary Society of the Evangelical Association when it was organized in 1884. From 1892 to 1922, she was its president and then president of the Women's Missionary Society of the Evangelical Church from 1922 to 1924, a total of thirty-two years. During the church's Centennial Celebration in 1940, a $50,000 Memorial Chair of Missions was established at Evangelical Seminary, Naperville, Illinois, in recognition of her missionary zeal.

—Excerpt from *They Went Out Not Knowing*, 9

bounds," they announced, but added "under the direction of the Board of Missions. ... "[2] The women dismissed the pronouncement. Shortly after, Mrs. D. H. McGavock of Nashville, who was later to be corresponding secretary of the society at the national level, submitted a timid memorial to the General Conference of 1874 asking for authorization for an independent and church-wide society. It was referred to a committee on missions and never heard of again. The women had been rudely dispatched.

Unshaken, they set to work as if their proposal had won hearty approval. They organized new societies in southern churches and lobbied to win influential friends. Before the General Conference in 1878, funds were in hand for a year's work, and a young female missionary candidate prepared to set sail for China. Though some of the more chivalrous gentlemen feared for the future of womankind, the Conference gave its assent. One historian suggests that three bishops, whose wives were missionary society partisans, had more than a little to do with the Conference action: they were voting for domestic harmony. But even the most diffident men must have been aware that the church's weak missions program desperately needed the impetus the women had handily proved they could bring to it.

Not all churches were so ready to grant women the right of independent action—and not all church women wanted that right. The Evangelical Church, still steeped in its Germanic tradition, was slow to permit the organization of even an auxiliary society. When the women petitioned their Board of Missions in 1878 for permission to start local societies, they were informed "that the interests of the whole church opposed such an organization."[3]

Two years later, Miss Minerva Strawman, the young daughter of an evangelical missionary leader, discouraged after several rebuffs, finally succeeded in securing the assistance of two males in drawing up a new appeal to the Board; 50 women signed. It was given a polite, if less than rousing welcome. In fact, the Board was in debt and needed the women's fundraising acumen. For the same reason, the General Conference agreed to allow the founding of local societies, and after a bitter debate, finally authorized a churchwide organization in 1884. Even then, all control remained in the hands of the men, local societies were placed under the supervision of the preacher-in-charge, and all proceedings of the Woman's Missionary Society were submitted annually to the Board for review. Despite continual frustration, the women bought themselves a persuasive role in mission policy with their genius for feathering the nest. In 1894 they were finally given one representative on the Board of Missions.

In striking contrast, the women of another church of German origin suffered almost no official opposition. Instead some of the eminent brothers of the United Brethren Church were the first to encourage women to organize a mission society. Nevertheless, until the issue was decided, not everyone felt kindly towards the idea, and many of the clergy were reluctant to see the women freed from their tutelage. Contention seethed in the pages of the *Religious Telescope,* the church periodical.

The Woman's Missionary Association was formed early in 1875. By October of that same year, one of its outspoken adherents wrote a blunt letter to the *Telescope:*

> We want something or nothing. We are tired of standing in the anteroom, waiting for admittance and recognition. We are tired of asking for your sympathy or aid. We are tired of being asked what we want. We now turn to you and ask: "What do you want?" We are ready to work with you for the Master. We come to you and say, "Give us work."[4]

A month later the same woman took issue with the *Telescope's* editor when he "inferred" from the Association's constitution that the women would initiate no new missions but would instead follow where the Board chose to lead them.

Lizzie Hoffman
Women's Missionary Association
United Brethren Church

The organization of the Women's Missionary Association first took form in the heart and mind of one woman, Miss Lizzie Hoffman, a young school teacher in Dayton, Ohio. She struggled to know God's will for her life. Finally she spent a night in prayer, and near dawn the answer came as she perceived that she should enlist the women of the church in mission work. Miss Hoffman was a member of the United Brethren Church which was organized during the period of the missionary awakening in America. A call was issued in *The Telescope* for a meeting of the ministers and women of the Miami (Ohio) Conference to meet for the purpose of organizing a woman's missionary society. The call received a good response, and on May 9, 1872 "a number of ministers of the conference, general officers and women not a few" met in Summit Street Church, Dayton, and organized the Miami Conference Branch. Lizzie Hoffman was elected corresponding secretary. Her first minutes were written on meat wrapping paper.

—Excerpt from
Along the Journey, 11

Whether the original Board shall put in the sickle first, or whether this new Board, full of zeal and enthusiasm, shall outrun it, as did Mary of old when visiting the sepulcher, remains to be seen. We do not propose to wait for any "Board" or for any authority, save that of General Conference.[5]

Brother Hoke, a preacher from Pennsylvania, viewed these ideas of independence with alarm. Claiming endorsements for his position "from several parts of the church among whom are more than one of the highest official position," he maintained that "as an independent organization, acknowledging allegiance to nobody, other than the General Conference, it (the Woman's Association) will inevitably fail." But its failure was not what concerned him—the competition of the women for contributions to missions was the real calamity. "Already some of our interests have suffered from this division," he claimed. For good measure, he added one more argument he hoped would clinch his case—that "it is proposed to hand over part of this work to inexperienced persons who must inevitably follow in the wake of all boards, and squander much of their means for want of the necessary knowledge as to the methods of operation."[6]

Brother Hoke found an audience. Churches in Virginia responded, resolving that they would prefer a Woman's Association that was auxiliary to the Board of Missions. But others, men and women contending with all the "Brother Hokes," pointed to the success of women's societies, especially the Methodist. Of the more specific charge—that the Association's collections had already brought about lower contributions to the Board in one section of the church, Salome Kumler Rike, a Dayton, Ohio, socialite and a devoted church woman, replied, "Oh dear, I had to pray for grace when I read that."[7]

The urbane and witty Mrs. Rike represented the Woman's Association before the General Conference in 1877. By that time, the women had demonstrated that their work resulted in increased contributions to both men's and women's societies. Mrs. Rike's eloquent, but appropriately modest appeal, was the finishing touch to their long campaign. The opposition fell away and the Woman's Missionary Association was recognized by a unanimous standing vote. Within the year they took over the support of a woman missionary in Africa.

The women of the Methodist Protestant Church began their organization on a hopeful note. Some of them had been involved in women's missions for years, contributing money through the Methodist Episcopal Woman's Foreign Missionary Society and through the interdenominational Woman's Union Missionary Society. When they finally organized their own society in Pittsburgh in 1879, the Board of Missions of the church was amenable, and even helped pay the expenses of the women's first missionary in 1880. The General Conference of 1880 recognized their independent status, and the future was promising.

But in 1882 the Board of Missions grew uneasy in its new partnership and suggested that the Woman's Foreign Missionary Society become an auxiliary. Tensions increased when the women proposed to buy or build a missionary home in Japan. The Board not only rejected the idea, but proposed that the Society drop its work in Japan and start a new mission in India. The men were jealous at being outdone by the "ladies," who evidently were not subtle enough about their intentions: "The Society's wish to be independent of the Board of Missions," one woman commented later, "was that it might be able to push its work abroad with more rapidity than the policy of the Board seemed to favor."[8]

In 1884, seeking to resolve the controversy, the Woman's Foreign Missionary Society petitioned the General Conference for recognition as one of the Boards of the church, including all work with women and children under its direction. In response, the Committee on Missions drew up a statement of "Rules for Governing the Woman's Foreign Missionary Society of the Methodist Protestant Church." Twenty minutes before the report was to

Woman's Foreign Missionary Society
Methodist Episcopal Church,

"For the purpose of engaging and uniting the efforts of the women of the Church in sending out and supporting female missionaries, native Christian teachers and Bible women in foreign lands."

In order to retain their independence as a separate mission society, the women were forbidden from raising funds at church services or other public meetings. The Society was forced to rely on a two cents a week contribution from each of its members as the base for funding its entire operation, including eventually hospitals, schools and orphanages.

be read and voted on, it was shown to three representatives of the woman's society. Then the confused women watched as the gentlemen explained to the conference that the report had the Society's approval. After it was voted on, the women found themselves an auxiliary cut off at the knees with no power over their own funds or missionaries. The women did not acquiesce. Four years later, having learned a hard lesson in church polity, they won back their independence. As one of them put it, in the understated and courtly parlance of the time, "We were shown through many perplexities, how to manage that doubtful problem, the reluctant brethren."[9]

Though the women in the mission societies "managed" the brethren, they could never relax their guard. Their access to annual meetings and general conferences remained indirect and slight. Restrictions on Society activities, and even revisions of their constitutions, could occur without their knowledge or consent. A Methodist woman wrote in 1881:

> Let us only think our evening secure when suddenly a telegram from Dr. Rust, Dr. Fowler, Chaplain McCabe, or some of the other comets or meteors of the great connectional work of Methodism moves us out of our inheritance, and puts us in a less desirable corner. ... But we are *only* women, you know, and have been used to it for ages and ages."[10]

The embarrassments men caused were frequent, and sometimes comic. Shortly after the formation of the Methodist Episcopal Society, Mrs. Clementina Butler was invited to speak at a Sing Sing camp meeting. The room was crowded with pious women in long, full black silk gowns, their little bonnets perched on top of smoothly parted coiffures. But Mrs. Butler was distressed to see that there were also a few men in the audience. Because of her inexperience in public speaking and the timidity natural to a "lady," she pleaded with the men to leave. Most of them stubbornly kept their seats.

After some time an impressive woman in widows' weeds rose and asked, "Mrs. Butler, would you like to have me put them out?" Everyone looked at her incredulously. She left the hall, and a short time later reappeared with the camp's one policeman, and the audience burst into laughter as the distinguished gentlemen, some of them in clerical collars, were escorted to the door. As soon as the merriment had died down, Mrs. Butler gave her address. The impressive widow, Mrs. William B. Skidmore, made a generous contribution and joined the society. A commanding presence (a eulogist pronounced her a "woman born to control"), with a broad-featured, rugged face, she became one of the Society's most influential leaders.[11]

Later Mrs. Butler had an argument with Dr. Durbin (the secretary of the Board of Missions) about the meeting. A collection had been taken, even though the women had promised to refrain from raising funds at public assemblies. Mrs. Butler asserted, presumably with a straight face, that the meeting was not public since no men had been present.

Clementina Butler soon got over her fear of "public" speaking and, like other Society organizers, took every opportunity to enlist women in the cause. At one time she spoke at 17 meetings in nine days. Julia Lore, later a missionary to India, described those days:

> Mrs. Butler took me all about in a long visitation of the little places which Mother had planned for her. ... What a large part of my education it has been to know the beginners of the Woman's Foreign Missionary Society. Mother in her gentle, brave way doing what she had never done before and doing it calmly, sure it was right—Mrs. Skidmore, Mrs. Alderman, and the incomparable Mrs. Warren—and how it brought out the utterly unrevealed possibilities of so many quiet women in country churches—and how *one* was the spirit![12]

On passenger and freight trains, buggies and stagecoach, or road wagons and by foot, women were crisscrossing the country with their message. For some the traveling required of a missions society organizer was traumatic.

> Tell them not to be afraid to attempt big things for God. Tell them to be faithful and keep at it!
>
> —Minerva Strawman Spreng, Woman's Missionary Society, Evangelical Association, 1924

One Georgia woman, who had never ventured any distance unescorted before, was delegated to attend a meeting a few miles distant. Arriving at her destination, she discovered that no one was at the railroad station to meet her. Panic-stricken, she took the next train home.

Mrs. Juliana Hayes, president of the southern Methodist Woman's Society, was well over 60 years old when she went "from Maryland to Texas" in "rough conveyances and over rougher roads ... to churches that seemed to her almost on the outskirts of civilization."[13] Late one night she found herself at a deserted Arkansas railroad station. There were no more trains expected until morning, and when she inquired, she learned the nearest house was a half-mile away. Following a station attendant with a flashing lantern down the railroad tracks, she saw at last a crude cabin. Answering her knock, a man inside offered to give her his place in bed, and she was ushered into a room with three chairs and the proffered bed. A woman, who lay there with a baby, welcomed her: "Come, lie down by me." Mrs. Hayes wearily assented, took off her shoes, spread her traveling shawl over the vacant place on the soiled, rumpled looking bed, and sank down. Incredulously, the woman asked, "Are you going to sleep in your clothes?" "It's so late I shall not undress," replied the embarrassed churchwoman.

The strangeness of her situation kept her awake for some time until she hesitantly asked her bed partner: "Are you a Christian?" The answer came, "I'm a Methodist, what's left of me." Later, the hearty gentlewoman remarked, "These words acted like a charm on my feelings; they were a benediction of peace. I dropped to sleep at once, and never slept better in my life."[14]

Missionary organizers not only endured the tedium and mishaps of travel, but also the distrust and occasional hostility of those who believed that, being women, they should have stayed home to preside over the tea table. At a meeting in Florida, a gentleman was asked to introduce Mrs. Hayes, but refused to do so on the principle that women should be seen but not heard in public. After listening to her speech, he relented and later became an outspoken partisan of women's work in missions.

Perhaps nothing was as difficult for the ladies of the 19th century as speaking in public. Dr. Elizabeth Blackwell, America's first woman physician, overcame the mockery of journalists and catcalls of children on the street to earn her medical degree in 1849. But when she was asked to march in a procession and appear on a platform to receive the honor, she refused because it would be "unwomanly." Thirty years later the Methodist missionary, Isabella Thoburn, on furlough from pioneering education for Indian women, was determined not to make speeches for the same reason. In the beginning, women who were to become famous for their eloquence were terrified of the speaker's platform. At times their trepidation could reach absurd proportions. A Texas historian commented about a conference Society meeting: "Noting the excessive timidity of the duly authorized delegates, the brethren graciously consented to lend their assistance by frequently nominating the officers."[15]

What the women suffered and how they overcame their fear was recounted by a New York missionary society leader who was asked to speak before an audience of ministers and upper echelon clerics. At the church door, clinging to her husband's arm, she found herself murmuring repeatedly, "There is no use talking; I cannot do it." The proceedings of the meeting were a blur to her until the assembly knelt in prayer. Then she dropped to her knees fervently beseeching, "Oh God, if ever you helped me, help me now." Finally it was her turn to face the black-coated assembly:

> ... and the whole scene changed. The brethren vanished from sight and instead were hundreds of millions of heathen women pleading, "Just a word for us, sister!" and there was a victory—instantaneous, complete, and permanent, for God did it; to Him is the glory. I doubt not that in its essential features many women have had similar experiences. God thrust them out and empowered them to do His bidding.[16]

If most women were reluctant to speak, many were no more overjoyed to assume leadership. At the first meeting called to organize the Methodist Protestant Society, one woman after another declined office, "each pleading, 'I pray thee have me excused.'"[17] In one small town society in Kentucky, no one would consent to be president until a 14-year-old girl volunteered. She turned out to be an able leader.

The leadership on the conference level was no more polished. The president of the North Georgia Conference Woman's Society was 70 years old when she was elected, and she served for five years. Her granddaughter described her first actions in that office:

> At one of the early meetings over which grandmother presided she would rise early and study a little slip of paper which my father had prepared to help her in her duties as chairman. As she pored over this piece of paper, she said in confidence, "I do not know a thing about parliamentary usage, but I would not have these women to know it for the world!"

Mrs. W. D. Williams ... was another elderly woman who became a conference officer. She was for years our treasurer. During this time she lost her sight, but with the help of her son she continued to keep the books, and a more faithful and accurate treasurer we never had.

Woman's Missionary Society
Evangelical Association

"I will win one to the Woman's Missionary Society to an awakened interest, to wider horizons, to a deeper sense of responsibility, to a deeper consecration. I do this because I have a responsibility to carry out the Great Commission (Matthew 28:19).
I believe in the Woman's Missionary Society as one of the most helpful avenues to build the kingdom of God. There is a place for every woman in the Woman's Missionary Society, and I want to help her fill her place. I believe that the Woman's Missionary Society affords exceptional missionary educational advantages. Each new member means added prayers, gifts and service. So work with God—then nothing's lost; who works with Him, does best and most."

Imagine the consternation of the Entertainment Committee at Quitman, where one of our early conferences was held, when these instructions came with the names of the delegates: "Please provide a home near the church for Mrs. Walker, the president. She is old. Please see that Mrs. Williams is near the church. She is blind. The Secretary of the Thomasville District must be near the church. She is lame." No wonder that someone confidentially whispered, "The officers at this meeting consist of the lame and the halt and the blind!"[18]

Alice Cobb, the dean at one of the South's first women's colleges, a missionary organizer in Georgia and later an officer in the national organization, instituted a course in parliamentary practice in the college curriculum determined to produce a generation of women who would be able to "rise to a point of order." But most women, like the elderly Mrs. Walker, learned by trial and error and with the help of a friendly male.

Old and infirm, or young and uncertain, the women struggled on in their crusade. Their dedication could beggar all description. One pastor's wife in Mississippi found it impossible to interest the women in her church in forming a society. Each month her husband announced a meeting from the pulpit. "Promptly, at the appointed time, she went into the parsonage parlor with family Bible, hymn book and purse and held the monthly meeting by herself, sending her report and dues regularly to the Conference society."[19]

Such extraordinary consecration was needed. Elders and bishops might be won to their side, while preachers and husbands remained unconvinced, and their antagonism could be churlish. Women would come long distances to churches and find the doors bolted; many meetings were held on church steps. Sometimes husbands simply forbade their wives to become involved, and failing that, locked them in their bedrooms for the duration of any meeting.

In at least one instance the women's "difficulties" were mysteriously "removed." A conference historian reported, presumably with tongue-in-cheek:

> In these early meetings, when a society did not flourish, an investigation was made. At this time, Leitchfield, laboring under some disadvantages, asked to be dropped from the roll. A motion was carried that prayer be offered for the removal of the difficulties, whatever they proved to be. It was finally revealed that certain husbands of members of the Society were opposed to the work being done by their wives. The prayer must have been answered, as a certain pastor to that church declares that never in a long pastorate has he served a church in which there were so many widows.[20]

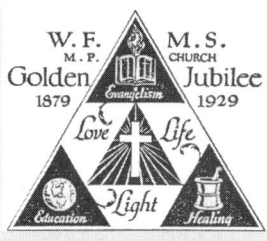

Woman's Foreign Missionary Society
Methodist Protestant Church

"The purpose of this Society is to unite the women of the Methodist Protestant Church in efforts to send missionaries, Bible readers and teachers to women in heathen lands, and in employing native Christian teachers and Bible readers."

"The payment of one dollar shall constitute annual membership, and the payment of ten dollars at one time, life membership, and fifty dollars, a honorary manager for life."

"The funds of the Society shall not be raised by public collections in our churches, but by securing members, life members, honorary members, and in such other ways as the Society may determine, and which shall not conflict with the regular collections for the Board of Missions."

Not all husbands tried to thwart their wives' new ambitions. When a young woman was asked to become a society treasurer in New York, she refused, saying she was not competent. When she reported the incident to her husband, he responded, "But, my dear, I did not marry an incompetent person." She took the job—and held it for the next 28 years.[21]

Every missionary society had its male friends who fought its battles in general conferences and before boards, in the pages of religious periodicals and in the local churches. Many of the women were interconnected with the church power structure through husbands, brothers, fathers and even sons. Mrs. Rike's father and grandfather were United Brethren bishops, and Mrs. Skidmore's husband had been one of the founders and leaders of his church's general missionary society.

The women who organized the mission societies were the elite of the church. In their homes, the luminaries of church and society gathered for tea and conversation. Upper middle-class and educated, some of them even accomplished the unheard of feat in their day of combining marriage and a career. And, like Mrs. Cobb, married and a pioneer in education for southern women, they also found time for a profusion of other activities. Alice Cobb was active in history and literary clubs, a current topics club, the Woman's Christian Temperance Union, the Daughters of the American Revolution, an alumnae association, the National

Geographic Society and at least three other organizations.

But nothing animated them like the missions societies. As one woman commented: "... it was said that 'every woman who takes hold of this Woman's Foreign Missionary Society becomes at once an enthusiast, and these Heathen Women (as they were called) can think and talk of nothing else.'"[22] They took their excitement to the nation, determined to "sow the country knee-deep with missionary literature."[23] They had no money to spend on the solemn and weighty tomes of the general missionary societies. For that reason and because they were appealing to women and children, they created and gave away (or sold for a few cents) hundreds of leaflets and tracts with stories and poems; and thus began the great popularization of missions of the 19th century. One of the most spirited and enthusiastic writers for missions called for lively literature, "not prosy columns of close print with spiritless rills of statistics oozing through them." Another woman declared, "people want information, but information on fire."[24]

Just as important were the women's missionary magazines. They not only helped thousands to identify with the missions cause, they made money. While other church periodicals went bankrupt or were heavily subsidized, subscriptions swelled to magazines such as *The Heathen Woman's Friend, The Evangel, The Woman's Missionary Advocate,* and *The Woman's Missionary Record.* These journals were to be found in parlors and drawing rooms, in parsonages and churches throughout the country. Women read them avidly and, through them, participated vicariously in the work of the missionaries. Knowing they were significant in the Christian mission's success and even sharing a sense of responsibility for its defeats, they felt like neighbors to the missionaries—and sisters.

The missionary societies did not stop with the publication and distribution of literature: they worked out programs of study. At meetings members were expected to read prepared papers on subjects like Buddhism or the caste system of India. For many women a whole diverse world filled with unexpected possibilities opened up while they listened wonderingly in parlor or pew. Others were more hesitant. One local president reported, "When I first invited the ladies to write and read, they thought me wild."[25]

The involvement of women in missions was expected to find expression in their everyday life, especially their prayer life. In Kentucky, for example, Methodist women could be discovered on their knees each day at twilight, praying on Monday for China; Tuesday, Japan; Wednesday, Mexico; Thursday, Brazil; and Friday for the American Indian. On weekend evenings they prayed for missions in general.

Women's Mission Publications

From our missionary society beginnings in 1869 to the present day, women organized for mission have been producing magazines to tell the mission story. *The Heathen Woman's Friend*, published from 1869-1896 in Boston by the Woman's Foreign Missionary Society of the Methodist Episcopal Church, was the first of sixteen mission magazines to be published in the history of Methodist missions. The Society also printed or initiated journals in other languages (German, Japanese and five vernacular Indian languages) as well as a children's journal. *The Heathen Woman's Friend* underwent a name change in 1896 and was published until 1940 as the *Woman's Missionary Friend*. A descendant of *The Heathen Woman's Friend* and the *Woman's Missionary Friend, Response* began publication in 1969 after organization of The United Methodist Church and the merger of the Woman's Society of Christian Service and the Women's Society of World Service. Today, *Response* is the official voice of women in mission and United Methodist Women of The United Methodist Church.

Meetings were also prayerful occasions. Even the minutes of business proceedings were full of exclamations about the "waves of feeling" that passed over those assembled, or "the nearness of God" suddenly experienced after a report of some success in Africa or China. In the middle of a dry discussion on organization, a recording secretary could find good reason to interrupt her record with the words of a hymn. The meetings most moving to the women featured one or more returned missionaries with stories to tell and exotic costumes to show.

All this inspired women to give—and often, to give sacrificially. Barred for many years from collecting offerings at church services and assemblies, the societies devised other means of raising money besides dues (which were slight—perhaps a few cents a week), and finally most of the money that filled the coffers was secured in more imaginative ways. Individual women and societies were invited to support special projects and persons. Whether or not a school in China was to have desks or a church in India an altar came to depend on them. They adopted, fed, clothed and took over the support of native evangelists and orphan children alike. Children were often given the names of their benefactors or some deceased saints the women wanted to honor with their gifts, a practice that was finally ended: it proved impractical and sometimes took on bizarre aspects. One poor Japanese child, for instance, was baptized with the name "Indiana Maize" by a group of Indiana women.

The power of this custom to engage the women, and its tendency to exaggeration, is shown in the example of a "little woman in rusty black" who beseeched a missionary to allow her to support a girl who would take her name. Later she wrote:

> Now I feel I have a substitute who can fulfill my long cherished desire to be a missionary. Just as soon as we begin to do for anyone how different we feel towards them! I feel that she is very near to me and my prayers for her and in fact for all the missionaries have a new interest. They who do now have this personal touch do not know what happiness they have missed. When I tell you I am in my seventy-second year, have a house full of boarders, three shut-ins, and two are cripples, and a sister in her ninety-second year, three doctors coming here during the winter and no nurse but myself for any of them and only one incompetent girl to help me, you will see the demands upon my time, but feel that I must have another girl to bear my married name, as this one does my maiden name.[26]

Women earned money in more orthodox, though scarcely less original, ways. Fairs, socials, flag festivals, quilting parties and bake sales were held; waste paper and rags were collected and sold. Farmers' wives raised begonias and chickens, and many communities had their "missionary calves." One society published a cookbook, and a mother, in concert with teaching her family table manners, raised money by charging her offspring a penny for each spot on the tablecloth after meals. At every society meeting were the ever present "mite boxes," and the women filled them.

Some could only afford to give "mites," but others gave fortunes. Wealthy women left thousands of dollars in their wills. A New York woman worked eight months embroidering a fine coverlet and sold it for $1,500. Mrs. D. H. McGavock secretly gave the diamonds that had been pinned to her wedding veil to a China missionary: a school was built.

Children were also enlisted in the cause—and their pennies added to the treasury. Mrs. Cobb started a juvenile society in Macon, Georgia, and one youth later recalled being a child in the missionary crusade:

> What a pride we felt when the roll was called, and we responded to our names by going forward and placing our earnings on the marble-top table! ... The money had to be earned, and each child had to tell how it had been done! It was considered a disgrace for a mother to have to *give* the money to her child. I

Justina Lorenz Showers
Women's Missionary Association
United Brethren Church

Justina Lorenz Showers was elected the first secretary of Young Women's Work of the Women's Missionary Association of the United Brethren Church, after graduation from Bryn Mawr College in Pennsylvania. This organization was the forerunner of the Otterbein Guild for girls. She was on the Association's Board of Trustees for twenty-five years, and served as its president from 1941–1946. When the Evangelical and United Brethren Churches united to become the Evangelical United Brethren Church, she was elected the first president of the Women's Society of World Service and served from 1947–1954.

recall that one little girl had refrained from sucking her thumb, one had nursed the baby, one had kept the wood-box full, and another had waited on the table. Our little hearts would swell with satisfaction as our leader [Mrs. Cobb] praised us for these small tasks. She made us feel that we were a real force in the world.[27]

They all—women and children—felt they "were a real force in the world." The freshness of their vision gave new impetus to the missionary endeavor, and the general missionary boards had to work harder in order not to be outdone by the women. (Impatient Methodist Protestant women started work in China 18 years before the men were financially able to join them.) Women's societies frequently found themselves initiating projects that men were slow to approve. One historian wrote in 1892:

> Surely in this department the women are going far in advance of the men, and were a competitive examination in order on the program of the missions of their own denominations, they would come out victorious. In too many cases the men are in the position of the good deacon who, when called upon at a prayer meeting to pray for one particular field, refused, on the ground that he did not know enough about that mission field to pray for it intelligently.[28]

The success of the women's missionary enterprise won it grudging, and occasionally joyful, acceptance in church councils. The piety, prudence and efficiency of the societies persuaded the most dour of sceptics that what the women were doing was to be included in their narrow definition of "women's work." But the most convincing argument of all to the doubters was the decorum of their new partners in mission: the women still behaved like ladies. As a Kentucky newspaper reported of a Society meeting: "Two things can be affirmed of this gathering of women; it was not in the interest of woman's rights nor suffrage, nor had they a crank among them."[29] Churchmen sighed with relief: women still knew their place.

Program Guide

WORSHIP CENTER

Prepare a simple worship table or designate a space for some candles and an opened Bible. You will need matches to light the candles at the appropriate time.

FOCUS STATEMENT

This is a story of Protestant Christian mission and women's involvement. It is the story of the struggle for women's rights in church and society. "If it can give [you] some sense of [your] own history (or herstory), some feeling for [your] beginnings, then it will have fulfilled its aim."[30] We are here to communicate the struggle of our foremothers in the Methodist tradition and to gain a new perspective on their life and work. As we read, study, discuss, reflect, pray and worship, may we come to appreciate the course they have charted for our future as women organized for mission and accept our role to continue the story and the journey toward women's full and equal participation as partners in God's mission.

OPENING WORSHIP

CALL TO COMMUNITY FOR STUDY AND REFLECTION:

As the leader reads the focus statement (see above), one member of the group lights the candles on the worship table. Another member then reads the Scripture.

SCRIPTURE: Romans 16:1–15

LITANY ON THE PURPOSE OF UNITED METHODIST WOMEN[31]

For this litany, you will need someone to read the part of the "Leader" and divide the group into two smaller groups to read the parts for "Group 1" and "Group 2."

Leader: As members of United Methodist Women,

Group 1: Involved in our families and involved with our neighbors,

Group 2:	Involved in our communities, our country; and yes, involved in our world!
All:	**God calls us to be in mission!**
Leader:	We are a community of women.
Group 1:	Women seeking new ways of thinking.
Group 2:	Women searching for new ways of learning about being in mission.
All:	**God calls us to be in mission!**
Leader:	Our PURPOSE is to know God.
Group 1:	To know God is to love God and to be in relationship with God.
Group 2:	To know God is to love each other and to be in relationship with others as an expression of that love.
All:	**God calls us to be in mission!**
Leader:	Our PURPOSE is to experience freedom as whole persons through Jesus Christ.
Group 1:	Where the dignity of all persons is upheld.
Group 2:	Where all cultures can be celebrated.
All:	**God calls us to share the good news of God's love for all people in every land.**
Leader:	Our PURPOSE is to develop a creative, supportive fellowship.
Group 1:	To become partners, to be linked together in God's mission.
Group 2:	To understand more about ourselves and each other and to have fun together.

All:	**We are called to be partners in God's mission!**
Leader:	Our PURPOSE is to expand concepts of mission.
Group 1:	To be educated about and for God's mission.
Group 2:	To learn and tell the stories of God's mission.
All:	**God calls us to affirm God's love for all creation.**
Leader:	Our PURPOSE is to participate in the global ministries of the church.
Group 1:	By working for social justice and becoming advocates for the oppressed and dispossessed.
Group 2:	By providing clean water, food for hungry children and spiritual nurture.
All:.	**God calls us to be in mission! Let us share the good news of God's love with all creation!**
Leader:	Join me in reciting the PURPOSE of United Methodist Women.
All:	**The organized unit of United Methodist Women shall be a community of women whose PURPOSE is to know God, and to experience freedom as whole persons through Jesus Christ; to develop a creative, supportive fellowship; and to expand concepts of mission through participation in the global ministries of the church.**
HYMN:	"Help Us Accept Each Other" *(The United Methodist Hymnal,* #560)
PRAYER:	"From Fear"[32]
Leader:	From fear of staying still,
All:	**O God, deliver me.**

Leader:	From fear of surrender,
All:	**O God, deliver me.**
Leader:	From fear of decision,
All:	**O God, deliver me.**
Leader:	From fear of losing respect,
All:	**O God, deliver me.**
Leader:	From fear of facing my fear,
All:	**O God, deliver me.**
Leader:	But from the fear that marks your presence,
All:	**I beseech you O God, do not deliver me. Amen.**

QUESTIONS FOR DISCUSSION AND REFLECTION

Together, reflect on these questions. List examples from the third chapter of Conduct: *"Oh Dear, I Had to Pray for Grace When I Read That," and make any obvious connections with previous chapters.*

1. What impact did the "Woman's Rights" movement have on the formation of women's missionary societies? What impact did the formation of women's missionary societies have on the "Woman's Rights" movement?
2. How did the male contingent react to the formation of women's missionary societies? What conditions or restrictions were placed upon these societies?
3. What were the men really afraid of or concerned about? How did the women respond to these situations?
4. What obstacles and challenges did the women face as they took an active role in telling the mission story?
5. Men were not always the antagonists of the women's missionary societies. How did some men lend their support?

A VOICE FROM THE PAST

Share this quote with the group and invite brief reflections.

There is a serious question before you. ... Dare this conference stand before the omen given by God and frustrate his will for the upbuilding of his church by your prejudices? ... The question of the future is whether you will have power to conquer the forces of sin, and I tell you it will need every woman that can be found to stand side by side with the good-minded men in this work if the church is to be triumphant.

—Eugenia St. John,
from the debate over seating women delegates at the
1892 Methodist Protestant General Conference
quoted in *Methodist Recorder,*
June 4, 1892

RISING TO THE CHALLENGE

For this portion of the session, you will need to gather back issues of Response *and* New World Outlook *magazines, 4" or 6" squares of colored construction paper or card stock, glue stick, markers and any other items you want to make available as the group creates "quilt" squares. You can also choose to use actual fabric squares and sew the quilt, but this option will take more time. You will continue to add quilt squares and patch it together over the next four sessions.*

Ask the group to write, paint or draw the names on a "quilting" square— one name per square—of a biblical, historical or contemporary woman who they believe exemplifies and/or challenges "conduct becoming to a woman." Include names of women from international leadership, Bible stories, U.S. history, United Methodist tradition or personal history. To depict these women's contributions to our work as women organized for mission and for leading the way toward full and equal participation of all women as partners in God's mission through church and society, gather photographs and clippings from the magazines or other artwork and add these to the squares. While the group is making the squares, engage in conversation about these women's lives and their significance for each group member. Remind the group that you will continue to add to this "quilt" and patch it together over the next four sessions.

CLOSING WORSHIP

SCRIPTURE: Luke 1:39-56

Leader: We stand with generations of women who know that the Lord their God is One God; who love the Lord with all their hearts and minds and strength; who established the legacy of Sarah and Deborah and Ruth.

All: **Our souls magnify the Lord, and our spirits rejoice in God our Savior.**

Leader: We share the news with those first women at the tomb who went forth to proclaim the gospel of Jesus Christ; who served the early Christians with zeal; who were named Mary and Phoebe and Priscilla.

All: **Our souls magnify the Lord, and our spirits rejoice in God our Savior.**

Leader: We remember those women who shaped the church in cloistered community and civil court; who listened to inner voices and pursued mystical union; who mothered and married the "fathers of the faith"; who loved the church when it was most unlovable.

All: **Our souls magnify the Lord, and our spirits rejoice in God our Savior.**

Leader: We honor women who defended the reformed faith and supported the reformers; who gave up comforts and family for their convictions; who were sometimes called witches and often became martyrs; who arrived in the new world and took new responsibilities.

All: **Our souls magnify the Lord, and our spirits rejoice in God our Savior.**

Leader: We recall those women who came to this land not on deck, but in the dark hold of a slave ship; who preserved an African heritage and understood the liberating message of the Christian gospel; who nurtured a church under Jim Crow and Daddy Grace; who knew the double jeopardy of being black and female.

All: **Our souls magnify the Lord, and our spirits rejoice in God our Savior.**

Leader: We listen to those Native American sisters whose people were here long before anyone came to this country; who remind us of the interrelated fabric of earth and sky and sea; who know the pain of displacement and betrayal; who have much to share with all women.

All: **Our souls magnify the Lord, and our spirits rejoice in God our Savior.**

Leader: We read in history of missionaries who heard a call to teach and heal in the name of Jesus; who shared their faith with women and children throughout the world; who exercised authority with charity, if not always wisdom; who widened the horizons and expanded the vision of the church.

All: **Our souls magnify the Lord, and our spirits rejoice in God our Savior.**

Leader: We know strong women who stayed at home and worked in groups and churches to change American life; who founded anti-slavery societies, Sunday schools, peace movements, suffrage organizations and temperance halls; who saved and raised money for mission at home and abroad; who were proud of "women's work" and kept the churches going.

All: **Our souls magnify the Lord, and our spirits rejoice in God our Savior.**

Leader: We are enriched by the influx of Pacific and Asian women who bridge the cultural gulf between East and West and raise our global awareness; who come from islands where women have valued tradition; who know the problems of multicultural and multilingual communities in our urban society.

All:	**Our souls magnify the Lord, and our spirits rejoice in God our Savior.**
Leader:	We are heirs of those women who challenged the status quo and pioneered in new roles; who insisted on a woman's right to preach the gospel, to practice medicine, to defend the law, to hold public office; who refused to let tradition and custom stifle their gifts; who call the church to accept new forms of leadership even today.
All:	**Our souls magnify the Lord, and our spirits rejoice in God our Savior.**
Leader:	There are women who have worked in the churches as wives of pastors; who although too often unacclaimed and unnoticed, have given themselves in a faithful and dedicated ministry.
All:	**Our souls magnify the Lord, and our spirits rejoice in God our Savior.**
Leader:	We are learning to love those women who are variously called Latina, Hispanic, Chicana, Mexican, and Puerto Rican; who speak Spanish in our church; who know the journeys of employment and the waste of unemployment; who add yet another culture and language to the church.
All:	**Our souls magnify the Lord, and our spirits rejoice in God our Savior.**
Leader:	We are all of these women who seek to serve you, our God. We are many, and yet we are one. We are bound together and joined together by women. We are members of the church of Jesus Christ. We are empowered for mission because of these women.
All:	**For all of these women, and all women everywhere, we give you thanks, O God. Amen.**[33]
HYMN:	"Here I Am, Lord" (*The United Methodist Hymnal*, #593)

PREPARING FOR THE NEXT SESSION

Before the group is dismissed, the leader should highlight the following opportunities for study and reflection beyond the session. Remember to select a leader and make any assignments, as needed, in preparation for the next group session.

1. Continue to reflect on the questions from chapter three, "Oh Dear, I Had to Pray for Grace When I Read That," and make additional notes in your journal.
2. Read the next chapter, "Grit is Needed as Well as Grace," in preparation for the next session.
3. Review the questions for discussion and reflection in the program guide that follows chapter four, "Grit is Needed as Well as Grace." Begin to make notes on your thoughts and feelings related to the material in this chapter.
4. Continue to explore your own history (herstory) by working on your personal timeline. See "Suggestions for Individual and Group Study" on page xi for details.
5. Continue to work on your "quilt" squares, if you choose, between the sessions.
6. Select one woman from the list on page 96 of the next chapter's program guide and prepare to tell her story as if it were your own. *Note: The group leader for the next session may wish to "assign" one woman to each group member to avoid overlap.*

SENDING FORTH

Leader: Our benediction is one we will act out, not only here with hand motions, but also as we leave this place to live in faithful service. We will repeat three motions three times—twice, as I say the words of benediction, and the third time, in silence. Please stand as you are able and join in this benediction.

The first time, give instructions about the motions as you say the words of benediction and demonstrate each motion.

First, hold hands with the persons beside you, as a sign that we stand in solidarity with each other, united in Christ, the Prince of Peace. *Pause*. Then, raise your hands to shoulder height, in the shape of fists, but palms forward, as a sign of our determination to witness boldly, to act with courage and to take risks as we work for peace and justice. *Pause.* Finally, extend your arms with open hands, reaching out to the sky, as a sign of your commitment to reach out with the compassion of Christ, to embrace the world with God's love.

The second time, say the words of benediction as you do the motions.

Let us enact this benediction as I say it for the second time. *Holding hands.* Stand in solidarity with each other, united in Christ, the Prince of Peace. *Fists raised to shoulders.* Go in determination to witness boldly, to act with courage, to take risks as you work for peace and justice. *Arms extended upward.* Commit yourselves to reach out with the compassion of Christ, to embrace the world with God's love.

The third time, do the benediction in silence.

And once more in silence.

Lead the sequence of three motions, with a brief pause between each motion to allow time for silent prayer.

Amen.[34]

As the group disperses—sharing signs of God's peace, if desired—the leader extinguishes the candles.

Grit is Needed as Well as Grace

After a long, uncomfortable voyage, related Clementina Butler's daughter, her mother and the rest of the ship's party were overjoyed at their first sight of the Indian coast: they were about to begin their missionary labours. On the ship, anchored some distance from shore, Mrs. Butler was startled to hear shouts that a man in a boat was approaching.

> Everyone crowded to the side of the steamer to see the first man of India, but when he came near, the ladies retired to the other side of the deck, for this representative of the people among whom Clementina Butler expected to pass her life was a man almost nude, his body bearing the marks of the devil worshiper. His appearance was so revolting that Mrs. Butler wondered if she could endure to live among people like that.[1]

Thousands of women who followed Mrs. Butler had the same experience. They had come out of pity and duty, but their first emotions were repugnance and horror. Most of them tried to squelch these feelings as quickly as possible. As a missionary to Mexico reminded herself, "Christ died even for them. Yes, for the very lowest."[2]

The woman missionary was not a peculiar creature of her time. Breeding dictated that she feel revulsion at immodesty and dirt, and, as a lady, she was also suitably trepidatious about stepping beyond the bounds of "woman's sphere." But that sphere had expanded to embrace nearly every action that could be interpreted as "service" to mankind (and especially to womankind). The challenges the woman missionary faced in her new understanding of her role would defeat some, but transform others into heroines and pioneers in the liberation of women.

Dr. Leonora Howard, who later became famous as a physician to the aristocracy of China, was supported through medical school by the Methodist Episcopal Woman's Foreign Missionary Society. On the eve of her graduation

The Woman's Missionary

The stereotype of the woman missionary has ranged from the long-suffering wife, characterized by the epitaph: "Died, given over to hospitality," to the spinster in her unstylish dress and wire-rimmed glasses, alone somewhere for thirty years teaching "heathen" children. Like all caricatures, those of the exhausted wife and the frustrated old maid carry some truth: the underlying message of the stereotypes is that missionary women have been perceived as marginal to the central tasks of mission. Rather than being remembered for "preaching the gospel," the quintessential "male" task, missionary women have been noted for meeting human needs and helping others, sacrificing themselves without plan or reason, all for the sake of bringing the world to Jesus Christ.

—Dana L. Robert, *American Women in Mission*, xvi.

she went to a member of the Society in tears: "I will have to give up graduating after all," she lamented. Asked why, she went on to reveal the ladylike values survived her poverty and rigorous medical training: "My class [has] decided to wear silk, and I can't possibly get a silk dress." Yet, several years later, this same woman, on the basis of having lost an eye on a chaotic Peking street, formally requested the right to ride a horse to her house calls. Despite male fears that the outrageous sight of a white woman on horseback would be greeted by the Chinese with derision and threats, Dr. Howard got her way. Riding through the tumultuous city, she gamely ignored the children who shouted after her, "See the foreign devil riding a horse."[3]

Most gentlemen missionaries were only gradually (and never altogether) convinced that the ladies were their equals on the mission field. James Thoburn, one of the first Methodist missionaries to India and later a bishop, was relatively educable. When his sister Isabella first came to India, she stayed with him. He recalled later:

> A few days after my sister had commenced work I found myself pressed for time and asked her to copy a few letters for me. She did so cheerfully, and very soon I had occasion to repeat the request. The copying was again done for me, but this time I was quietly reminded that a copyist would be a great assistance to her as well as to myself. The remark made me think,

and I discovered that I had been putting a comparatively low estimate on all the work which missionaries (male) were not doing. Woman's work was at a discount, and I had to reconsider the situation and once [and] for all accept the fact that a Christian woman sent out into the field was a Christian missionary, and that her time and her rights were as sacred as those of the more conventional missionaries of the other sex. ...[4]

There was no "typical" woman missionary—they were strikingly individual. Nevertheless, they shared certain kinds of experiences. The prospective missionary usually grew up in a pious home where novels were a forbidden pleasure and the Bible, resting in its special place and reverently pored over at family devotions, held every secret for living and dying. Influenced by the godliness of her home, the budding evangelist sometimes played "missionary:" Mary Porter Gamewell, who was to go to China, transformed the chairs in her room into heathens and preached to them; Layona Glenn, later a missionary to Brazil, went further and held a revival meeting with some of her playmates—until the game became shockingly real with the tearful conversion of one of the children.

Hard work and self-discipline were honored, even in wealthy homes. In this atmosphere children were expected to strive for perfection, which for girls meant a special degree of obedience and submission. Probably the trauma that followed (when their inevitable human imperfection was reflected back in scriptural readings and Sunday sermons) was greater for the incipient woman missionary than for her brother because any show of independence or strength could be interpreted as a lack of female modesty *and* Christian humility. But to be "deeply convicted of sin" was to be on the threshold of conversion.

Conversion was an essential part of nearly every missionary's biography. It was so customary that James Thoburn, in a life of his sister Isabella, felt compelled to write an apologia, explaining why she apparently never experienced it—or showed any need for it. For most churchwomen it was what made them Christian. Long nights and days, sometimes months, of anguished prayer, accompanied by a crushing consciousness of unworthiness and futility, would suddenly be followed by release—an awareness, sometimes reinforced by visions, that sin was forgiven and that all life, including theirs, was in the hands of God. The only thing required of them was to surrender to God's direction.

For missionaries, conversion and the "divine call" to missionary service were frequently simultaneous. Though the "call" was no more universal than conversion, it was actually included among the qualifications for missionary

Primary Functions of Women's Missionary Societies

To found institutions and deploy personnel throughout the United States and the world;

To raise, budget, administer and publicly account for the expenditures of millions of dollars;

To supervise the construction and maintenance of buildings in which the work of evangelism, education and ministering to ill people took place;

To publicize their causes through magazines, leaflets, and other publications; and

To make policy for the further development of the program and financing of their organizations.

work by some societies. The experience of Carrie McMillan, a missionary to India, was unusual only because it occurred when she was seven years old:

> All alone, out in the fields, I wept and prayed until the light and love of the justified and pardoned came into my soul. Long as the cycles of eternity roll I think I can never forget the joy of that hour. At night, when alone in the darkness, I seemed to see the loving angels hovering over me, with wreaths of flowers in their hands. I cannot tell you how early this one thought entered my heart and filled my whole soul—that my lifework was in India![5]

She couldn't remember any influences or associations that might have stimulated this inspiration, and it led to a missionary career of more than 50 years.

At least one missionary was skeptical of "divine calls." The irrepressibly censorious Mary Sharp, impatient when the Methodist Episcopal woman's society hesitated to send her or any missionary to Africa, protested (in a letter to a bishop) some of the "apologies for women" that had been sent abroad.

> A few years ago I should have said, "I felt divinely impressed to go." Now I should not even say that. I have seen too much inefficiency professing to be divinely called. An absorbing desire "to do good both to the souls and bodies of men," and an ability and adaptation to a

certain work is sufficient call for me.⁶

Call or no call, women missionaries often met with opposition from their families. The angry father of one of Mrs. Butler's proteges threatened her with responsibility for his daughter's life should anything happen to the young woman. Mary Sharp was disowned, and Layona Glenn and her father were estranged for several years after he discovered her missionary ambitions. Public opinion did not always hold missionaries in high esteem either. In 1875 Milwaukee newspapers featured stories with headlines like "Bouncing Satan," "The Good Ladies Who Wrestle Among the Heathen," and "Strike the Hydra-Headed Monster Straight from the Shoulder."⁷ Julia Lore, about to leave for India, met a woman who looked at her quizzically and said, "Say, are you the one who is going as a missionary, and why? You haven't a wry neck or a crooked nose."⁸

Even the critical and the scornful agreed with devotees to missions on one point: lady missionaries were extraordinarily virtuous. On the field they were expected to navigate a contradictory course where they assumed authority, but remained retiring; spoke out strongly, but in soft modest tones; behaved with extravagant courage, but without ostentation. Under the weight of this ambivalence, few women had the unabashed self-confidence of a Mary Sharp. The healthiest missionaries were those who could feel honestly (at least most of the time) that their lives were in the hands of God, and who could forgive themselves their supposed failures because they believed that God had done as much. Failure on the mission field was more common than success, and the emotional, mental and physical demands on missionaries were enormous. They had to be prepared to live—and die — with Christian composure!

In the spring of 1898 word of a violent uprising of Africans reached a mission station in Sierra Leone. Five missionaries (three single women and a married couple) of the Woman's Missionary Association of the United Brethren Church were living there at the time. An English visitor recalled that the mission was "homelike, with an American air of 'go' and sincerity about the place."⁹ Though the group was warned of possible danger, they didn't really believe anything would happen to them. The rebellion was against the British government; they were Americans, and they were there for the good of the African. In addition, one of the women, 47-year-old Dr. Marietta Hatfield, was ill.

By the time the gravity of their situation became apparent, they were unable to secure the assistance of frightened boatmen or hammock men to carry the ailing Dr. Hatfield. They sent the mission children away to their homes,

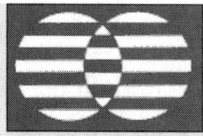

Undesignated Giving

From declaring to "walk the streets [of Boston] in calico dresses" to charging her children 1¢ for every stain on the dining room tablecloth, members of United Methodist Women and its predecessor organizations have been raising undesignated dollars for mission since the early 1800s. Today nearly 800,000 members pledge and raise over $20 million a year to support mission in the United States and 100 countries around the world. Undesignated giving, symbolized by the logo above, is comprised of five channels: the Pledge to Mission, the Special Mission Recognition, the Gift to Mission, the Gift in Memory and the World Thank Offering. When members ask, "What happens to my pledge-to-mission dollar?" they only have to look as far as the next issue of *Response* magazine or visit a nearby National Mission Institution (there are 103 nationwide). The undesignated giving of members of United Methodist Women touches the lives of many people around the world. The total program of United Methodist Women is mission, including mission education, spiritual growth, outreach and action. Look for the symbol for undesignated giving to see the variety of programs that are funded through your gifts to mission, and share the mission story of women organized for over 130 years.

except for one orphan who was like a member of the family, and hid out in the bush overnight, praying and imagining every rustle of leaves to be a grim-faced, spear-bearing enemy.

At dawn the group attempted to flee. Thomas, one of their young African parishioners, carried the small, wiry Marietta Hatfield on his back. The other women stumbled over the rough terrain in their long dresses, but none of them had gotten far when the war party caught up to them. Excitedly shouting threats, and dragging and kicking their captives, the warriors brought them back to the mission compound. Intent on their white victims, no one paid any attention to Thomas who crept like a shadow after them.

Terrified, peering through the bushes, Thomas witnessed the slaughter. Dr. Hatfield was hanging or leaning on a wire fence in front of the mission house, while a few yards away the others were stripped of their clothing. The warriors only had sticks and crude spears, so a London newspaper description of the missionaries being "literally hacked to pieces" was probably no exaggeration of what Thomas saw. All the while, the staid, self-controlled Dr. Hatfield looked up towards the cloudless sky and prayed, while Thomas burst into tears. The missionary became aware of him. "Don't cry, Thomas, it's all right." A few minutes later she was pulled to the middle of the road and killed.[10]

A far more common cause of death than "weapons-brandishing heathen" was disease. Lochie Rankin described her and her sister Dora's exposure to contagion in China:

> When we returned to the boat to go home, the woman's child cried so much that Dora inquired if the child was ill, and the woman indifferently replied: "No, not ill; he only has the smallpox." We got out, you may be sure, as soon as the boat could be pulled to the bank, and walked home, some four or five miles.[11]

In India, cholera and varieties of dysentery were common, and few missionaries, with the notable exception of the indomitable Mary Sharp, went to Africa without contracting "African fever." Health furloughs were inevitable, and many times the sufferer died on the journey home. Emma Michener went to Liberia at the same time as Mary Sharp, but lasted barely a year and a half. Her short career was crowded with troubles. On the voyage over, the ship foundered off the coast of Wales, and she spent hours in a drifting lifeboat. Finally arriving, the fragile young school teacher stayed in Monrovia for a few months, but soon went off into the interior, carried by African bearers over jungle trails. She was the only white person for 40 miles in every direction. Months later, back on the coast, she grew ill and almost died, but after being nursed by a black Baptist woman missionary, she was eventually well enough to teach an hour each day. When she got sick again, she steadfastly refused to leave the country, but finally consented to be taken back to Monrovia. She died on the way.

While the missionary society at home reverently recorded Emma Michener's last days, a Liberian churchman wrote to church officials that she was "in great affliction ... I think she is fast losing her mind, but she will not consent to leave the country."[12] "African fever" frequently affected the mind. When *The Heathen Woman's Friend* eulogized an early black woman missionary to Africa, Mary Sharp (always quick to relay unpleasant news) responded that it was rumored that the woman's last days were spent in mental affliction and drug addiction.

Mental breakdowns were not always related to disease. After two years Dr. Kate Bushnell returned from China suffering from "nervous prostration" caused by "anxiety and overwork."[13] Though she failed as a missionary, she was to become an important figure in the White Cross movement in the United States (organized for the protection of young girls). Dr. Harriet Woolston was not so fortunate. After only a year in India, she was pronounced "not satisfactory;" she died, insane, only a few years after her return.[14]

There is no concrete evidence as to what went awry with Dr. Woolston; it was not the kind of thing the woman's societies publicized. However, it is

Elida García de Falcón
Woman's Society of Christian Service
The Methodist Church

Elida García de Falcón was orphaned at the age of ten in Guerrero, Tamaulipas, Mexico. She made her home with her only sister, Rosaura, who had married one of the first Mexican Methodist ministers, Pedro Grado. With them she itinerated and attended mission schools, including Holding Institute in Laredo, Texas. She attended what is now Southwest Texas State College, taught in Texas public schools, was a writer and poet, and contributed to many of the Spanish newspapers published in Texas. From 1943–1964, Mrs. Falcón translated the *Program Book* into Spanish for the Woman's Division of Christian Service. Until illness intervened, she wrote out the translation, which was then typed by her daughter, Clotilde Falcón Nañez. Her daughter continued the work, and mother and daughter together spent twenty-six consecutive years translating. Mrs. Falcón also translated many of the hymns in the *Himnario Metodista,* the official hymnal of Hispanic Methodism in the United States. Her pastor wrote of her upon her death: "She is truly a saint. Many of the people of our city have gone to her home seeking a word of counsel, inspiration, and guidance. Her home has been the shelter for the sick and the needy."

—Excerpt from *They Went Out Not Knowing,* 15

likely that she suffered more than the usual degree of pressure to succeed, since she was a cousin of the eminently successful Woolston sisters of China. Her letters to *The Heathen Woman's Friend* tell of "an indescribable feeling of loneliness and pain, when I think of the distance that separates me from my loved ones." She was disappointed in the appearance of the country and upset by "toads, lizards, snakes that infest our houses. ... Will you laugh when I tell you I never pick up a shoe without examining it to see if there be a scorpion in it, or enter my dressing room, but I look around for a venomous snake, of which I have heard so much. ..." When Harriet Woolston was replaced, there were only a few patients straggling in occasionally, the medical records were in disarray, and the shelves were nearly bare of medicines.[15]

Another failure counted by the female missionary societies, though not necessarily by the missionaries, were the "hindrances and discouragements" created by matrimony.[16] Many single women married on the field, depleting the ranks of the woman's societies and adding to those of the general mission societies. Mrs. McGavock, president of the southern woman's organization, went out of her way to keep her workers single. On one occasion she disrupted plans and juggled schedules in order to send five young women out on a different ship from three male missionaries who were sailing at the same time. But, like so many best laid plans, this one "gang-aft agley": the men were stubborn and they were waiting on the wharf when the women arrived in [Asia]. Several years later they took wives from this group.

Occasionally, women missionaries turned out to be "ne'er-do-wells." Bishop Thoburn complained bitterly of a missionary who called on his sister Isabella for help. When Miss Thoburn, at some risk to her health, arrived to assist her, it was discovered that the woman was "more anxious to be rescued from some of her troubles than to do right." A few years later, while Isabella Thoburn was engaged in deaconess work in Chicago, she caught sight of the same woman on a city street,

> but the poor creature turned abruptly down another street to avoid recognition. It has been reported since that she was there awaiting the action of a divorce court, with the intention of contracting a so-called marriage with the husband of another woman as soon as the wicked farce of a so-called divorce could be enacted by a heathenish Chicago court. As a fitting sequel to the career of such a woman, it remains only to add that she is now engaged in lecturing on the beauties and profundities of Hinduism, and is said to have many admirers.[17]

Moral earnestness was required of a missionary. Certainly the work had few attractions except the joy of helping and converting others. Salaries were just barely adequate; hostility, disease and dirt made life, at best, uncomfortable; and excellence at tedious routine jobs was more in demand than romantic courage. To the missionary fell a vast array of duties—from marketing and planning meals for hundreds to supervising the construction of buildings, from keeping account books to administering schools and hospitals. She taught, she nursed, she counseled and reproved. She learned impossibly difficult languages like Chinese—"a work for men with bodies of brass, lungs of steel, heads of oak, hands of spring steel, eyes of eagles, hearts of apostles, memories of angels, and lives of Methuselah."[18] Moral earnestness was necessary, but as Mary Sharp put it, "grit is needed as well as grace."[19]

Another important qualification was a quick common sense in situations where the usual remedies were not available. When a child in the Woolston sisters' Chinese school fell and knocked out a tooth, Sarah Woolston speedily picked up both child and tooth, put the tooth back in its place and bandaged the child's mouth shut until it grew back again.

Common sense also required that missionaries live in healthful, even comfortable, situations. Mortality rates were high enough without trying to live under the same conditions as the majority of their charges. And so, homes

Mary Q. Porter Gamewell
Woman's Foreign
Missionary Society
Methodist Episcopal Church

In 1871, Mary Q. Porter Gamewell was appointed as one of two women sent to China by the Woman's Foreign Missionary Society of the Methodist Episcopal Church. She arrived in Peking, China, in April of 1872; and she and her missionary partner, Maria Brown, agreed that if they were able to begin a school, they would require that the girls unbind their feet. By August, they took in the first girls for the Peking Boarding School. Foot-binding was widespread among the Han Chinese upper and aspiring classes as a sign of beauty and virtue. The feet of little girls were bound so tightly with bandages that the bones broke and grew deformed so that the foot remained approximately six inches long or less. Girls suffered excruciating pain in the process and were crippled, made unable to work or even to walk. Porter's school was the first in China to require the unbinding of feet as a condition of admission. The difficulties of maintaining the unpopular position were so great that even though 150 girls applied for admission to the free school during its first two years, at the end of that time only seven girls were enrolled. By the 1880s, following the lead of Mary Porter, progressive Chinese and Chinese Christians increasingly joined women missionaries in efforts to ban social customs detrimental to women.

for missionaries were frequently the Virginia manse or the New England cottage transplanted to the heart of the Chinese empire or the African bush. Mary Sharp, who had money of her own, built herself "a handsome house, the showiest in the Republic,"[20] replete with Victorian gingerbread. But the practice of making real American homes in foreign lands exaggerated the tendency of some missionaries to stay aloof from cultures they could not easily comprehend or approve.

There were missionaries who, literally and figuratively, rarely got outside the walls of the mission compound. Layona Glenn in Brazil became "somewhat disgusted with those who hesitated and sometimes downright refused, to speak the [English] language or to use it in prayer."[21] Mary Porter Gamewell refers to a missionary "who all her life in China had suffered from fear of the Chinese, though she was devoted to those with whom she was well acquainted."[22] Mrs. Gamewell also complained that "even in providing ordinary comfort we give the impression of wealth ... the money we use seems to stand between us and the people we would reach, by force of the bad motives it creates. ..."[23] Again and again, she found that the hope of gain lay behind supposed conversions.

Mary "Q." Porter (discovering that there was another Mary Porter in Peking, she had whimsically given herself the middle initial "Q," for the Latin *quo* or what), who later married a fellow missionary, Frank Gamewell, was a pioneer with the Methodist Episcopal Woman's Foreign Missionary Society in southern and western China. Approximately 30 years in China left the Chinese people strangers to her, and her a remote figure to them. But even friends could write of her that she "seemed aloof and reserved until you got to know her."[24]

Mary Q. Porter's mother was a doctor, and she imparted to her daughter a sense of worth as a woman and as a person. But in spite of her strengths, and because of the comparative richness of her background, it could not have been easy to be "shut in a little world behind a twelve foot gray brick wall with eight of her countrymen, blue sky obscured by dust."[25] Outside, she and the other missionaries were hated and considered repulsive. Children ran from them and mothers shielded their offsprings' eyes, fearing the "foreign devils" would bewitch them. When the missionaries started a girls' school, the first child fled on her little bound feet as soon as she saw her teachers. They were the only foreigners she had ever seen, and she found their appearance terrifying.

Itinerating through the countryside was not much better. There were constant dust storms. Journey by canal boat was torturously slow and sometimes dangerous; overland travel could be worse. The story was told of "the man who left Tientsin in a cart and with the first propelling jerk of the mules, left his seat on the bottom of the cart and never landed there again until he reached Peking."[26] The inns were grimy and smoky, with a layer of grease over everything: dirt floors, brick platforms for beds, and as an extra attraction the smell of animals and their shuffling registering clearly through rice-paper-thin walls.

In the country the hostile Chinese were transformed into garrulous, curious crowds of women who chattered in "high-pitched, grating voices,"[27] picked at the lace at Mary Porter's wrists, asked her age and where her husband was, and eyed her every move closely. "I have been amused to notice," the missionary wrote, "that the expression with which some watch my movements and listen to my words is identical with the expression I have seen on faces intent on the antics of a monkey."[28]

Missionaries were expected, even under these conditions, to give unremitting attention to their work. Within a few years of Mary Porter's arrival, four women broke under the strain. Despite the fact that she worked at least as hard as any of them, she was able to survive to establish a successful school and church and to begin a Christian crusade against foot binding. Though she never grew to love China or the Chinese, she had enough imagination to understand their reluctance to accept the Christian message.

She also had pity, and a peculiarly strong, almost mystical faith. Writing to

Dora Rankin   Lochie Rankin

Dear Lord,
we pray for the men on the Board of Missions. Thou knowest how they have troubled and worried us. They have been hard to bear sometimes, but we thank thee that they are better than they used to be.

—Maria Gibson, Woman's Home Missionary Society, Methodist Episcopal Church, South

a friend, she described an experience of feeling "beaten" and "undone" that had begun with an awareness of the futility of her efforts to help others and ended with a fatigue and emptiness, overwhelming and entire; she sat inert, unable to cry or even pray. In this situation, with "every possibility of resistance gone," she was given peace and rest, an awareness of God's presence so palpable it was almost a vision, and an assurance that:

> All is well ... About serving God: *total* surrender is one condition. When you put yourself into his hands, and assert *no* will of your own as to what he shall do with you, then wait and trust; he will empty and fill again. He will show you by his spirit what to do and how to do it.[29]

Dora and Lochie Rankin, southern Methodist missionaries in Nantziang, China, had as strong a faith as Mary Porter Gamewell, though they were less reflective about it. They also had a genuine affection for the Chinese—and a sense of humor. Dora, the younger and more buoyant of the two, found the chopstick a special source of amusement when she first came to China as a novice missionary: "I always laugh when I see the Chinese eating," she wrote in a letter home.[30] Even when a sporadic war between French and Chinese sputtered around the mission home, both sisters found the Chinese soldiers more comic than threatening, with their "long, unkempt hair, wound loosely about the head; a uniform, the pattern of which would delight the heart of the crazy quilt maker, and dirty enough to frighten a regiment of French. They come to church and sometimes watch us play tennis."[31] Neither Dora nor Lochie ever recorded Chinese impressions of the two white ladies in their long, flowing dresses, batting a ball across a net, but they were well aware that the Chinese thought the foreigners just as peculiar. One evening when Dora sneezed, she overheard one man say to another: "They sneeze just like a native, but when they talk, it is different."[32]

In fact, it was a wonder that the white missionaries and their [Asian] neighbors achieved the close relationships they did. Chinese women felt a pity that bordered on contempt for the aliens born outside of the Celestial Kingdom. Even the most enlightened missionaries, dismayed by dirt and poverty, were slow to respect the Chinese or their culture. But Dora Rankin was fast on her way to becoming a Sinophile before her short career ended. On visiting a public garden, she described it as:

> a marvel of Oriental taste and skill, showing a decided difference between Eastern and Western ideas of beauty. I have been here so long that my ideas have become Easternized, no doubt, as of many things which I thought quite pretty and unique, new arrivals said: "Yes; they do very well for China."[33]

Dora and Lochie's pupils were devoted to them and they, in turn, were at least fond of the children. But disappointed like Mary Porter Gamewell by false converts, they distrusted many of their Chinese acquaintances. They were isolated most of the year from other missionaries and found that "living among Chinese unfits us for intercourse with society ... it is quite enough to make hermits of us."[34]

The sisters were passionately devoted to each other. When Dora died suddenly, Lochie wrote:

> From the first I was as one scarcely awakened from a fearful dream. We never paraded our love, but she was intertwined with every fiber of my being, and all my thoughts flowed out to her. Just before coming upstairs tonight a trifling incident occurred, and swiftly came the feeling: "I'll go and tell Dora." Do you wonder that my heart breaks anew every hour, almost every moment of the day?[35]

Immediately after Dora's death, Lochie went back to work. When someone suggested a possible change, she replied: "Dora was one half of my life; the

Laura Askew Haygood
Woman's Foreign
Missionary Society
Woman's Home
Missionary Society
Methodist Episcopal
Church, South

Born in Watkinsville, Georgia, Laura Haygood moved to Atlanta at age seven, received her early education from her mother, enrolled at Wesleyan Female College, Macon, Georgia, at age sixteen, and graduated in two years (1864). She established a private school for girls in 1866. In 1872, she was appointed teacher, and later principal, at Girls' High School, the first Atlanta public school for girls. During these years, her roots were deeply entrenched in Trinity Methodist Church in Atlanta. She pioneered there, in the organization of the Trinity Home Mission, a church home and industrial school to serve the poor and needy that later became a model for city mission projects. In 1883, she assisted in organizing the women's home mission work of the Methodist Episcopal Church, South. In her writings and speeches, she addressed issues of women's rights and the needs of the poor. In 1884, she decided to go to China. The McTyeire Home and School in Shanghai, completed and dedicated seven years after her arrival, remains today a visible symbol of her work. The Laura Haygood Normal School, built in 1916 in Soochow, China, also honors her work. She died in Shanghai, and was buried there.

—Excerpt from *They Went Out Not Knowing*, 5

work at Nantziang is the other. I cannot leave that."[36] For more than 30 years she continued her mission alone.

In 1891 Laura Haygood, in what could have been a reference to Lochie Rankin, wrote that living alone had helped her:

> to understand more thoroughly and to sympathize more tenderly with my fellow-workers who have become one-sided, or eccentric, or narrow, from living long in isolated places; apart from companionship that could help or strengthen. ... I see now that, given the same conditions, I might become as peculiar as any of them—I almost surely would.[37]

Laura Haygood's own loneliness was of another sort. Hers was the isolation of the administrator who made plans for others to enact. Not typical of the young teachers who became missionaries, Miss Haygood was the middle-aged sister of a bishop, a noted woman educator in the South, and the guiding light of city mission in Atlanta before she went to China. An impressive and authoritative figure, she was needed in China for her executive abilities and expertise in school administration. Perhaps no other missionary accomplished so much, and yet had so little intimate contact with the people she had come to help.

Not that she wasn't appreciated: "The Chinese pay great deference to my age and *size* and spectacles," she observed with amusement.[38] Other missionaries looked up to the poised, cultured woman even before she had learned the language or understood much about China. But like any leader, she suffered criticism from many who, in disagreement with her ideas, decided she was ambitious and dictatorial. At one point the criticism was so vociferous that she almost despaired: "For a while God even seemed to turn away from me. I felt that 'all His waves and billows had gone over me.' It was then that my heart had almost broken."[39]

Laura Haygood was one of those people others always called on for help. They could never imagine that this "larger-than-life-sized" woman could have any needs of her own. "I am troubled about much serving," she wrote, "and have so little time 'to sit with Mary at the Master's feet' that I am slowly starving while I am trying to feed others."[40]

Her isolation was intensified by a homesickness that grew less with the years, but never totally disappeared. Though she gradually became more comfortable in China, it was never home to her. For a while a close friendship with another missionary, Anna Muse, made mission life more enjoyable ... until Miss Muse left to be married. She brooded:

My heart is still too sore about Anna's new plans to say much about them. ... I cannot yet be glad about it. I have been trying to think for the past two weeks that my sorrow was all for the sake of "the work." I still think it is chiefly so, for I love her so well—this child of my heart's best affections—that I could but be glad for anything that brought such joy to her, whatever personal loss it might involve for me. Today I have been conscious that there is more of the personal—hence the selfish—in my grief than I knew before. ..."[41]

Towards the end of her short life in China, Laura Haygood spent a season itinerating by boat with a Chinese Bible woman. She relished the experience, but her health, which was never good, soon forced her to relinquish this happiness. Even this heightened contact with individual Chinese could not provide a satisfying relationship for a cultured American woman—for a reason Laura Haygood understood very well:

It is almost impossible to find congenial companionship with the Chinese. We may have Christian fellowship with them, and we often do; we may feel a warm affection for them, and for many we do; we may enter in some measure into their lives, because we make it the business of our lives to do that, and study them and their language and their literature to that end—but, save that part of our lives which has been given to work for and with them, our lives are closed

Isabella Thoburn College
Lucknow, India

In 1870, Isabella Thoburn, along with other devoted missionaries, established a school in Lucknow, India, to bring education to women and girls in Asia. Sixteen years later, there was a demand for higher education from its students, and the school grew into a college which opened as the first Women's College in India in 1886. Since its humble beginnings, the college has contributed richly to the leadership of Indian women. The first woman Indian Administrative Service officer, the first woman doctor, several women scientists and women in politics and positions of authority in education are the products of Isabella Thoburn College. Today, Isabella Thoburn College accepts the challenge that changing times can offer to educated women—the challenge of achieving without losing cultural moorings by balancing the demands and expectations of a traditional family culture and society. Isabella Thoburn College understands its mission to be that of empowering women to envisage for themselves the path and choices which will enable them to overcome existing cultural and societal constraints and be pacesetters in the future. Hence, its motto rings true: "We Receive to Give."

to them. All our past, our language, our literature—are blank to them. Can you imagine what it means to live in a Chinese city with not one of your own race near you?"[42]

After 10 years as a missionary, Laura Haygood died of cancer in Shanghai. Until it was too late to leave, she refused to return to the United States. There were still ways in which she could be useful. "I have tried to live for duty these many years," she answered her sister's pleas that she return.[43]

Just as Laura Haygood struggled with feelings of failure and loneliness, another missionary, in self-imposed isolation high in the Himalayas, suffered the same emotions. The rugged mountains suited Dr. Martha Sheldon's personality; she needed hard challenges. Her life was devoted to climbing both figurative and real mountains. The more difficult ascent was the one to Christian perfection. Her frailties troubled her so deeply that once she was on the verge of handing in her resignation.

But Dr. Sheldon's strong sense of her own flaws enabled her to identify and sympathize with the people she had come to convert: "Talk about the faults of the heathen! In myself, I find them all. But just as I know how the gospel of Christ helps me by giving me hope and courage, so do I know it will help them, my brothers and sisters. ..."[44]

Dr. Sheldon was not the only woman missionary living in the mountains. The English-born Annie Budden and her corps of Indian Bible women were evangelizing villages and nursing the sick. At Chandag Heights, Mary Reed lived with a colony of lepers. Miss Reed's loneliness was unique. She herself was a leper. But she was not subject to the anguish of Martha Sheldon because the leprosy was a "magic circle," a setting aside by God. She believed God had marked her for a clearly defined and circumscribed vocation. Even when some medical experts, noting her apparent health in the mountain environment, questioned the diagnosis of leprosy, she kept her faith in her peculiar call.

Mary Reed had no need or reason to scale mountain passes with Dr. Martha Sheldon and her sometime-companion, Eva Browne. Like that sturdy doctor, she could tend the sick, plant fields and orchards, and build homes for her new community. But Martha Sheldon was not content to serve and preach to her hill people; she had to press on. The same woman who read books in trees as a child was now able to climb formidable trails by horseback and foot, while frightened native coolies balked. Determined to reach "the forbidden land" of Tibet, she scrambled up a nearly perpendicular pass where the only path was a trail of goat and sheep manure. When she reached the barren, snow-covered top, 17,000 feet above sea level, she looked over into a Tibetan landscape lying "in a glare of sunshine" with "bare golden mountains and plains."[45]

Time and again the Tibetans refused her entry, fearing the pollution of an alien on their sacred land. Finally, in 1911, at the age of 51, her reputation as a doctor having preceded her, she was invited into that country to perform cataract operations. She took advantage of the opportunity to preach and sing the gospel.

On her last furlough to the United States, Martha Sheldon longed for her mountains and her tent. She was homesick for India. She, Annie Budden and Mary Reed all died and were buried in their beloved highlands, mourned by their large families of hill people. Annie Budden's death even prompted funeral orations from Muslim Moulvis and Hindu priests. Martha Sheldon, anxious over debts, stoically and silently suffering, but still laying plans for the future, died alone one morning as the sun rose. Her bed was half outside on the verandah, facing the mountains.

To all appearances another solitary missionary, Mary Sharp never suffered. Her pugnacious faith in herself was too strong. When Dr. Durbin (of the Methodist Episcopal Church's general missionary society) told her he did not expect any more missionaries to be appointed to Liberia for the time being because of the high mortality rate, she replied, "But doctor, I can live there."[46] She was 42 when she went to Africa, and she did *live* there—to the advanced age of 78.

Martha Ann Drummer
Woman's Foreign
Missionary Society
Methodist Episcopal Church

Martha Ann Drummer, one of seven children, was born in Barnesville, Georgia. Following her father's early death, her mother moved the family to Griffin, Georgia, to secure better educational opportunities for the children. Martha's minister secured a tuition scholarship for her to Clark College in Atlanta, and, while at Clark, she decided to become a missionary. Following graduation in 1901, she entered the Northwestern Deaconess Training School in Boston, majoring in nursing, and graduated in 1904. She was the second black missionary accepted for service by the Woman's Foreign Missionary Society, and sailed for Quessua, Angola, in 1906, after serving briefly with the Woman's Home Missionary Society. She served sixteen years in Angola and Portuguese West Africa. At her death, one who remembered her arrival in Africa twenty-nine years earlier stated: "It was a joy to know that a new missionary was coming, but our surprise and delight was [especially] great when we saw the new missionary was one of us, for she was black." Miss Drummer is remembered as a "true friend," "a firm teacher," "an evangelist," and a "healer of sick bodies."

—Excerpt from *They Went Out Not Knowing*, 16

Mary Sharp had little difficulty adjusting to Africa or to the African people. She was too sharp-tongued for friendship and too stringent to maintain any relationship but one of "boss," "teacher," or—as her "boys" called her—"mammy." She won their affection and respect with her single-minded devotion to their moral and intellectual cultivation; what she felt for them was the attachment of a superior for her inferiors.

But Mary Sharp had little respect for most people. During the first years of her career, the situation of the mission in Liberia was chaotic. There was an inordinate amount of scandal and Miss Sharp liked nothing more than scandal. In an age when most people emphasized the positive and virtuous to the total diminution of the negative, she kept a critical eye out for the worst in everyone. Most disturbing to those around her, she was usually accurate.

Mary Sharp worked with the Kroo tribe in the environs of Monrovia, establishing a large and mostly male congregation. She found the women difficult to reach. They made a broad distinction between the men's salvation and their own and were apathetic towards the new religion. Needless to say, the Woman's Foreign Missionary Society was not pleased that Mary Sharp was converting only males. But that was not the only reason they recalled her—they could not have helped but take offense at the woman who once remarked to a bishop: "The 'Women's Board has sometimes struck me as a sort of big kindergarten affair, rather than an enterprise bent on the conversion of the world."[47] She brooked no timidity, no hesitation, no failure.

Not at all discouraged by the recall, and with no intention of heeding it, Mary Sharp, who had an independent income, went on with her work. She was almost a legendary figure among her followers; she built churches and made converts, and enthusiastically outlasted and outlived everyone with the same efficiency with which she finally emptied Krootown of Catholic missionaries, "My voice that helps greatly in the work (not from its melody, but from its force) came in good. After three years and no following they abandoned the field, and left me sole possessor."[48]

When she finally died, Mary Sharp was not buried in the cemetery with the other white missionaries, but among some of her Kroo converts. On the gravestone was the inscription: "Mary A. Sharp, 1837–1914, Erected to Honor the Memory of Our 'Mammy' By Her Boys and the Kroo Church."[49]

Mary Sharp was not the only woman missionary who found herself working with men instead of women. One early Methodist Protestant Woman's Society missionary "had to be restrained from evangelizing efforts among men and boys."[50] The Society later relented, and both the Methodist Protestant and United Brethren women sent out missionaries of both sexes who worked for the conversion of men as well as women. Lochie Rankin once wrote, "The men of China must be reached. It is worse than nonsense to talk of elevating the women of any country while the men remain ignorant, superstitious, and prejudiced against everything good and ennobling."[51] It was impossible that woman missionaries limit their ministry to women. Nevertheless, most of them focused their energies on their foreign sisters.

Isabella Thoburn was one of the most impressive female educators in India. To hundreds of Indian women she was a friend and a parent. It was difficult to imagine that she had ever been a child. She was robust, always dignified, with a simple, direct manner, as if she had been born venerable. A motherly woman, her own mother was a pivotal figure in her life. When asked once why she had come to India, she replied, "It was my mother. She made us feel that we must help those who need us most."[52]

In the first half of the 19th century, one of the leading missionary educators of India declared that "to attempt female education in that country was as hopeless as to try to scale a wall five hundred yards high."[53] At Lucknow in April 1870, Miss Thoburn opened her first school in India. The only building she was able to find was one room standing on a noisy thoroughfare "in sight and in dust of all the passersby."[54] A boy with a stout bamboo stick stood guard at the door while six girls, duly chaperoned by relatives, began their

Bible Women

Bible women, or indigenous women hired to do evangelistic work, were a product of the late 19th century woman's missionary movement. The use of indigenous women as evangelists was not seen as a priority for denominational boards prior to the advent of the woman's missionary movement. The first Bible woman hired by Methodist women in India was paid for in 1861 by the newly-formed Woman's Union Missionary Society. While the role of "evangelist" was open to women missionaries in the Woman's Foreign Missionary Society, its implications were problematic because of the bias toward employing indigenous women to do most of the evangelistic work. Bible women were both cheaper to support and more effective as evangelists than western women. Methodist women were more likely to find themselves training Bible women than serving as evangelists themselves. By 1909, the woman's missionary movement had employed 441 missionaries as "evangelists," but it had hired 6,154 Bible women. The Women's Division has revitalized the training of Bible women in recent years in many countries in Asia based upon our foremothers' principles and mission philosophies.

first lessons.

Though it was expected that Hindu and Muslim men would be hostile to the education of their daughters and child-wives, many male English and American missionaries proved no more encouraging. But gradually, with the skill of a diplomat, Isabella Thoburn went about breaking down their prejudice. She said in a speech in 1882:

> Ten years ago missionaries who were preparing boys for the university degrees insisted that their sisters would be spoiled if taught English. Less than half of ten years ago I have myself turned a blackboard to the wall to hide a geometrical diagram, when visitors were announced who would be grieved, if not shocked, at what they considered wholly out of place in a girls' school. When the girls had matriculated, and had brought up the whole tone of the school, lifting the ambition of its pupils from idleness and dress to work and study, observers were convinced, and it was no longer necessary to avoid argument by concealing the unfinished work of the upper classes.[55]

In 1871 Lal Bagh (or Ruby Garden), the former home of a royal treasurer, was offered for sale at a low price to the Methodist mission. Shortly after, Isabella Thoburn's school was moved onto the exotic estate. By 1880 there were 132 pupils—and in 1887 Miss Thoburn started the first Christian woman's college in Asia.

At first there was no money for staff or materials, and only a few college level courses were offered. On a health furlough in the United States, Miss Thoburn finally convinced the Woman's Society to give her its official support—but fundraising was left up to her. In *The Heathen Woman's Friend* she pursued her goal:

> We have taught them that, though women, they have minds that are capable of receiving education and that they require it. Shall we now teach them that they require less, and are less capable than their brothers? For them missionary societies provide schools of all grades, and not only for these Christian brothers, but for those who are still idolaters. In all Eastern countries, missionary societies supplement the work of the governments by establishing colleges for young men. But in all Asia there has not been one for young women until now, and even now there is little sympathy with the attempt that is being made. "It is too soon," they say. "The expenditure required is too great for the number asking the benefit. Such a high degree of education is not needed yet."[56]

Lal Bagh flourished, and was followed by other women's schools, like Laura Haygood's McTyeire College in China. These schools and other Christian institutions produced women who were to change the almost universal opinion of the inferiority of their sex. In 1900 Lilivati Singh, one of Miss Thoburn's first pupils, came to the United States with her teacher. By that time, the young Indian woman had a master of arts degree and was a teacher at Lal Bagh. On hearing her speak, former President Benjamin Harrison remarked, "If I had given a million dollars to foreign missions, and was assured that no result had come from it all except the evolution of one such woman as that, I should feel amply repaid for the expenditure."[57]

Miss Singh and Isabella Thoburn were intimates. The Methodist educator had a faculty for making friendships with people of every age and from every stratum of society. Without seeming in the least strained, she always had time for everyone. She would nurse an old woman with smallpox or prepare the body of a dead girl for burial, tell fairy tales to children, make wedding clothes, entertain at leisure and still perform her regular duties which ran the gamut from administration to teaching to editing a magazine for Indian women. Lal Bagh came to be thought of as the unofficial headquarters of Methodism in India: "The latch-string was always out … and the head of the house was always at the door to greet those who came her way."[58]

It was as a teacher that Isabella Thoburn excelled. "She taught us English

Virginia (Jennie) Atkinson
Woman's Foreign
Missionary Society
Methodist Episcopal
Church, South

Virginia "Jennie" Atkinson was a Methodist Episcopal Church, South, missionary in China from 1884–1940. After graduating from LaGrange Female College in Georgia, she went to China in October 1884 with Laura Haygood. Working primarily in the Shanghai and Soochow regions, Atkinson taught, was instrumental in establishing several schools, and involved in women's work. In Soochow she was placed in charge of the city day schools under the Woman's Board and later established a center in the western part of the city which accommodated four of the schools. She founded the Atkinson Academy for Boys in 1896 and the Davidson Girls' School. When the Boxer Rebellion erupted, she took many Chinese Christians to Japan. In 1901 Jennie returned to Soochow and continued her work with the day schools. During this period of her work another center, the Embroidery Mission, was opened, providing evangelistic work, teaching and housing many Chinese women. Upon her retirement in 1927 with emeritus status, she received special permission to stay in China near Soochow, remaining through the Japanese invasion, ministering to the Chinese. Due to poor health and the growing threat of war, Atkinson eventually left China in 1940. She was later buried in China.

literature," remembered Lilivati Singh, "and I can never forget how her enthusiasm for heroes and poets kindled a like enthusiasm in us." They learned the names of flowers and how to tell the age of a tree ... "these are simple things for educated people, but O what a world they opened to us!"[59]

For centuries women had accepted the judgment that they were subhuman. In an area of China, missionaries found that nearly all of their female converts had disposed of one or more daughters before becoming Christians (there was an instance in which a woman discarded nine out of the 10 girl children born to her). The historian Helen Barrett Montgomery wrote in 1900:

> Twenty years ago the boys in mission schools were fond of arguing that women had no souls and could not be saved, much in the same line that slaveholders used to argue about blacks. The sight of girls actually doing what their brothers do, and that equally well, is mentally disturbing, is, in fact, a social ferment of the most violent kind.[60]

Through education, example and even legislation, women missionaries helped to transform the lives of women on every continent. Dr. Nancy Mansell agitated successfully in India for a law forbidding the marriage of girls under 12. China missionaries freed the bound feet of their female converts. Female doctors and hospitals not only relieved the suffering of women whose customs strictly forbade their being attended by male doctors; they gave women a sense of their own value as human beings. "The world was made for women also," rejoiced a Hindu woman after a month's stay in a hospital where she had seen caste and outcaste women treated with equal respect.[61]

In many places just the sight of unescorted women missionaries, whose actions showed them to be anything but "loose," had a positive effect on both men and women. A missionary in Rosario, Argentina, did "an unheard of thing" by attending courses of lectures on the natural sciences; local women soon joined her, "and the men, seeing women present, sat the whole evening without lighting a cigar."[62]

Girls' schools produced a new kind of woman—independent, educated and even physically stronger because of being saved from too early marriage and childbirth. These lively institutions also inspired innovations in teaching methods. Reported Mrs. Montgomery:

> In fact these missionary school-ma'ams may fairly claim to be the pioneers in the New Education. While the schools in the home land were still bowing down in blind worship to the three R's, these progressive ladies, spurred on by necessity, were finding that hand-work seemed a powerful stimulus to brain-work, and that children taught to do things actually learned better than those who pored over their books the whole time. Hence object-lessons, expression work, manual training, domestic art, were flourishing in missions before ever fads and frills began to agitate a scandalized and belated public at home.[63]

But the missionaries not only opened schools—they went to women in their homes. The isolated "zenana" women of India, who were rarely permitted to leave the dark, secluded chambers reserved for them, were visited by foreign missionary women who brought them word of a larger world. Despite strict caste laws that sometimes required long fasts and purification rites afterwards, the women emerged from their walled-in prisons to attend "zenana parties." Hindu, Muslim and Christian women mixed for the first time, shyly talked together, and perhaps took a stroll in the mission garden—well out of sight of the contaminating gaze of unfamiliar men. One Muslim woman, after viewing stereopticon slides at a party, told her family that she had seen "buildings, animals, flowers, trees, men, women, the moon, the stars, the sun, clouds, lightning; that there was nothing more for her to see but God. If she saw Him, her life would be finished."[64]

The women of remote cultures were not the only ones who were being educated. Both the missionaries and the women's societies were growing in

Olive Hodges
Methodist Protestant Church

I desire, then, that in every place the men should pray, lifting up holy hands without anger or argument; also that the women should dress themselves modestly and decently in suitable clothing, not with their hair braided, or with gold, pearls, or expensive clothes, but with good works, as is proper for women who profess reverence for God. Let a woman learn in silence with full submission. I permit no woman to teach or to have authority over a man; she is to keep silent. For Adam was formed first, then Eve; and Adam was not deceived, but the woman was deceived and became a transgressor. Yet she will be saved through childbearing, provided they continue in faith and love and holiness, with modesty.

—I Timothy 2:8–15

understanding and foreign women were no longer merely pitied, they were now respected. Symptomatic of this transformation was the change in title of *The Heathen Woman's Friend*. In 1893 the ladies redesigned the cover so that a vine wound about and across the word "Heathen," making it less conspicuous. By 1896 so much objection was taken to the word, especially by missionaries, that the periodical was renamed *Woman's Missionary Friend*.

The missionary had come to honor her adopted home. Lilivati Singh recalled that she once affected Western dress, but later discarded it: "… She (Isabella Thoburn) made me love India; she planted true patriotism in me, so that I gave up foreign dress myself."[65]

Not only did the missionary respect her alien home—she loved it. When Laura Haygood was on her deathbed, she spoke to her Chinese students through a translator. A few years later, Lilivati Singh witnessed Isabella Thoburn's death.

> In her pain and agony she kept speaking Hindustani. It nearly broke my heart to hear her. She had lived for us, and she was dying for us; she was so one of us that in her last moments she forgot her own tongue and spoke in ours. There was no one like her—our dear, devoted friend.[66]

Perhaps no missionary belonged more to her second country than Virginia (Jennie) Atkinson. "As I saw it," a friend remembered, "the Chinese respected the missionaries in general, but they loved Jennie Atkinson."[67]

At the age of eight Jennie was sent by train to her father's cousin with a label pinned to her coat. She had already lost a mother and a stepmother, and a prospective third mother didn't want her. No one was at the station to meet the child. The cousin didn't really want her either—he had been promised a boy. In spite of his reluctance, he took her in, provided for her, and gave her an education.

Despite deeply-rooted feelings of inferiority, Jennie Atkinson, out of conscientiousness and devotion to her church, volunteered to go to China as a missionary. She went out at the same time as several other women, including Laura Haygood whose poise and eloquence left her feeling more inadequate than ever. In Denver, on their way to a ship bound from San Francisco to [Asia], they met a Chinese man on the street. "I was so frightened that I had to step back and let the others meet him first," Jennie remembered. She was afraid of nearly everything—strange people, storms, boats, water. ..."[68] In Shanghai Laura Haygood was to write, "I simply do not know what to do with Jennie Atkinson."[69]

The frightened Miss Atkinson became an able missionary and lived 56 of her 80 years in China. Her timidity and self-deprecation (what Mary Culler White called her "pernicious humility," a "rare" and "absolutely incurable" disease), fitted with Chinese ideas and propriety.[70] They liked her, and she liked them. She proved to be an efficient teacher and administrator—and brave, though she may have shown more tremulousness than the garden variety of brave women.

In Soochow, an extremely conservative city with a bias against foreigners and education for girls, she and a Chinese friend, Mrs. Zah, limped through the crowded streets from school to school (Jennie had bunions and Mrs. Zah had bound feet). Learning that Mrs. Zah, in desperate need, had sold her daughter some years before becoming a Christian, Jennie set off to buy the girl back. It was an unheard-of venture, but she succeeded. The daughter and Jennie became close friends, and a long time after the grateful daughter bought a burial plot for the missionary next to her own.

Every time Jennie Atkinson was called on to take a furlough, she balked. She could not face the public speaking engagements she would be expected to undertake, although if she could have spoken in Chinese instead of English, it might not have seemed so impossible. Her second furlough came as a shock to the Chinese as well as to the missionary. By then they had forgotten that she was a foreigner: "they thought she belonged to China in the same way that they did."[71] Other missionaries got farewell gifts and parties, but her send-off was spectacular. Forty-five boys in navy suits headed up the parade, followed by Jennie in a mandarin's chair with a red umbrella, a mounted escort and a line of sedan chairs stretching a city block. By then her hair had grayed and she'd put on weight, characteristics the Chinese honored (and on her— revered).

The first half of the 20th century was a tumultuous time in China, filled with war and anti-foreign feeling. Nevertheless, Virginia Atkinson fought another furlough in the 1920s; she was 65 years old, and she feared she would be forced into retirement if she returned to the United States. At the 50th anniversary celebration of southern Methodism's Woman's Board of Foreign Missions, she and the unhappily retired Lochie Rankin, who was also homesick for China, went off between sessions to comfort each other with their memories.

Virginia Atkinson got to go back to Soochow again. This time, the Chinese, intent on keeping their "spiritual mother" with them, built her a house. But when the Japanese occupied the city, she was finally persuaded to go back to America "for the good of the Chinese." Fraternizing with Americans was frowned upon by the invaders. Feeling out of place and like an alien in the land of her birth, she died in Memphis, Tennessee, still begging to be allowed to return to the only real home she had ever known.

Jennie Atkinson was not unique in her love of her missionary home. When the

The Missionary's Bride

Who'd be a missionary's Bride,
Who that is young and fair
Would leave the world and all beside,
Its pomp and vanity and pride,
Her Saviour's cross to bear?
None—save she whose heart is meet
Who feels another's pain
And loves to wipe from sorrow's cheek
The trickling tear—and accents speak
That soothe the soul again.
She who feels for them that need
The precious bread of life.
And longs the Saviour's lambs to feed
O, such an one would make indeed
A missionary's wife!

—written in the album of Abigail Smith by Betsey Learned, 1832 and quoted in Mary Dillingham Frear, *Lowell and Abigail: A Realistic Idyll*, New Haven: Privately Printed, 1934, 22

Japanese came into Mary Culler White's section of China, she, like many others, ran. "But I was careful to run *inward*—toward China's great interior—rather than outward toward one of the port cities. I wanted to remain with my Chinese friends, and I fondly hoped to find a place so small that the Japanese would overlook it. ..."[72]

Olive Hodges, a tall, austere woman, originally a missionary of the Methodist Protestant Church, stayed in Japan as long as she could during World War II. Interned, she was finally repatriated in 1943, and worked with the Nisei in Washington, D.C., for the duration of the war. Used to Japanese restraint, she was disconcerted by the Americans' open display of affection and had adopted the habit of bowing from the waist on being introduced. In 1950 she returned to Japan and lived there until her death.

They were myriad—these women whose best affections lay in the land of their missionary labors. An evangelist educator, Laura Mauk, stubbornly refused to leave Japan and was interned throughout the war. She weighed only 50 pounds on her release, but she had converted the internment camp's directors. Lottie Spessard, a United Brethren missionary to the Philippines, dodged the invading Japanese army in the mountains until 1945, when she was commissioned a second lieutenant in the Philippine army.

The lady missionary had metamorphosed. From her first shocked gaze at a foreign race, she pursued her ideal of service into alien hamlets and cities, bush and mountains, and discovered she was capable of heroic labors. She wanted to change the world, but found the relation could only be reciprocal: the world changed her. Pity and duty were transmuted into love and respect—and sisterhood was no longer a rallying cry. It was a reality.

Program Guide

WORSHIP CENTER

Prepare a simple worship table or designate a space for some candles and an opened Bible. You will need matches to light the candles at the appropriate time.

FOCUS STATEMENT

This is a story of Protestant Christian mission and women's involvement. It is the story of the struggle for women's rights in church and society. "If it can give [you] some sense of [your] own history (or herstory), some feeling for [your] beginnings, then it will have fulfilled its aim."[73] We are here to communicate the struggle of our foremothers in the Methodist tradition and to gain a new perspective on their life and work. As we read, study, discuss, reflect, pray and worship, may we come to appreciate the course they have charted for our future as women organized for mission and accept our role to continue the story and the journey toward women's full and equal participation as partners in God's mission.

OPENING WORSHIP

CALL TO COMMUNITY FOR STUDY AND REFLECTION:

As the leader reads the focus statement (see above), one member of the group lights the candles on the worship table. Another member then reads the Scripture.

SCRIPTURE: I Corinthians 12:12–27

Leader: We share our stories.

All: Each of us brings a unique story and gifts from God.

Leader: Our stories are about journeys of faith.

All: We walk a path of righteousness.

Leader:	We share our path with all creation.
All:	**We are all related.**[74]
HYMN:	"The Golden Rule She Has Pursued" (*Global Praise 1*, #53)
PRAYER:	"God of Power and Joy"[75]
Leader:	God of power and joy, of calling and vision and hope, you have endowed us with limitless desire, and sisters with whom to sing. Let us bless our sisters: whose greeting fills us with joy; whose presence gives us speech; whose love we acclaim with pride; with whom we need hold back nothing.
All:	**Blessed is she who has believed. God's promise will be fulfilled.**
Leader:	Let us bless our sisters: whose yearning leaps to greet our own; who are not diminished by our power; whose wisdom discerns our soul; who embrace what we shall become.
All:	**Blessed is she who has believed. God's promise will be fulfilled.**
Leader:	Let us bless our sisters: who have stirred us to new vision; whose courage lets us act; with whom we proclaim on the housetops the dreams we have held in secret.
All:	**Blessed is she who has believed. God's promise will be fulfilled. Amen.**

QUESTIONS FOR DISCUSSION AND REFLECTION

Together, reflect on these questions. List examples from the fourth chapter of Conduct, *"Grit is Needed as Well as Grace," and make any obvious connections with previous chapters.*

1. What were the main reasons why the women's missionary societies established foreign missions?
2. What characteristics and attributes were needed to be a woman missionary?
3. For those women who accepted the "divine call" to missionary service, what challenges and obstacles did they experience? What effect did these have on them?

4. What were the basic qualifications and duties of the woman missionary?
5. How was the woman missionary received and perceived by those she went to serve? How did she respond to these receptions and perceptions? What effect did these have on her and her mission?
6. What impact did the woman missionary have on those she served? On the church and its overall mission work?

A VOICE FROM THE PAST

Share this quote with the group and invite brief reflections.

Can one love God and yet believe that he is right in attempting to restrict his neighbor's knowledge—the growth of his mind—to that which will restrict his neighbor's livelihood? His neighbor's share in the conduct of the community? Can one love God and serve him with open mind and open heart and still wish for his neighbor less than he has for himself? Consider his neighbor to possess less human dignity? To be worthy of less courtesy and respect? To need fewer physical comforts and cultural opportunities? No! Surely none of these things are the love of God, nor are these the acts of brotherhood.

—Mary McLeod Bethune,
"We march forward to brotherhood,"
sermon given at Riverside Church, New York City, November 13, 1949

RISING TO THE CHALLENGE

For this portion of the session, you will invite each member of the group to select one woman from the list, review her story as it is presented in the chapter and retell her story to the rest of the group in first person, narrative form—as if the story were her own. Each group member will also create a "quilt" square of the woman she is representing to the group and add it to the "quilt."

- Mary Q. Porter Gamewell
- Dora and Lochie Rankin
- Laura Haygood
- Martha Sheldon
- Mary Sharp
- Isabella Thoburn
- Jennie Atkinson

CLOSING WORSHIP

SCRIPTURE: Luke 10:25–37

Leader: For over 130 years, United Methodist Women and its predecessor organizations have been organized for mission. Will you covenant with me to know and tell the story of mission with excitement and enthusiasm?

All: **Yes! Count me in!**

Leader: United Methodist Women is an organization of women moving the world in Christ's direction. Will you participate in the continuing vision to involve women of all ages in the ongoing story of United Methodist Women organized for mission?

All: **Yes! Count me in!**

Leader: We are a community of women who are faithful to God and to our history as women organized for mission. Will you remain faithful to our Christian mission heritage?

All: **Yes! Count me in!**

Leader: We are a community of women who are purposeful. Knowing God, experiencing freedom as whole persons through Jesus Christ, developing creative supportive fellowship, and expanding concepts of mission through participation in the global ministries of the church are central to our organization. Will you interpret the PURPOSE of United Methodist Women?

All: **Yes! Count me in!**

Leader: We are a community of women who are supportive: offering Christian friendship, seeking diversity in age, family situations, race, income, language and employment. Will you be a supportive community for all women?

All: **Yes! Count me in!**

Leader: We are a community of women who are unique: more than a million women organized in local units across the United States, circling the globe with networks, combining each person's unique gifts and journey to ensure ministries with women and ministries with children and youth around the world, supporting missions through five channels of undesignated giving. Will you tell the unique story of United Methodist Women?

All: Yes! Count me in!

Leader: We are a community of women who are global: supporting mission personnel with prayers and offerings and joining with women worldwide to fulfill God's mission. Will you support the global mission of United Methodist Women?

All: Yes! Count me in!

Leader: We are a community of women who are responsive: celebrating the joys and responding to the hurts and pains of others, engaging in the study of social issues, breaking down the barriers that separate us, advocating for legislation that affirms every person's human rights, and working with other organizations for the common good. Will you respond to the needs and concerns of all people in God's world?

All: Yes! Count me in!

HYMN: "You Are the Seed" (*The United Methodist Hymnal*, #583)

PREPARING FOR THE NEXT SESSION

Before the group is dismissed, the leader should highlight the following opportunities for study and reflection beyond the session. Remember to select a leader and make any assignments, as needed, in preparation for the next group session.

1. Continue to reflect on the questions from chapter four, "Grit is Needed as Well as Grace," and make additional notes in your journal.
2. Read the next chapter, "They Carried Flowers Day by Day into Malodorous Abodes," in preparation for the next session.

3. Review the questions for discussion and reflection in the program guide that follows chapter five, "They Carried Flowers Day by Day into Malodorous Abodes." Begin to make notes on your thoughts and feelings related to the material in this chapter.
4. Continue to explore your own history (herstory) by working on your personal timeline. See "Suggestions for Individual and Group Study" on page xi for details.
5. Continue to work on your "quilt" squares, if you choose, between the sessions.
6. Select one woman from the list on page 134 of the next chapter's program guide and prepare to tell her story as if it were your own. *Note: The group leader for the next session may wish to "assign" one woman to each group member to avoid overlap.*

SENDING FORTH

Leader: Now to God who by the power at work within us is able to accomplish abundantly far more than all we can ask or imagine, to God be glory in the church and in Christ Jesus to all generations, forever and ever.

—Ephesians 3:20–21

All: **Amen.**

As the group disperses—sharing signs of God's peace, if desired—the leader extinguishes the candles.

THEY CARRIED FLOWERS
DAY BY DAY INTO
MALODOROUS ABODES

In a small Kentucky town one evening, a policeman knocked at the door of a church. Two women responded, and at his request they left with him and walked to a ramshackle boardinghouse. There, he took them to a squalid room where they were introduced to a young unmarried mother who explained tearfully that she could not support her baby and wanted to give it away; the churchwomen took custody of the infant. The memory of that night never ceased to trouble them. They had discovered a wrong, and they yearned to right it. And like women all over the country in the second half of the 19th century, they decided to organize in order to accomplish their ends. A Woman's Christian Association was formed, and within a few years they were able to build a refuge for "unfortunate women" and their children.

Home missions happened like that—naturally, inevitably. Long before women ventured to alien corners of the world, they were visiting the impoverished and sick and collecting clothing and money for their own neighborhood poor as well as for American Indian mission stations. But their ultimate aim was to evangelize. Since poverty was associated with sin and prosperity with righteousness (though a few were thought to have combined wealth and wickedness), what was required to restore the indigent to society was the Christian gospel, and every other form of help was considered incidental. When the inner man was converted to godly living, then hard work, cleanliness and punctuality would bring their ultimate economic—and spiritual—rewards.

The years were to transform radically this simplistic analysis. The country grew larger and more complicated, and women emerging from their homes into a world electric with social change found themselves grappling with the most intricate moral issues of their day. Through educational and welfare institutions, temperance crusades, woman's rights and minority rights struggles, they tried to recreate America in their own image. The cultured

Alma Mathews House

Immigrant Girls' Home originated in 1888 as one of the earliest projects of the Woman's Home Missionary Society. The Society provided money to start the Home to assist the large number of girls arriving in the United States without sponsorship, frightened in the new surroundings, without friends or family, and not speaking English. Opened in temporary quarters in New York City, it moved in 1891 to a five-story building and later to its present location in the two brownstones in Greenwich Village, New York City—purchased in 1927 and 1957. The name change occurred in 1928 to honor the retirement of Miss Alma Mathews who had worked among the immigrant women for almost 40 years. During her unwavering years of service, Miss Mathews distributed clothing and religious tracts, wrote letters and sent telegrams to help the women find placement, and brought young women to the home for temporary lodging. For many years 500 to 800 young women were sheltered each year. As immigration patterns changed in the 1930s, Alma Mathews House was a cooperative residence for business and professional women in the lower salaried group. In the centennial year of Alma Mathews House, the Women's Division contracted with the National Parks Service, U.S. Department of Interior, to display the Immigrant Girls' Home plaque at the Ellis Island Museum. Since 1982, Alma Mathews House has served as the Women's Division Conference Center for the many volunteers who come to New York to conduct the business of The United Methodist Church.

Christian lady was the bulwark of the family, and the Protestant family was the heart and soul of America. They succeeded in feeding, clothing and schooling hundreds of thousands who were then sent out into society to work and make homes and churches. But while this effort went on to press the world into an idealized 19th century Protestant mold, two unexpected shifts occurred: the women were changed, and the mold broke. Protestant America became a polyglot of languages and cultures, of religions and irreligious. The "lady," who had existed only in the public mind, began to disappear altogether when the actual individuals who tried to exist in her image grew too busy with their real work in the world to pay homage to fantasies.

The early foreign missions organizers were also involved in home missions. The first business of the New York Female Missionary Society was to make collections for work with the American Indian, and Mary Mason, its president, was only one of a number of prominent Methodist women who distributed tracts in city slums and visited the city prison. In 1844 some of these women started the New York Ladies' Home Missionary Society with the object of supporting a missionary (male, of course) "to preach the gospel, visit the poor, the sick and friendless in lanes and alleys of our city to converse and pray with them."[1] In 1850, at the instigation of Mrs. Phoebe Palmer, a famed Methodist revivalist and author, the women undertook support of the Five Points Mission in one of the city's bleakest neighborhoods. A precursor of later settlement houses and community centers, the mission contained a chapel, schoolroom, baths and 20 rent-free apartments. Besides Phoebe Palmer, its founders included some of the women who later organized the Woman's Foreign Missionary Society: Mrs. Wright, a "bonnet-maker for the elite" as well as the widow of a man who was both governor and senator of Indiana, and the dignified Mrs. Skidmore. (History has it that the two women had frequent differences of opinion.) So involved was Mrs. Skidmore in the work of the city mission, that she at first refused to join the Foreign Missionary Society. She never skimped on any of her duties to spare herself, and in time her hands were gnarled from long hours of such activities as sewing children's clothes.

Home missions were not always popular. At the eighth annual meeting of the Methodist Protestant Woman's Home Missionary Society, there were no officers present, and foreign missions leaders presided. The report given of the meeting was short and succinct, noting a budget of around $200 and "a clear lack of some definite purpose."[2] Though domestic missions in other denominations fared far better, the Methodist Protestant assembly displayed symptoms of an extraordinary turnabout in public opinion. For years there had been voices in the churches decrying foreign missions and declaring there were more than enough souls in need of salvation at home. But after the foreign adventure was securely entrenched as a natural and incontestable part of the church's destiny, home missions took on an unwanted aspect. The women who organized the societies not only had to contend with apathy and male opposition, but with the hostilities of those who feared competition with foreign missions. One Missouri pastor, noting the demise of a home missions society in his church, sarcastically pronounced, "I can only say, 'Peace be to its ashes.'"[3]

Nevertheless, large numbers of women had a part in foreign and home fields. The United Brethren and Evangelical societies worked in both. Organizers in home missions in northern and southern Methodist churches were frequently active in foreign missions programs as well. The same methods of raising funds were employed, literature and periodicals were published, and local societies were organized by hardy travelers. And though missionaries in the United States were never as glamorous to the public as those abroad, the home missions societies, once established, grew swiftly and involved thousands of women.

The greatest impetus to women's activities came about through a secular, not a religious agency. The Civil War thrust women into the management of

Sarah Ann Dickey
Woman's Missionary Association
United Brethren Church

Born near Dayton, Ohio, Sarah Dickey had almost no schooling until she was 16, but her determined progress thereafter was rapid, and at the age of 19 she secured a teacher's certificate. After six years of teaching in her native region she went to Vicksburg, Mississippi, to teach in a freedmen's school operated by the United Brethren Church. After three years, she went to Massachusetts to attend Mount Holyoke Female Seminary and graduated in 1869. She then returned to Mississippi and taught a year in the freedmen's school in Raymond. In 1871 she moved to nearby Clinton, where she opened an academy for African-American students.

Dickey secured support among the local black community, despite threats from the Ku Klux Klan, and enrolled a board of directors of prominent Mississippians. In 1873 a charter was granted for the Mount Hermon Female Seminary, which opened in October 1875 in a large brick house. In addition to her teaching and fundraising activities, Dickey reared a number of African-American children left in her care and was active in her community. In 1896 she was ordained a minister of the United Brethren Church. Mount Hermon Seminary passed into the hands of the American Missionary Association, which closed it in 1924 in favor of its own Tougaloo College.

organizations for raising and distributing aid to soldiers—and they discovered capabilities in themselves of which they and the nation had been unaware. In the decades following the war, hundreds of clubs and societies sprang up, most of them with the avowed purpose of serving humanity and advancing civilization. Women were determined to *do something* in the world.

Hardly had the last shots been fired when northern women set out with their brothers to meet the most perceptible need of the day—the education of the newly freed slaves. It was a popular cause. Many of the crusading teachers had grown up in homes where the anti-slavery position was staunchly defended and where the "underground railroad" ran through their barn or their neighbor's basement. With emancipation the next move was obvious, and so they, like Mary Sharp who headed a school for blacks in South Carolina for 10 years before going to Africa, devoted themselves to helping the freed men secure their new citizenship.

In the South before the war, the minute secular or religious training the slave acquired was left to the discretion of the plantation wives. In 1861, not long after the hostilities had erupted, one woman wrote:

> The field, of all others, for the care and labor of southern women is the mission to the colored people, because in the nineteenth century, if there is a people to whom they should be grate-

ful, it is these people. They nurse her and her children, in sickness and health, relieve her of the hard toil that makes a drudge of the New England wife, and withal she daily learns lessons, in her association with them, of patience, thoughtfulness, forbearance, and charity. ...[4]

But these kindly feelings were largely forgotten in the aftermath of the war. The bitterness of the defeated South was exacerbated by invading hordes of northern opportunists who came to take advantage of the economic and social chaos. The teachers and evangelists, with their outspoken confidence in the righteousness of their cause, were no more welcome. The education and elevation of blacks, whose inferiority many believed a God-given fact of life, enraged the beleaguered southerner, and lynchings and riots became the order of the day. White women with other views could only wait for a better time and direct their energies elsewhere in the meanwhile.

Even before the war was over, a young school teacher named Sarah Dickey, among a small party of United Brethren missionaries, went by steamer down the Ohio and Mississippi Rivers to Vicksburg. The city had surrendered to Union armies only months earlier. Thirty thousand freed slaves, ragged and bewildered, swarmed the streets and crowded into bullet-ridden buildings; in some places six at a time could be found living in dingy, windowless huts no more than a few feet square.

The intrepid missionaries established their school in a deserted Baptist church with shattered windows and unhinged doors, bloodstains on the floor and a shell hole in the wall. Sarah Dickey and two other women taught simultaneously in an often cold and drafty chapel, overstuffed with 300 pupils. In a year's time they reported that 100 had learned to read readily in the New Testament, 50 of those making good progress in penmanship, geography, English grammar and arithmetic. The ambitious teachers also noted improvements in manners and cleanliness.

Sarah Dickey left Vicksburg after 19 months when the mission was forced to close, but by then she knew what her life's work was to be and she went north willingly. She wanted a deeper education for herself before she returned to educate the freedwomen of the South. Schooling had never come easily to her. Displaced as a child by her mother's death, she was farmed out to various relatives whose design for her always included hard work, but not of the academic kind. At 13 she was illiterate; at 16 she could read and spell a few words, but could not write. It was then that she announced her determination to become a teacher, at which point, she was mocked, discouraged and apprised by her relatives of the fact that she was commonplace. But for the

Toki Nakasone Akamine
Woman's Society of
Christian Service
The Methodist Church

Toki Nakasone Akamine is one of the most dedicated women in the work of United Methodist Women in Hawaii. As a youth, she was active in the choir, Epworth League, young adult group, and as a church school teacher in the Japanese Methodist Episcopal Church in Lahaina, Hawaii. Toki was a teacher and vice principal in the Hawaii public schools for thirty years. She and her family are members of Wesley United Methodist Church, Honolulu, where she has been a teacher, choir director and leader in many other areas of church activity. In 1947, she was elected the first president of the Woman's Society of Christian Service in her church. She was also the first Asian to serve as vice president and president of the Territorial Woman's Society of Christian Service of Hawaii from 1954–1959. In 1970, Toki received the Mayor's Merit Award for her service to the community, which included serving on the Board of Directors of Susannah Wesley Center from 1963–1968, and on the Model Cities Program of Honolulu from 1966–1970. Since 1981, she has been a volunteer English teacher of Laotian and Vietnamese immigrants. Toki Akamine is a respected member of the church and community in Honolulu, Hawaii.

—Excerpt from *They Went Out Not Knowing*, 41

first time the stolid, uncommunicative girl took charge of her own life. Boarding with a family of 14 members, she got herself up at four every morning to perform the tasks they assigned her and then proceeded to go to school. After classes, from four in the afternoon until 10 at night, she sewed, cooked and cleaned; and when the family retired, she set about preparing her lessons and washing and mending her own clothes! In three years, at the age of 19, she won a teaching certificate.

Even apart from her relatives, no one ever seemed to have thought the young Sarah Dickey brilliant, or even particularly bright. Only one sister supported her in her ambitions for higher education when she returned from Mississippi, and several schools refused entrance to the 27-year-old penniless woman. But something else sustained and guided her at the decisive moments of her life—an audible voice answered her prayers and plainly told her what to do. In this instance the instructions were: "Go to Mount Holyoke Seminary."

It was an impossible idea. The school was one of the most prestigious in the country and she had only $10 to her name. But she borrowed money for the journey to the famous Massachusetts school and started off. The money failed to take her the whole distance, and she left her trunk as collateral for a ticket the rest of the way. Arriving two weeks after the start of the fall term with 35 cents in her purse, she went directly to the surprised headmistress. In two more weeks she had passed the entrance examinations, found a job, and begun the four-year college course. She was one of 38 out of the original 100 in her class to graduate in 1869.

During Sarah Dickey's first month at the seminary the "familiar voice" gave a further direction: she was to build a "Mount Holyoke" in the South for black girls. Shortly after graduation, she returned to the troubled state of Mississippi. The breach between blacks and whites seemed to have grown, and while some blacks held important state offices in the reconstruction government, the majority were living in extreme poverty and dying from plague. Their white countrymen were lashing out bitterly at the new order with every means at their command.

A year after Sarah Dickey's arrival, she took charge of a public school for black children in Clinton. Threatened and shot at by the Ku Klux Klan, still she felt secure enough in the divine origin of her mission to ignore the savagery around her. Harder to overlook, and more painful, was the social ostracism. No one would rent her a room except a black state senator (an unusually fearless man who was to die violently a few years later). Women on the street pulled their skirts away from her when she passed, as if to avoid contamination. In church everyone she took a seat near would get up and find another pew.

She staunchly disregarded the heckling of white college boys until her sister visited and was subjected to their taunts of "nigger teacher." *Then* she wielded an umbrella to good effect!

In 1873 Sarah Dickey started her school. As usual she had no money, but she traveled from place to place soliciting funds from small black churches in the South and from school friends and white churches in the North. For over 30 years the summers were taken up with long journeys to keep Mount Hermon—"the Mount Holyoke of the South"—a going concern. Her relationships with the United Brethren Church remained close, if unofficial, and some money was forwarded by individuals and agencies within that denomination. An excellent businesswoman as well as a tireless worker, she bought and sold property to advantage. And Mount Hermon students raised their own food, sewed their own clothing and made most of the repairs on the property. Nevertheless, Mount Hermon was always in debt and some years after the death of its intrepid, vital founder, the school closed.

But this fantastic stubborn woman from the North had made a difference to black Mississippi. Many of the black women she educated went on to become teachers, and thus her influence was multiplied. (When, at the beginning of her career, the Clinton public school for blacks was shut down, Sarah Dickey

**Jennie Hartzell
Woman's Home
Missionary Society
Methodist Episcopal Church**

Jennie Hartzell began work among the freedwomen in New Orleans in 1876. Her work was approved by officials of the Methodist Episcopal Church and reported through the Freedman's Aid Society. With Bishop Wiley and Dr. and Mrs. R. S. Rust, she raised funds; and a school with three teachers was established. A memorial was sent to the 1880 General Conference noting approval of Mrs. Hartzell's work in New Orleans and recommending that it be incorporated into the regular efforts of the Freedman's Aid Society throughout the South. The report was adopted, and seemed to signal general church approval for work among freedwomen and girls. Within a week women met in Cincinnati, and the Woman's Home Missionary Society was formally organized. Mrs. Hartzell was present to report on her work in New Orleans. She was appointed recording secretary of the WHMS and worked to get the organization recognized by the Louisiana Conference. She later served as conference president. Ill health caused by earlier strenuous activity prevented her participation in the wider organizational activities of the Society.

—Excerpt from *They Went Out Not Knowing*, 5

took over; for years hers was the only school for black children for miles around.) Eventually, Mount Hermon became the center and the pride of the black community. On Sundays men, women and children attended church there, and at the yearly commencement exercises they came by buckboard from every part of the state.

Miss Dickey seems to have been one of those rare individuals with no race prejudice. While Clinton's whites were never persuaded to her attitudes, they came to trust and respect her. She was often the mediator between blacks and whites, and from the beginning she saw to it that the school's board of trustees was composed of equal numbers from both races. Always ready to assist the helpless, she supported children and old women on the Mount Hermon property, but some of her other projects approached contemporary concepts of "self-help." Purchasing a large tract of land, she inspired blacks without property to build their own homes in a new community. The district later came to be called "Dickeyville."

While Sarah Dickey was establishing Mount Hermon Seminary, another northern woman, Mrs. Jennie C. Hartzell, found herself drawn into efforts to help freedwomen in New Orleans.

Her first work was in response to a call to visit a dying girl in a disreputable house. A minister had been asked for, but none dared to go. Dr. Hartzell was out of town, and she went alone; went again and again for two weeks, and saw the girl happily converted, and willing to die. Once, on coming out of this place, the proprietress of another such house waited on her and asked her to come the following Sabbath, and speak to her young women as she had talked to this dying girl. She went, and had twenty of those poor women, whom no one seemed to care to save, intently listening to her words, so hungry were they for help and comfort.[5]

For several years Mrs. Hartzell acted on her own—visiting homes, attending and organizing mothers' meetings, distributing literature and encouraging church work. But by 1880, aided by contributions from church men and women in the North, she had seven missionaries in her employ, and day schools and five industrial (sewing) schools in operation. Soon, as many as 500 girls and women were under the mission's influence, with many converted and others in possession of at least a minimal education and useful skills.

The success of Mrs. Hartzell's work was a catalyst to the creation of the Woman's Home Missionary Society of the Methodist Episcopal Church. Over the years a number of women had been looking for some means by which to perform home missions work. A proposal that the word "foreign" be dropped from the Woman's Foreign Missionary Society and its activities extended to include programs within the borders of the United States was rejected. In 1875, a mass meeting of women in Baltimore appointed a committee to petition the Freedman's Aid Society for female representation on its Board of Managers. Safeguarded by the terms of its incorporation which contained a clause restricting membership to men, the Society turned the women down. Mrs. Rust, one of the petitioners, found that even her husband, who was the organization's president, was not to be persuaded.

However, women were invited to participate as advisors and counselors, and they immediately proceeded to the task. They advised and counseled the creation of a woman's department auxiliary to the Freedman's Aid Society. Once more, they were refused, but this time the men budged an inch and offered Jennie Fowler Willing the job of proselytizing, collecting funds and organizing local auxiliaries for them.

The gentlemen had been indulgent toward the wrong person. Jennie Willing was a strong woman's rights advocate, and she had no intention of raising money for a men's organization that permitted her no say in the nature and direction of its programs. Then, too, she was one of a small group who believed women should start their own independent society. But no immediate action was taken, and the whole matter appeared to have been dropped.

Lucy Webb Hayes
Woman's Home
Missionary Society
Methodist Episcopal Church

Lucy Webb Hayes was an ardent, loyal Methodist—a woman of culture, rare judgment and convictions. She attended Cincinnati Wesleyan Female College, graduated in 1850, and married a young lawyer whose career eventually led him to the White House. Throughout his career, Lucy Webb Hayes played a vital role both as his wife and as a leader among women. During her years as First Lady, she was known as "Lemonade Lucy" because of her refusal to serve alcoholic beverages. On July 10, 1880, Lucy Webb Hayes was nominated, without her knowledge, to be president of the newly-formed Woman's Home Missionary Society. At the urging of friends, she accepted the nomination on January 8, 1881, with the stipulation that her college friend, Mrs. John Davis, be her first vice-president and chair the Executive Board. This saved Lucy the monthly train trip to Board meetings. She served as president until her death. The Lucy Webb Hayes Training School for missionaries and deaconesses in Washington, DC, was named in her honor. The name has been carried forward and today the undergraduate and graduate schools of nursing at American University bear the name of Lucy Webb Hayes.

—Excerpt from *They Went Out Not Knowing*, 2

In 1877 Dr. and Mrs. Rust visited New Orleans. Deeply impressed by Mrs. Hartzell's work, Elizabeth Lownes Rust returned north to seek out donations for the mission; she was also determined to see a women's society organized to provide permanent support. When the General Conference of 1880 expressed its appreciation of the New Orleans project, she and her companions in the cause called a meeting. On June 8, a week after the Conference, 50 women assembled at Trinity Church in Cincinnati and agreed to form the Woman's Home Missionary Society with "a recommendation for special attention to the southern field."[6] Probably at Mrs. Rust's instigation, some of them still sought an affiliation with the Freedman's Society, but a month later the issue was decided and an independent constitution adopted.

Like the women who organized the Woman's Foreign Missionary Society, these pioneers in home missions were in the upper strata of society and were influential members of the church. The wives of university professors and eminent churchmen, most of them were in their 40s and 50s, well-educated and social leaders. Mrs. Rust, notwithstanding her efforts to keep the Home Missionary Society connected with her husband's work, had lived much of her life as a single woman and artist, studying and painting for some years in Europe. But the brightest star in the new organization was its elected president, Lucy Webb Hayes, the wife of the recently retired United States President

Rutherford B. Hayes.

Mrs. Hayes was one of the more famous "first ladies." (The title is said to have been coined specifically in reference to her.) She was the first to be college-educated, and the first teetotaler. Nicknamed "Lemonade Lucy" by her detractors, she brought total abstinence to her domain which created consternation in diplomatic and congressional circles. Sunday evening entertainments were turned into hymn-sings during the occupation of the White House by this staunch Methodist couple.

Lucy Webb Hayes was a Republican *and* a Methodist heroine of her day. Before the election of Lincoln and the start of the war, the Webb family had freed their slaves, and she continued to take an interest in their welfare until her death. During the war she followed the Union armies to the front, nursing her husband and others in camps and hospitals. Her stand on temperance gave the cause new impetus and endeared her to a generation of crusading women.

Perhaps no social struggle attracted as many women to its ranks as temperance. It was at root a campaign to save the drunkard's wife from abuse and the American family from the results of his dissolute behavior. Woman's Foreign Missionary Society meetings were frequently cancelled in the early 1870s to permit members to join thousands of their sisters in an effort to destroy the liquor industry. They haunted big city saloons and harassed male consciences with hymns and prayers. Many of them were subjected to the insults of the exasperated drinkers but some, like Mrs. Clark, a leader in foreign and home missions and the dignified wife of a bishop, met with outrageous misfortune—she was sloshed with a pitcher of beer.

While many mission society women were active in the movement for prohibition and eventually added the issue to their own work, Jennie Fowler Willing was one of the founders of the most influential of temperance organizations, the Woman's Christian Temperance Union. And one of her friends, Frances Willard, a Methodist briefly connected with the Woman's Foreign Missionary Society, became a president of the WCTU and one of the luminaries of the 19th century. (After her death Congress put her statue in its rotunda and voted her "the first woman of the nineteenth century and best-loved character of her time.") Miss Willard brought women from every hamlet and city of the country into the temperance movement and passed them along, in time, to the struggle for woman's rights.

Nothing showed the power of Frances Willard's personality more clearly than her trip into the South in 1882. Cut off from the rest of the nation by the war and the disaster and humiliation of reconstruction, the southern states were slow to afford enthusiasm for the popular causes of the day. Moreover, the

**Frances Willard
Woman's Foreign
Missionary Society
Methodist Episcopal Church**

Frances Willard is known as an American temperance leader and reformer, well-known lecturer, writer and educator. She was born in Churchville, New York, and graduated from Northwestern Female College in Evanston, Illinois, in 1859. She was president of Evanston College for Ladies and dean of women at Northwestern University. After leaving the university, she helped organize the Chicago Woman's Christian Temperance Union in 1874, and became president of the National Woman's Christian Temperance Union in 1879. In 1891 she was elected president of the World's Woman's Christian Temperance Union. Willard turned away from a solid career in education to devote herself to the temperance crusade. For many years she worked for the Temperance Union with no pay, living on money made at speaking engagements. She was instrumental in the formation of the Prohibition Party, and was later elected president of the National Council of Women, largely for her belief in women's right to vote. Frances Willard is remembered among Methodists for her strong stance in favor of women's participation in the church. She was elected by the Rock River Conference as a lay delegate to General Conference in 1888, but was denied the seat.

General Commission on Archives and History, The United Methodist Church

women below the Mason-Dixon line were predisposed to distrust the agitators for temperance and woman's suffrage, whose careers began in opposition to slavery. Finally, of course, there were those traditional ideals of womanhood—so entrenched in southern society. But despite this negative atmosphere, Frances Willard was received, and with accolades! As one biographer wrote:

> She is a northern temperance woman, and a woman who addresses large audiences from platform and pulpit. This was something decidedly heretical, but clergymen of the most fastidious ideas, bishops who had hitherto agreed with Paul about woman's keeping silent in churches, and cultivated southern ladies who had been strongly secession in their sympathies during the war, all extended to Miss Willard the most cordial greeting, and her visits to the South have been one long ovation. ...[7]

At the same time that Frances Willard traveled from the Carolina coast to Texas, founding nearly 50 WCTU auxiliaries, Laura Haygood, (another more sedate worker for woman's place in the world) was organizing what would become a model for home missions work in the South. Miss Haygood, not yet a foreign missionary, was not content with being the head of a girl's high school, as well as teaching, and performing the typical activities of a churchwoman. She established for unchurched Atlanta citizens Sunday school classes that in time were to become independent churches; at the same time, she conceived the Trinity Home Mission Society. Her group of nearly 60 women was determined to help the poor, and to show them how to fend for themselves. Like many other societies, they founded an industrial school to teach sewing skills, but they also created a market for selling their pupils' work and allowing them to retain the proceeds. When someone suggested to Miss Haygood that it would be easier to just give the money to the poor, she replied: "Quite true, but in giving them work we increase instead of diminish their self-respect; we encourage them in habits of industry; we do a little toward lifting them out of the chronic pauperism into which so many of their lives have fallen. ..."[8]

When the school opened, only three or four students appeared—an hour late, and looking doubtful. But they were warmly welcomed and involved in activity. Eight months later 76 women and 50 children were in attendance. At the end of the first year 1,560 garments had been made and sold, and the school was almost self-supporting. Religion was not forgotten either:

> While the work is being received a young lady at the organ leads the singing of gospel hymns. Then a Bible lesson is read with very simple exposition and practical suggestions as to ways in which we may serve God in everyday life, or the old and yet new story of Jesus' love is told, and we pray together. Another hymn or doxology, closes the service. ... Then individual audience is given to any who have stories of special troubles, with attention and sympathy when nothing else is possible.[9]

Often the women made certain that something else was possible. Not only did they start a Sunday school in the poor section of town, but they also created a day school for the children who could not be persuaded to attend public school. They loaned and gave money, and finally built a temporary shelter for homeless women and children. No one was as diligent in her efforts as Laura Haygood.

> Nothing that would help was too lowly. How merrily she used to laugh over a license to peddle on the streets of Atlanta issued by the City Council to Laura Haygood, with the privilege of transferring it to some poor woman. No home was ever too repulsive with poverty, dirt, disease or shame to be brightened by her presence and cheered by her gifts and words of counsel. ...[10]

In the same year that Miss Haygood began her Atlanta mission, the Board

Lucinda Helm
Methodist Episcopal Church, South

God made woman with her faculties, her traits, her way of looking at all great questions from the highest to the lowest, and He made her to be a helpmeet for man, and He made man to be a helpmeet for her; He made them to stand side by side, sun-crowned; He made them to stand in a republic, as I believe, bearing equally its magnificent burdens.

—Francis Willard, from an address before the International Council of Women, 1888 and quoted from her book *Glimpses of Fifty Years: The Autobiography of An American Woman,* Chicago: Woman's Temperance Publication Association, 1889, 594

of Church Extension of the Methodist Episcopal Church, South, was formed, and a Kentucky churchwoman, Lucinda Helm, went to its secretary and asked if she could be of any help. Miss Helm and her sister Mary were daughters of one of the South's most prestigious families. Lucinda was wan, fragile, sweet-natured and a semi-invalid most of her life; but her energy and ambition for woman's work in the church transcended her poor health. Mary, who had been the livelier of the two when they were children, was badly injured in an accident as a teenager, and though she recovered, she lived with pain most of her life and was slightly hunchbacked.

Lucinda Helm was put to work preparing literature for the Board, but she soon set about expanding her job. Moved by the struggles of itinerant pastors and their families in the still untamed West, she devised plans for a woman's department to build parsonages. Dreaming a little, she included home mission work in her designs. When the Board had reviewed the scheme, the woman's department was left with one function: to collect money for preachers' homes.

Lucinda Helm didn't argue the point—it was a beginning. At the end of two years she had organized 214 auxiliaries, and in four years, the department had raised $33,642. Reducing her accomplishments to an impressive list of statistics, and engaging the support of a few influential male allies, she got what she wanted. The Parsonage and Home

Missions Society was recognized by the General Conference of 1890, and after some argument, the home missions work was placed under the direction of the women. In 1892 Lucinda Helm resigned as head of the Society to devote herself to editing the organization's periodical, *Our Homes*. When she died a few years later, her sister Mary replaced her as editor. In 1898 another prominent woman in southern society, Belle Bennett, was elected president of the newly named Woman's Home Missionary Society.

One of the first projects the women undertook was the construction of Sue Bennett, a school for impoverished Kentucky mountain children as a memorial to Belle Bennett's sister, who had been enthusiastically involved in mountain work at the time of her death. The first of many institutions that followed, the school opened in 1897 with 75 pupils. For years it functioned in place of a public school; this was not unusual—the schools run by mission societies were often the only means of education for those they served. In Mississippi, the last state to establish a school system, northern Methodist women were credited both with filling the gap and providing a model for future public schools. Though mission schools tended to emphasize industrial skills, most of them had at least a rudimentary academic program and some, like Sue Bennett, eventually became colleges. In many instances, the industrial school was attached to a university so that more promising students could continue with their education.

Not everyone welcomed the prospect of education. The American Indians, not unnaturally, were suspicious of the white representatives of church and government who so often turned out to be identical. The missionary who wanted to reach them required diplomatic skill; two northern women had that knack. Arriving at sunset on the border of a Navajo reservation, they went about the business of pitching their tent and preparing their evening meal while two Indians wrapped in blankets sat and watched. They continued their silent observation until the women closed the flap of the tent, said their prayers and extinguished their lamp. The next day the Navajos came to inspect the tent, bringing with them an interpreter who asked how large a building they intended to erect. One of the missionaries marked out a space 16 by 16 feet, and the Indians smiled and left satisfied. It would not be room enough for a school house. Time passed and the women built their small house. They won friends with medical aid, and soon began to teach cooking and sewing; they also acted as intermediaries between Indians and whites and demonstrated new agricultural techniques. Ultimately, their school was established, *and* a hospital, *and* a church.

Spanish Americans—Cubans in Florida and Mexican Americans in the

Mellie Perkins
Women's Missionary Association
United Brethren Church

Deaconess Mellie Perkins first saw the Española Valley of New Mexico from a mule-drawn wagon. She was dismayed to find isolated Spanish villages in need of churches, health care and schooling. When these concerns were brought to the attention of the Mission Board of the United Brethren Church, the Board appointed Mellie to New Mexico. Upon her arrival in Velarde in 1912, she set up classrooms in the abandoned buildings bought by the Board, taught school, held Sunday services, and visited and cared for the sick. With love and determination, she endured hardships, ill health and fierce opposition to evangelical Christianity. More missionaries came and other villages implored the church to help them. Miss Perkins started a day and boarding school in Santa Cruz in 1915. It was named Edith McCurdy Mission School (now McCurdy School) in memory of her friend and Spanish teacher whose parents contributed toward the school. Mellie Perkins retired in 1918 because of ill heath, leaving well-established schools and churches that grew to have wide and permanent influence in northern New Mexico. As was said of David Livingston, "She gently lived, she greatly loved and died right mightily."

—Excerpt from *They Went Out Not Knowing*, 14

Southwest—were still another people the missionaries tried to help, with varying success. When Mellie Perkins, a United Brethren deaconess working in Texas and Oklahoma, went to New Mexico for an annual meeting, she saw her "first Spanish Americans closely and heard about their spiritual neglect, superstition, and ignorance, and the advantage the Roman priests were taking of them."[11] A devoutly religious woman, whose poor health had frustrated her childhood ambitions to be a foreign missionary, she felt called by God to work among these people. She immediately set about getting the support of her church, and two years later she returned to New Mexico.

With another young woman as an assistant, she left Santa Fe by train to go to her new mission station at Velarde:

> I must confess that things did not look very bright, and the nearer we came to our destination the drearier grew the scenes, and when we landed across the Rio Grande and found we had to walk the ties on the railroad bridge in order to cross, we felt quite uncomfortable, but I did not dare to show the white feather as I saw the tears in the eyes of my friend. ... As I walked that mile to the mission and saw nothing but dark-faced Mexicans staring at me, I felt that I was in a country far from home and kindred and that my desires were fast vanishing, but I called on One who gives strength and courage when needed most and my spirits soon rose.[12]

What the women found at the end of their trek was no more encouraging. The house had not been used for four years; the floors were warped and covered with mud and the walls crumbling. For the next year, in addition to teaching and preaching, visiting and caring for the sick, writing hundreds of letters and doing the necessary housework, Mellie Perkins renovated the property. Weeds were cleared, fallen buildings torn down and carted away, and broken-down fences replaced. Her assistant left after a few months, and she was left alone with her diverse and arduous tasks. Though a large, big-boned person with a loud voice, who gave the appearance of great strength, she was never healthy and her diary recorded continual physical complaints: "cramps very bad at night," "headache," "nervous," "back hurts," "pleurisy," "neuralgia," "awful dreams," "terrible pain in shoulder and chest."[13]

After several years at Velarde, Mellie Perkins was directed by the missions board to move 18 miles away to Santa Cruz and begin again. Before she could begin she was called home to tend to a sick sister. Even on this enforced furlough, she devoted time to the work, speaking in churches and auditoriums to raise money and recruits. She reached at least one woman, Lillian Kendig, who was to follow her a few years later as principal of the Santa Cruz school. More than a half century later Lillian Kendig Cole recalled: "When I first met her I was a student at Bonebrake Seminary. She was dressed in a deaconess habit, perfectly tailored, which emphasized her commanding appearance. Her message was thrilling, making you want to help."[14]

When Mellie Perkins returned to Santa Cruz, Mary Brawner, another assistant, was with her:

> I remember riding over the country in a wagon. The wind was strong—I had on a hat with a feather on it and wind whistled through the feather like a flute.... When we reached Española we were dumped from the train to the station platform waiting for another wagon to take us "home" to Santa Cruz. We had a rented adobe home, pretty well on the downgrade. Seems to me there were but three rooms but there might have been four. ....[15]

During the first year they were so crowded for space that the two women taught at the same time at either end of the room. "Both learned to moderate their voices, which was not bad for either."[16] In the absence of Mellie Perkins a Catholic bishop had visited Santa Cruz, ridiculed the Protestant invaders, threatened those who trafficked with them and called down the curses of God on the troublemakers. Opposition grew in the following months and children were warned against "the devil and her spirits." The hostility finally resulted

Jane Addams

Born September 6, 1860 in Cedarville, Illinois, Jane Addams was the eighth child of a successful miller, banker and landowner. Jane did not remember her mother, who died when she was only three years old, and was devoted to and profoundly influenced by her father. Jane attended Rockford Female Seminary in northern Illinois, from which she graduated in 1881. Religion and the classics dominated the curriculum, but she developed an interest in the sciences and entered the Women's Medical College in Philadelphia. After six months, illness forced her to discontinue her studies permanently and undergo a spinal operation; she was never quite free of illness throughout her life. During a tour of Europe, Jane visited Toynbee Hall in London and realized an outlet for her talents and energies. As a result, she established Hull House in one of Chicago's most poverty-stricken immigrant slums to service young women desiring more than a homemaker's life. Hull House soon developed into a great center for the poor of the neighborhood, and it became a source of inspiration for dozens of similar settlement houses in other cities. In December 1931, Jane Addams was awarded a Nobel Peace Prize for her work in labor organizing, social and political reform, peace, freedom and women's suffrage. She was an author, renowned speaker, advocate and adviser to several American presidents.

in a public book-burning, including not only the mission's tracts and volumes, but also the Protestant Bible.

Mellie Perkins was a force in her students' lives. Mrs. Cole noted that "in the school room she had no trouble with discipline. You followed her directions or else. ... The young feared her but many of the older ones—especially boys in their later teens—received impetus to become successful."[17] In 1917 Miss Perkins retired because of her health. She had organized churches and schools at three mission stations. (One of them, McCurdy School, still continues to flourish.) She returned home, worked briefly for the WCTU and taught, and died in 1924.

One of the more exotic, if troubling, fields of missionary endeavor, was the work among [Asians] on the West coast. In many places public education was denied the Chinese and Japanese, poverty and corruption thrived in their communities, and an extensive "slave trade" (importing and buying of immigrant girls for prostitution) was routinely practiced. Many missionaries found themselves "kidnapping" terrified girls and pursuing complicated litigation to establish the young women's legal status. But even the simplest visiting required a certain daring.

> None but brave women would venture down those alleys and slums of darkest Chinatown, where are hard-looking white men drunk with Chinatown whiskey. It is anything but pleasant for

refined gentlewomen to enter houses where girls (slaves and worse) are to be seen with chalked faces, gaudy silks, and bejeweled headdress, singing lewd ballads, while Chinamen play mora and drink samsha. Day after day Miss L. and her interpreters are seen climbing rickety stairs leading into sunless homes and windowless rooms, where patient women, with babies strapped to their backs, drudge from morning till midnight sewing overalls for ten cents a dozen. They have carried flowers day after day into malodorous abodes, and God's comfort to desolate hearts. They have nursed the sick and comforted the dying. They have gone down into ghoulish chambers of silence and found sick girls left to die between coffined corpses, and boxes of dead men's bones. They have conducted every week Sabbath schools in squalid tenements, where human beings lived packed like sardines. ..."[18]

The work with [Asians] was only one small part of the women's mission to burgeoning cities and industrial centers. Immigrants were pouring into urban areas and crowding into slums, and were isolated by their language and customs as well as prejudice. A motley collection, they were terrifying to white Protestant America:

Superstition, idolatry, Sabbath-breaking and anarchy accompanied this great throng. People feared lest the poison entered there should spread throughout the life of the nation. After the assassination of President McKinley the additional motive of good Americans was self-preservation.[19]

Whether out of fear or sympathy, the missionary's aim was to evangelize and Americanize the immigrant. At ports of entry, reception centers were opened where a cup of tea, a prayer, a room for the night or general orientation to a puzzling new world could be offered to the stranger. Jane Addams' Hull House in Chicago stimulated secular as well as religious imitators to establish community centers and institutional churches where people could learn English or a trade, attend lectures on the arts of good citizenship, seek medical help or a kindergarten for their children, or just play Ping-Pong, talk and read. Boardinghouses were built for single working women. And prostitution and the liquor trade were vigorously attacked.

Living among the poor of the cities and rural areas, many missionaries began to understand poverty in new ways. The destitute were not always lazy or wicked, and when they were, they could not always be blamed. Unwholesome circumstances made problems for individuals. By the early 1900s churchwomen had joined women all over the country in appeals to employ-

Belle Harris Bennett
Woman's Home
Missionary Society
Woman's Missionary Council
Methodist Episcopal
Church, South

Belle Bennett was born in Whitehall, Kentucky, one of eight children in a wealthy, close-knit family that highly valued education and service to church and community. In 1886 she felt that God was calling her for a specific service through the woman's missionary work of the church. Belle led the women of her church in building a strong educational network and social service program at home and abroad. Because of her special concern for a training school for women Christian workers, she was commissioned by the Woman's Foreign Missionary Society to raise funds for building the Scarritt Bible and Training School in Kansas City, Missouri. It was relocated to Nashville, Tennessee, in the 1920s, expanded, and renamed Scarritt College. Memorial funds secured following her death built the Bennett Memorial Building and Wightman Chapel. Belle Bennett was president of the Woman's Board of Home Missions from 1896–1910, and president of the Woman's Missionary Council from 1910–1922. She was elected a delegate to the first General Conference that seated lay women (1922) but died before the Conference convened.

—Excerpt from *They Went Out Not Knowing*, 8

ers and Congressmen for improved wages and working conditions, for child labor laws and other reforms.

But no missions were more important, especially to northern women, than those that served black women and girls in the cities and towns of the South. Sarah Dickey, Jennie Hartzell, and many like them established schools and homes for freedwomen where instruction in "industrial" skills were emphasized. Eight or more girls would live together with a matron in a home near a school of the Freedman's Aid Society. Together they learned cooking and nutrition, homemaking and sewing, some agriculture and, of course, Christian doctrine. Academic education was provided by the Freedman's school. In time, some of the homes were built independently of the schools, and academic departments were added.

Like Sarah Dickey, many of the northern women found themselves surrounded by antagonistic southerners. (Integrated communities always provoked hostility and there were even instances of governmental pressure such as the 1914 Florida law forbidding whites to teach in black schools.) Despite continuing racial tension, southern women, led by Belle Bennett, finally extended their work to their black neighbors in 1901.

Belle Harris Bennett was "crowned with all the graces of southern womanhood." The daughter of one of the South's most illustrious families, she grew up in a home where piety and culture mingled easily, and where the arts and social consciousness were taken for granted like the lush Kentucky bluegrass and the elegance of life in southern high society. As a young and beautiful woman, she was pursued by suitors, "entertained and fêted," and celebrated as "a reigning belle at the Mardi Gras in New Orleans."[20]

But Belle Bennett was too intelligent and too serious to dance her life away at balls. She had ideas, a strong sense of social justice, and a need for hard, purposeful work. Her church provided a channel for her talents and ambitions, and Methodism in turn gained a stateswoman of unusual executive ability, eloquence and compassion. She was one of those individuals, ahead of her time but politic enough to know when those around her were ready to accept social innovations. And she was an egalitarian, not because of any special understanding of people outside her ken, but by birthright; she was so secure in her sense of who and what she was, she had no need to weigh people.

For at least 10 years before the Woman's Society addressed itself to the needs of blacks, Belle Bennett was doing it. Her friendships with black women and men went back even further, and at least one of her most intimate companions was a black woman, Josie Bates. Her public service to the people despised by most white southerners, began with Bible study classes for black pastors in Richmond, Kentucky, but it expanded over the years.

Working with black leaders in Richmond at the beginning of the century, she was instrumental in the organization of a "Colored Chautauqua," where prominent persons were invited to speak at convocations of black men and women. A state official reported:

> Through her committees she brought to Richmond a brilliant array of Negro talent from all parts of the country—Carver, Dubois, Proctor, Simmons—whose lectures, addresses, sermons electrified, uplifted, and enlightened the colored people of Madison County as well as people from adjoining counties. ... I think it was one Friday evening in August, 1916, during the Institute Chautauqua, that Dr. W. E. B. Dubois, famous scholar, orator, and sociologist, was to speak; 1500 people, white and colored, crowded into the ball park to hear the address. Someone decided to rope off a space for the exclusive use of white people. Miss Belle, noticing the roped space, inquired what it meant and when told its purpose she at once ordered it removed and gave orders for the space to be filled by whosoever desired a seat, and so far as I know no white person was in the least offended.[21]

Some time before her death a bond issue for a new white school to replace

Let the future bring what it may, "God is our refuge and strength, a very present help in time of trouble." The field is wide, the need is great. God loves us. Let us do the work he has committed to our hands, and let us be much in prayer for wisdom and guidance.

—Belle Harris Bennett, from an address to the Woman's Missionary Council, c. 1920 as quoted in the book, *Belle Harris Bennett: Her Life Work*, Nashville: Board of Missions, Methodist Episcopal Church, South, 1928 by Mrs. R.W. MacDonell, 272

one that had burned down came to a vote in Richmond. Belle Bennett judiciously suggested that to curry black votes some of the funds should be used to improve the black school; the bond issue passed. Shortly after she died, and when her will was read, it was discovered that she had made provisions to take care of the proposed improvements if the school board failed to live up to its agreement.

It was in 1899 that the subject of an industrial school for black girls at Paine Institute in Augusta first came to the attention of the Woman's Home Mission Society. The women refused to take on the project, pleading a lack of funds. The next year they were no wealthier, but something had changed. Mrs. J. D. Hammond of the Society explained:

> Miss Bennett wanted to begin work at Paine years before it was feasible. Finally, in answer to the argument that prejudice would die sooner if somebody fought it, she turned to God for guidance. There were three who prayed that afternoon in that upper room, and light was given. When the prayers were ended she rose from her knees and said, "We will begin tomorrow morning." And she did.[22]

There was opposition—public criticism and even threatening letters—but a start had been made. Schools soon multiplied, and within years white women and black women had begun a dialogue.

Belle Bennett had begun her work in missions in the 1880s with a crusade. Impressed by the poor preparation of missionaries for their life's work, she was inspired by Lucy Rider Meyer's experiment with a training school in the North. She felt called by God to follow suit for the southern church, and her conviction was strengthened when she became a member of a committee to examine missionary candidates. Questioning a young woman about her knowledge of the Bible, she was astonished when the aspiring missionary replied that "she didn't know anything much. She was a district schoolteacher and had always attended Sunday school and had heard of the wretched condition of the women in heathen lands, lands where there was no knowledge of Jesus Christ."[23]

In 1889, Miss Bennett presented her case before the Board of the Woman's Foreign Missionary Society. Young and inexperienced, she was so nervous that she remained sitting for most of her speech. But the women were stimulated and they resolved that a training school be built, and that she would be in charge of collecting the necessary funds. The job was not exactly what she had in mind for herself, and what's more, she hadn't the slightest idea how to begin. But in the next two years she wrote 3,000 letters, distributed 15,000 leaflets, and traveled over 20,000 miles. A location in Kansas City was chosen and plans for the building were being drawn up, when opposition arose. "Who is this Miss Bennett anyway? By what authority is she going through the church collecting money?" demanded one of the most powerful bishops in the church.[24] Much of the contention came from women in the Foreign Missionary Society who worried that collections for their mission work would be hampered by the demands of maintaining a school. But the arguments were resolved, and in the fall of 1892 Scarritt Bible and Training School was dedicated and opened for students.

Not yet hardened to the barbs of church politicians intent on winning their own way, Belle Bennett suffered during the controversy created by the school. She might have taken comfort from Lucy Rider Meyer's misadventures and discouragements, had she known of them. An enthusiastic young religious educator from New England, Lucy Rider had ambitious ideas, an eclectic mind, and a sense of humor. She needed all three—and a husband with a head for business—to start the Chicago Training School.

People were indifferent or opposed to a training school. Some were suspicious merely because it was a new idea; others firmly believed that Sunday school and church should be sufficient preparation for converting the most obstinate heathen; and a few thought women shouldn't be missionaries anyway. But to many, the most outrageous aspect of the proposed school was

Chicago Training School

In the earliest years, missionary candidates went to the field without special training. To this end, training schools for missionaries were established in several U.S. cities beginning in the late 1800s. The training school with the most impact on Methodist women missionaries was the vision of Lucy Rider and her husband, Shelley Meyer, a Methodist minister. Gaining the support of some local preachers and leaders of the woman's missionary movement, Lucy Rider Meyer held a meeting on the Woman's Foreign Missionary Society day of the Lake Bluff camp meeting in August of 1885. The assembly agreed to support a missionary training school, and Lucy Meyer agreed to lead the school for a year at no salary. The Chicago Training School for City, Home and Foreign Missions opened to four women in October, 1885. Lucy Meyer raised the first three thousand dollars for the school in nickels, and she wrote articles, circulars, and a small paper to publicize the school and raise money. The Chicago Training School continued to function as a major force in the education of Methodist missionary women into the 1920s; and in 1934, it merged with Garrett Theological Seminary and Northwestern University.

that the still feuding foreign and home missionary societies were both to have a share in it. "My dear!" exclaimed a wealthy New York woman. "That idea *alone* proves the absolute impracticability of your plan."[25]

In the summer of 1885, after a lot of talking, Lucy Rider Meyer finally got the tentative approval of three groups—the Preachers' Meeting, the Woman's Home and Woman's Foreign Missionary Societies. She was to go ahead, at her own risk of course. Two months before the school opened she could report that not half a dozen people really believed in its necessity or its feasibility, and donations to the work amounted to one month's rent.

Nevertheless, the Meyers rented a row house on a dingy Chicago street. They had scant furniture so they made desks of packing boxes covered with newspapers, with pigeonholes and drawers made of smaller boxes. When they invited the new Board of Trustees to dinner, they ordered chairs and a table on credit, and borrowed napkins and silver from their neighbors. Mrs. Meyer prepared oysters and coffee on the single-burner oil stove, and when the ladies and gentlemen sat down for their repast in the empty, echoing room, the Meyers discovered they were still short a spoon. After that meeting the Board was stirred to action; they all went home and combed their attics for old furniture.

Finally, on October 20, the school had its grand opening. The Meyers had worked for the event, and they waited expectantly for hordes of church dignitaries and eager students to arrive. Three guests made an appearance, and four students registered. Many months later Lucy Meyer admitted that two of their students were underage and one an invalid. Not to be discouraged, they tried again three weeks later with a "first annual reception." This time they decided to lure their guests with important speakers, and so distinguished names graced the program. They planned for 200 people; 12 came. (Mr. Meyer wryly pointed out that it was four times as many as at their last affair.) The weeks afterward were more memorable than the event itself: "We had sandwiches cold and sandwiches hot, and sandwiches steamed and fried and hashed," sighed Mrs. Meyer.[26]

The Meyers, their students and teachers constituted a kind of family—eating and laughing together, planning for the school and inventing ways to make and spend the next dollar. As much learning took place outside as inside the classroom. Fridays were saved for field work, at which time the students would range the neighborhood, helping people however they could and fathoming the profound problems of the hundreds of thousands of city poor. They shared their experiences over the dinner table, and everyone worried together over the unwed mother in the vermin-ridden third floor walk-up, or the delinquent boy with the pool hall friends and the drunken father.

The early Chicago Training School was far different from Scarritt Bible and Training School. The southern institution was housed in a spacious brick building with a small, but well-equipped hospital on the third floor for medical training. A cook, janitor and laundress were in residence, in addition to a disciplined corps of students to see to its upkeep. The principal, Miss Maria Gibson, had no complaints except for the lack of carpeting. That problem was soon remedied by a kindly Presbyterian donor, and she breathed more easily: "What a blessing to mind and nerves those carpets were, none but fellow sufferers from the noise of many feet on bare floors could fully appreciate."[27]

The disparity between the northern and southern schools was not only one between Chicago-tenement and Kansas City-institutional-brick. Long after Lucy Rider Meyer's school moved into its own concrete and mortar building, it continued to exhibit a free-swinging egalitarianism foreign to Maria Gibson. The two women principals were a study in contrast between Yankee experimentation and southern conservatism, and the schools were molded by their characters.

Maria Gibson was the epitome of ladylike decorum. And though she had earned a master of arts degree and traveled abroad, she had neither the love of learning nor the breadth of mind of Belle Bennett or Lucy Rider Meyer. Despite the fact that she was head of a school and for many years leader of

Scarritt-Bennett Center
Nashville, Tennessee

Scarritt Bible and Training Institute was established in 1892 in Kansas City, Missouri, as an institute for training young women being sent overseas as missionaries. It was Belle Harris Bennett's dream to create such a school; and on authorization of the governing body of the Methodist Episcopal Church, South, she raised the money for it. The College moved to Nashville in 1924 as Scarritt College for Christian Workers and became coeducational.

National College (previously Kansas City National Training School) in Kansas City, Missouri, also established by the Methodist Episcopal Church, South, to train U.S. and overseas missionaries, closed its doors in 1964 and all records were transferred to Scarritt College in Nashville. In its later years, Scarritt College trained many of the Christian educators, church musicians, and church and community workers employed in the Methodist and United Methodist churches. From 1980–1988, Scarritt College was known as Scarritt Graduate School and awarded master of arts degrees in Christian Education and Church Music.

In 1988 the college closed, and the Women's Division of The United Methodist Church reclaimed ownership of the campus. After significant renovations, the Scarritt-Bennett Center was opened in 1988 as a conference, retreat and educational center.

the southern Woman's Foreign Missionary Society, she had firm ideas about woman's place:

> In the providence of God, I, a woman, naturally dependent and lacking in self-confidence, have been called to do pioneer work in various lines, to undertake responsibilities and inaugurate enterprises which, unaided by the Spirit of God, it would have been impossible for me to accomplish. That he has used me to serve him and the Church for so many years is a cause of daily surprise and daily thanksgiving.[28]

Maria Gibson's rules for young ladies were strict; however, her pupils were not all that young. Layona Glenn, who at 26 was junior to most of the first 13 students, was outraged to learn that they were not permitted to go to town without a chaperone. Miss Gibson had an "old-fashioned" understanding of education—severity breeds discipline and minute attention to domestic niceties breeds ladies. A bureau drawer ajar or dust on the mantelpiece brought stern reprimands, and a small tear in a glove could become a reason for being denied an outing. The perfectly groomed Maria Gibson would have found Lucy Meyer an incorrigible student. The Chicago schoolmistress, her mind always grappling with some ingenious idea or other, had a habit of going to important assemblies with gloves mismatched and hat askew.

Layona Glenn was loquacious and

independent, and chafed under Miss Gibson's strictures, but she stubbornly stayed on for the full course while six out of seven members of her class left after the first year. She later recalled that she thought at her graduation: "The only thing I wouldn't miss about the place ... was Miss Maria Gibson. Much as I admired her, I would be glad to be rid of Miss Gibson."[29]

Scarritt students did admire their dignified principal and some, who got past her severity, grew to love her. In fact, Maria Gibson did enjoy festive occasions, and many serious young women were able to learn from her that fun was not irreligious. For others, the discipline worked, and when they got to the mission field they discovered new strengths in themselves because of the doorknobs they polished and the floors they scrubbed to a perfect sheen at the training school. "The mother of details," as she often called herself, also won their affection with her never-failing interest in everything about her students, no matter how trivial.

Their seemingly sophisticated principal had a simple faith, but it had not come easily. She was a proud woman who was nevertheless haunted by self-doubt. But by the time she became Scarritt's director, she was 47 and had developed, through constant application, a prayer life that was a day-by-day, relaxed dialogue with God. There was nothing in her or her pupils' lives that did not find its place—whether it was a parent's death, administrative minutiae, or a new coiffure. The women who became her friends were those she knelt with, empathetically sharing in their sorrows and joys through the medium of prayer.

Needless to say, Maria Gibson was conservative. Her natural reticence and her ideas about woman's place had been major stumbling blocks to her conversion as a young woman; she literally could not bring herself to speak or pray in public. Innovations in the school's curriculum were initiated by Belle Bennett and like-minded women in the missionary societies. (Miss Gibson balked when it was urged that sociology courses be added to Scarritt's schedule of classes, but once convinced, she acted with characteristic thoroughness.)

Lucy Rider Meyer, in contrast, was open to every idea. She feasted on books, and her active mind searched out any and all kinds of truths with complete confidence in their ultimate harmony with Christian faith. Science was a favorite subject; she had obtained a medical degree and wrote at least one scientific treatise that proved unpublishable. Though she had little occasion to make an issue of her views on woman's rights, she was clearly with the suffragists, and consequently her friends numbered women like Frances Willard and Jane Addams.

Occasionally, her enthusiasms created difficulty. In the school's first year,

Ruby Davis

Bertha Deen

The Deaconess Movement

The founder of the modern deaconess movement was German Lutheran pastor Theodore Fliedner who gathered and began to train released women prisoners for service to the outcast and needy. By 1884, there were over 5,500 German deaconesses in 56 communities. Deaconesses were organized for foreign missionary service, and all deaconesses received some nurses' training. The purpose of the deaconess movement was to revive the ancient ministry of Christian women to meet both physical and spiritual needs, in a Protestant rather than Catholic form. American Lutherans influenced by the German movement brought deaconess work to the United States, but the American Methodists fully developed the movement. Methodist missionary women used the concept of the deaconess on the mission field as early as 1871. The first generation of Methodist deaconesses served as pastor's assistants, nurses, travelers' aids, social workers and educators, roles deemed gender appropriate by church and state. The deaconess movement has continued to the present day where women work to allay societal urgencies: homelessness, youth violence, spousal abuse, disaster relief, child advocacy, AIDS. Today's deaconesses pursue their call in a dramatically expanded field of Christian social service.

Jane Addams taught a course on primitive Christianity on the grounds that the gospel interpreted in that light was the gospel for the poor. Mrs. Meyer invited the young teacher to join her Board of Trustees.

Jane Addams duly appeared at her first meeting, but she was quickly voted out. Hull House, Jane Addams' settlement house, had become notorious among church people for omitting religious instruction from its schedule of activities. The omission called down the anathemas of orthodox religionists, and much to Mrs. Meyer's consternation, her trustees wanted nothing to do with Miss Addams.

At the end of the second year of the Chicago Training School, many of the students were distressed at the prospect of disbanding. In their field work they had begun projects and made friends, and there was no one to continue what they had started. The boys' club would revert to the pool hall and the widow with many children would grow sicker. Some of them, with no means of support, stayed on through the hot summer months to try to cope with the unwieldy problems of the city streets. The next autumn four women paid a month's rent on a flat, and began to spend full time with the city's immigrant poor.

One of the women was Isabella Thoburn, home on leave from India, and the flat was the first Methodist deaconess home in the United States. Mrs. Meyer, appealing for funds for its support, recounted the year's donations: "money, rings, bracelets, old coins that had lain for years in treasure boxes, sewing machines, pianos, soap, postage stamps, toothpicks, wash tubs and cows. ..."[30]

But the response was not entirely positive. The dress and bonnet uniform of the deaconess was too reminiscent of the nun's habit for many sturdy Protestants. Working for nothing but a sustenance wage, the deaconess was "cheap labor" and an embarrassment to the good Christian worker who earned a decent salary. But the opposition went deeper:

> Woman might properly do dress-making, or devote her time to domestic service or teach school, pending her reception into the sphere to which she was born. Or, if fortune was unkind in exceptional cases, she might conceivably become a missionary. But that a door should be flung wide open into such an unnatural vocation by the final recognition of a Methodist sisterhood—What was the world coming to? Entrenched masculine rights and privileges took alarm, and at ministerial conferences one heard dark hints of "her-preachers" and a general up-heaving of ecclesiastical and time-honored customs.[31]

Largely thanks to Isabella and James Thoburn, deaconess work was recognized by the General Conference in 1888, and Miss Thoburn wore her costume back to India. In 1902, after successfully surmounting the same old arguments, the southern Methodist Church followed. In every church, women workers and deaconesses poured out of the Chicago Training School, Scarritt, and dozens of other schools that came after—and hospitals, orphanages, retirement and industrial homes, and community centers were the result. Though the Chicago Training School never became an official school of the Methodist Episcopal Church, 40 church institutions were founded by its graduates in Lucy Rider Meyer's lifetime.

When Mrs. Meyer retired with her husband from leadership of the Chicago school, the reason given was the very real one of ill health. But there was another unstated one. She and "Mr. Meyer" (she always called him by that name in public, and perhaps in private) could no longer work together, even though they were perfectly happy living together. Her ideas were liberal and far-reaching; he was conventional and even fundamentalist in his beliefs. And, after all the years of living with the intrepid Lucy Rider, he was also not converted in his estimate of woman's capabilities. He wrote in his "Memoirs:"

> Whenever I talked with her concerning a change, she insisted that a woman must succeed her as Principal; but I was definitely convinced that no woman

could be found to carry the responsibilities of that institution, maintain its finances, and provide the repairs and additions that were contemplated.[32]

He was stubborn, and she was ill, so they compromised and chose a man to succeed them whom they both trusted.

In the more conservative South, women were suddenly and rudely awakened to their subordinate position in the church. They had almost forgotten it in the rush of 28 years of activity in missions all over the world. But when the General Conference of 1906 suddenly declared its intention of uniting the home and foreign missions organizations without any consultation with the 100,000 women involved, they realized that they had no voice or vote in church polity.

Four representatives of the women's organizations, including Belle Bennett, rushed to the Conference meeting place in Birmingham. Being women, they were not permitted to speak on the floor of the assembly or even to the Committee on Missions. When they sent a memorial into the Conference suggesting a council composed equally of men and women to work out a plan, their action was so unusual that its announcement met with laughter. Finally a committee of nine men and four women was appointed to bring all of the mission societies of the church into some kind of union.

1906 made suffragists of southern Methodist women. Even Maria Gibson was to kneel at a missions meeting a few years later and utter the prayer: "Dear Lord, we pray for the men on the Board of Missions. Thou knowest how they have troubled and worried us. They have been hard to bear sometimes, but we thank thee that they are better than they used to be."[33]

PROGRAM GUIDE

WORSHIP CENTER

Prepare a simple worship table or designate a space for some candles and an opened Bible. You will need matches to light the candles at the appropriate time.

FOCUS STATEMENT

This is a story of Protestant Christian mission and women's involvement. It is the story of the struggle for women's rights in church and society. "If it can give [you] some sense of [your] own history (or herstory), some feeling for [your] beginnings, then it will have fulfilled its aim."[34] We are here to communicate the struggle of our foremothers in the Methodist tradition and to gain a new perspective on their life and work. As we read, study, discuss, reflect, pray and worship, may we come to appreciate the course they have charted for our future as women organized for mission and accept our role to continue the story and the journey toward women's full and equal participation as partners in God's mission.

OPENING WORSHIP

CALL TO COMMUNITY FOR STUDY AND REFLECTION:

As the leader reads the focus statement (see above), another member of the group lights the candles on the worship table.

Leader: The people perish for lack of vision.

All: We have come to tell the story of United Methodist Women and shape it into a vision for the future.

Leader: O God of all that was and is and is to come, carry us down the ages on threads of remembrance.

All: Connect us with our sisters and mothers of all times.

Leader:	Bring us their childhood innocence and their adolescent hope again.
All:	**Recreate the longings of our mothers and grandmothers, and touch us with the unfulfilled capacities of our foremothers.**
Leader:	Gather the light threads of anguish and hope that bind us together,
All:	**And weave for us a new memory in this time and place.**[35]
HYMN:	"Hymn of Promise" *(The United Methodist Hymnal,* #707)
SCRIPTURE:	Mark 5:25–34
PRAYER:	"God, Intimate and Fearful"[36]
Leader:	O God, intimate and fearful, who carried us with tenderness with in our mother's womb; who appointed us to speak when we were yet unborn: touch our mouths with your truth, and take away our fear, that we may proclaim you to the nations and celebrate your mighty acts.
All:	**Let the whole world see and know that things which were cast down have been raised up and things which had grown old have been made new.**
Leader:	Let us bless God for the women whose blood has flowed that others might have life; who have suffered at the hands of their allies; who have refused to accept shame; who have demanded healing.
All:	**Let the whole world see and know that things which were cast down have been raised up and things which had grown old have been made new.**
Leader:	Let us bless God for women who have boldly touched our lives; who have disrupted our use of power; who have made us see what was hidden and feel in our bodies what it means to be made whole.

All:	Let the whole world see and know that things which were cast down have been raised up and things which had grown old have been made new.
Leader:	Let us bless God for the women who know what has been done to them; whose courage leaves them exposed; who, in fear and trembling and steadfast truth, proclaim the whole truth of salvation.
All:	Let the whole world see and know that things which were cast down have been raised up and things which had grown old have been made new.

QUESTIONS FOR DISCUSSION AND REFLECTION

Together, reflect on these questions. List examples from the fifth chapter of Conduct, *"They Carried Flowers Day by Day into Malodorous Abodes," and make any obvious connections with previous chapters.*

1. What were the main reasons for the women's missionary societies to establish home missions?
2. What services did the women's missionary societies provide on the "home" front?
3. What shifts in society occurred to transform the image of a "woman" and her missionary work in the United States?
4. What challenges did the women face in undertaking home missions work?

A VOICE FROM THE PAST

Share this quote with the group and invite brief reflections.

Of all the fallacies ever concocted, none is more idiotic than the one indicated in the saying, "A woman's strength consists in her weakness." ... Let us insist first, last, and always that gentleness is never so attractive as when joined with strength, purity never so invincible as when leagued with intelligence, beauty never so charming as when it is seen to be the embellishment of reason and the concomitant of character. What we need to sound in the ears of girlhood is to be brave, and in the ears of boyhood to be gentle. There are not two sets of virtues; and there is but one greatness of character; it is that him (or her) who combines the noblest traits of man and woman in nature, words, and deeds.

—Frances Willard,
"Address before the Women's Christian Temperance Union," 1893

RISING TO THE CHALLENGE

For this portion of the session, you will invite each member of the group to select one woman from the list, review her story as it is presented in the chapter and retell her story to the rest of the group in first person, narrative form—as if the story were her own. Each group member will also create a "quilt" square of the woman she is representing to the group and add it to the "quilt."

- Belle Bennett
- Mellie Perkins
- Sarah Dickey
- Jennie Hartzell
- Lucy W. Hayes
- Jennie Willing
- Frances Willard
- Lucy Rider Meyer
- Maria Gibson and Layona Glenn

CLOSING WORSHIP

You may want to have a basket containing a variety of breads on the worship table and consider breaking and sharing these with the group at the close of this session.

SCRIPTURE: Acts 2:44–47

All: **We are a community of women.**

Leader: It is through the Bread of Life that community is nourished among us. Bread—the word brings many images to mind: whole wheat, rye with caraway seeds, pumpernickel, matzoh, biscuits, muffins, sweet rolls, bagels, long French loaves, plump raisin loaves, challah, white or dark, large or small, leavened and unleavened, freshly baked or day-old, so different, and yet, all bread.

All: **It is our PURPOSE to know God.**

Leader: The Bread of Life, God's Word incarnate, gives us the ingredients for our lives: grains of wheat, salt of the earth, living water,

	leaven. God kneads us, molds us, shapes us, forms us and wraps us in the warm blanket of love and lets us grow.
All:	**It is our PURPOSE to experience freedom as whole persons through Jesus Christ.**
Leader:	We ask each day for our portion of the Bread of Life. Toast for breakfast, donut at coffee break, sandwich for lunch, warm dinner rolls dripping with butter. Yet, millions of people, our brothers and sisters, go to bed hungry each night. They lack even a crust of bread. We, who have some bread, are called to share with those who have none.
All:	**It is our PURPOSE to develop a creative, supportive fellowship.**
Leader:	The Bread of Life empowers and sustains us to care for one another. The bread comes from the oven, fragrant and warm. Its aroma fills the house and passersby say, "Mmm, someone's baking bread." After it is cooled a bit, we wrap it gently and take it to our new neighbors. "Welcome to your new home. What can we do to help you?"
All:	**It is our PURPOSE to expand concepts of mission through participation in the global ministries of the church.**
Leader:	The Bread of Life calls us forth to tell the old, old story in new, new ways. As God is made known to us in the breaking of bread, the Body of Christ, given for us, may we, too, be blessed, broken, and scattered so that all may be fed.[37]

If desired, break and share the bread.

HYMN: "One Bread, One Body" *(The United Methodist Hymnal, #620)*

PREPARING FOR THE NEXT SESSION

Before the group is dismissed, the leader should highlight the following opportunities for study and reflection beyond the session. Remember to select a leader and make any assignments, as needed, in preparation for the next group session.

1. Continue to reflect on the questions from chapter five, "They Carried Flowers Day by Day into Malodorous Abodes," and make additional notes in your journal.
2. Read the next chapter, "Shall She Be Allowed to Preach?" in preparation for the next session.
3. Review the questions for discussion and reflection in the program guide that follows chapter six, "Shall She Be Allowed to Preach?" Begin to make notes on your thoughts and feelings related to the material in this chapter.
4. Continue to explore your own history (herstory) by working on your personal timeline. See "Suggestions for Individual and Group Study" on page xi for details.
5. Continue to work on your "quilt" squares, if you choose, between the sessions.
6. Select one woman from the list on page 159 of the next chapter's program guide and prepare to tell her story as if it were your own. *Note: The group leader for the next session may wish to "assign" one woman to each group member to avoid overlap.*

SENDING FORTH

Leader: May the God of hope fill you with all joy and peace in believing, so that you may abound in hope by the power of the Holy Spirit.

—Romans 15:13

As the group disperses—sharing signs of God's peace, if desired—the leader extinguishes the candles.

SHALL SHE BE ALLOWED TO PREACH?

In 1827 Harriet Livermore preached before the Congress of the United States; her "eloquence and musical voice" were said to have deeply stirred the assembled parliamentarians. She was no stranger to Washington. Many years before, as the daughter of a senator, "her dark-eyed beauty and brilliant conversation" thrust her into the center of the social whirl of the capital. But when her engagement to a young man was broken off by his parents because of her tempestuous displays of emotion, she viewed the disappointment of "all my hopes of sublunary bliss" as divine punishment for her "wild and irregular" disposition, and she turned to religion.

For several years Harriet Livermore pored over the Bible and wavered between one doctrine and another, finally settling on the Baptist interpretation. Her allegiance to that church was short-lived, and after a nervous breakdown in 1824 she became a "solitary eclectic" and began preaching and writing to broadcast her individual brand of religion. Her first book was called *Scriptural Evidences in Favor of Female Testimony in Meetings for the Worship of God,* and the proceeds went towards her evangelistic travels. As she grew more eccentric and alone, the self-termed "Pilgrim Stranger" became convinced that the millennium would soon be revealed in Jerusalem. She crossed and recrossed the Atlantic 10 times in visits to the Holy City. With an allowance provided by her father's will, Harriet Livermore continued to write and preach until 1869. Her last book was written in the vain hope of funding her return to Jerusalem to die; instead she died at the age of 80 in a Philadelphia almshouse.[1]

Harriet Livermore referred to herself as a "gazing stock" for other women to use as an example of their responsibility and usefulness to the church. More than 40 years later southern Methodist women, after amply demonstrating their "usefulness," were arguing for a vote in the affairs of their church while ardently denying any covert ambition for the rights of clergy. "The service of Christ in the Church never requires the abandonment of Christ's service in the

Phoebe Palmer
Methodist Episcopal Church

Born in New York City, the fourth of ten children, Phoebe Palmer was raised on a strict regimen of daily family worship. In her youth she showed signs of literary ability, writing poems as early as the age of ten. At the age of nineteen, she married Walter Palmer, a young homeopathic physician and a fellow Methodist who, like Phoebe, had been "powerfully converted" at the age of thirteen. Following an experience of "entire sanctification" at New York's Allen Street Methodist Episcopal Church in 1832, Phoebe began the "Tuesday Meeting for the Promotion of Holiness" which continued to meet in her home for 37 years. Phoebe Palmer's published writings and her work as a traveling evangelist made a still wider impact. She contributed frequently to the principal journal of the perfectionist movement, the *Guide to Holiness,* and wrote a succession of books. At her funeral, she was eulogized, "Twenty-five thousand souls saved under the instrumentality of Phoebe Palmer!"

home. The holy office and duty of motherhood is and should always be first with the true woman," wrote Mary Helm.[2] Once more the women were struggling against the proposition that any added degree of activity or power in the world would make them less "womanly" and remove them from their God-appointed bailiwick.

The specter of unladylike behavior grew more threatening as women emerged to assume what had been male prerogatives. Harriet Livermore was a curious phenomenon when she preached before Congress; when Isabella Beecher Hooker testified for woman's right to vote before the Senate Judiciary Committee in 1871, she was accused of shamelessness and promiscuity. For most women every step from the home out into the world only incidentally involved a move for rights and privileges equal to men's. To accomplish their duty as Christian women, they meant to extend their province to what they felt might be its preordained limit; they did not mean to break new ground. Content to concede that their role in society was not the same as man's, they believed that to argue for rights for their own sake was ambitious and unbecoming. But to pursue rights for a Christian motive was justified, and even righteous, wasn't it?

Even woman preachers challenging a traditional male bastion could be hearty advocates of "woman's place." Phoebe Palmer was credited with saving 25,000 souls in prayer and camp meetings and revivals in the United

States and England; and throughout her joint ministry with her husband, she completely overshadowed him. Nevertheless, she shunned the woman's rights movement, tried to avoid public prominence and even resisted allowing her name to be printed on the title pages of her books.

The Palmers began their work after two of their children died within a few weeks of birth. The couple took it as a sign that they were to concentrate their lives on spiritual things. In 1835 Phoebe Palmer instituted a weekly prayer meeting for women in her New York City home. The gathering, called the Tuesday Meeting for the Promotion of Holiness, soon attracted men as well as women. Over the next 37 years, some of Methodism's most distinguished leaders visited Mrs. Palmer's parlor, and by the 1850s the meeting drew laymen and ministers from many denominations. The famed lady evangelist also wrote eight books and edited the monthly periodical *Guide to Holiness* with a circulation of over 30,000.

Phoebe Palmer would have refused a license to preach on the basis of its being improper to her sex, but she could and did assume the role of an evangelist. In the revivals of the early and mid-nineteenth century, public testimony was invited from women as well as men, thereby greasing the way toward the more shocking concept of women preaching. The emphasis of the revivals was not on ordination by the church, but on the "divine ordination" of the Holy Spirit. If a woman gave evidence of a power to move and convert with her words and songs, who would dare insist that she go back to the kitchen?

But of course there were always scoffers, no matter what a woman's inspiration or reputation. Lydia Sexton, an early United Brethren woman preacher, recorded the reaction of one of her antagonists in her autobiography:

> I don't care what you say about women preaching. I know that God never called a woman to preach his gospel. He made roosters to crow, and not hens. My house is a preacher's home; but if that crowing hen should stop here I would not ask her in, but tell her to go home and wash dishes.[3]

Lydia Sexton was born in 1799 and raised in the backwoods of Ohio. A rude countrywoman, she had less reserve than the gentlewomen of the towns and cities. Her book is full of running commentary on the vicissitudes of a woman's life. She was the daughter of an itinerant Baptist minister and a mother with a forceful singing style:

> Mother was a remarkable singer, and contributed largely to his [her father's]

success in the good work, and barring the command to "keep silence in the churches," she sang so loud and so distinctly that the words of the hymn or song sometimes would be heard and understood half a mile distant.[4]

This memory gave reason for a long argument, based on scripture, against the offensive Pauline command. The battle for woman's rights was to be joined on this point again and again, sometimes with skillful exegesis and other times with a curt dismissal; Isabella Thoburn's mother refused to have Paul's injunction against woman's speaking read at family prayers in her home.

Lydia Sexton's life reads like soap opera. Her childhood was one of backbreaking work under hard taskmasters. She was widowed twice and left with two sons to support; sickness and poverty plagued her. Earning her living in tailoring and millinery, she met with constant discrimination: "I only mention this anecdote ... to show that whenever it can be done, even down to the matter of needlework, men are inclined to monopolize all branches of labor, as well as the professions. Ay, even into the kitchen they come, and immediately demand and receive double wages."[5]

At the age of 28, she married (for a third time) a man who was eight years her junior and a fiddler at country dances. Though she was happy for awhile, she was haunted by past misfortunes that left her bitter with God. Not long afterward, convicted of sin, she was

Lydia Sexton
United Brethren Church

Born to a Baptist preacher and his wife, Lydia Sexton struggled all her life with God's call. After two marriages ended tragically in the deaths of her husbands, Lydia met and married Joseph Sexton, and they moved from Ohio with the frontier to Indiana, Illinois and finally to Kansas. After hearing her speak at a love-feast, an elder in the United Brethren Church offered her a preaching license at once. Lydia refused the license, though she continued to preach. A year later she was offered a license and again she refused. Finally, in 1851, her class meeting took the matter into its own hands and voted to license her. They presented their decision to the quarterly meeting of the United Brethren Illinois Conference, and she was licensed. After renewing her license quarterly for seven years, Lydia asked that it be made an annual license, saving her a great deal of travel in renewing it. The General Conference, however, had decided to license no woman for fear that they would ask to be elders and even bishops. Yet they could not deny Sexton's gifts and the validity of her ministry so they "recommended" her as a preacher for life and gave her "credentials" as an approved pulpit speaker and a "useful helper in the work of Christ." At age seventy, Lydia became the first woman prison chaplain at the Kansas State Prison. Though she resigned a year later, she continued to preach and minister in the prison until her death, baptizing and giving communion to a class of inmates that eventually numbered nearly one hundred.

converted and baptized in the Miami River by the Disciples of Christ. It was one night at a dance that she received her call to the ministry, when she was suddenly seized by an irresistible urge to preach to the party-makers and incite them to repentance.

For 10 years Lydia Sexton debated her course. Shy of pressing her new ambition and fearful of ridicule, she only spoke up occasionally at prayer meetings. When she finally began preaching in earnest, her husband and relatives came to her support. They and most of her listeners were impressed with her ability to inspire congregations to revivalistic frenzy. With her husband accompanying her, she began to itinerate, preaching in rural churches of every denomination.

In the 1850s Lydia Sexton prevailed upon a United Brethren quarterly conference to give her a preacher's license. (The move was not without precedent. In 1849 Charity Opheral had been granted a license with some qualifications.) The General Conference of the church was more cautious, however. Concerned that legitimizing a woman preacher would lead eventually to woman elders and even bishops, the assembled dignitaries hedged. It was clear to all of them that the Bible proscribed woman's elevation in the church but it was just as obvious that Lydia Sexton's abilities should not be wasted. After a long debate she was voted "recommendations" instead of credentials, and given the title "pulpit speaker" instead of "preacher."[6]

Less than 15 years later, Margaret (Maggie) Van Cott became the first Methodist woman to receive a preacher's license. The "Widow Van Cott" began her soul-winning at Phoebe Palmer's Five Points Mission. Her successes there led to invitations to preach at local churches, and she soon became a popular revival leader. Annually, for over 30 years, she traveled from 3,000 to 7,000 miles, leading an average of 2,000 penitents to the altar.

Mrs. Van Cott was a colorful figure. Weighing around 200 pounds (her detractors said 250), she was famous for her elegant style. She was said to have "the dramatic fire of the true and natural actress."[7] A newspaper reporter's observations are instructive both for what they suggest about her appeal, and for the difference in description that would have been accorded to a male evangelist:

> The clerical toilet of the Rev. Widow Van Cott, as she stood up before the multitude, in Hudson St. Methodist Church, New York City, a few Sundays since, and dispensed the Word, is described as having been neat, and that she looked as blooming and blushing as a newly made bride. Her hair was nicely fixed and frizzed, and her face glowed with a modest but conscious splendor, as she stood

before the congregation in her rich but tasteful dress of bombazine. She wore a neat black jet ornament on her throat, and a handsome gold chain peeped from the black belt around her waist. Every word she uttered was delivered with function and force. There is considerable power and attraction in the manner in which the widow lifts her smooth white hand and nicely rounded fingers to the ceiling, and then brings them down with energy on the wooden shelf of the pulpit. When warmed to her subject her face seems lighted up and full of stirring animation. Her face in happy moments contracts and expands, and her handsomely shaped body sways to and fro with the excitement. Her elocution is natural and florid, and her sentences uttered in a bass tone voice.[8]

The democracy of the revival meeting was broad enough to include the fashionable Widow Van Cott and the black washerwoman, Amanda Smith. Of course the laundress had less cause to worry about her gentility, since no one at that time thought of black women as ladies. Born a slave on a Maryland plantation, Amanda Smith was freed as a child by the dying wish of her white mistress. She grew up poor, was educated minimally and married early. Her husband, who was something of a scoundrel, died in the Civil War. A second marriage proved no happier, and also ended in widowhood.

Amanda Smith had several children;

Margaret Newton Van Cott
Methodist Episcopal Church

Margaret Newton Van Cott was born in New York City. Though raised a strict Episcopalian, she joined the Methodist Church in her adult years and had an experience of conversion on the pavement in front of Old John Street Methodist Episcopal Church. Following her conversion, Maggie Van Cott issued her manifesto of independence by stating to her husband and the pastor of another Methodist Episcopal Church that "I believe my tongue is my own, and I will use it when I please, where I please, and as I please." In 1866 she made her first public address in a schoolhouse in Durham, New York, and made many other public addresses with many conversions to give divine endorsement to her efforts. In 1868 she received an exhorter's license which empowered her to conduct prayer meetings; and in 1869, she was granted a preacher's license by the quarterly conference of Stone Ridge, Ellenville, New York. By her 50th birthday, in 1880, it was said that she had traveled 143,417 miles, held 9,933 revival meetings, and preached 4,294 sermons. Her remarkable career as an evangelist lasted from 1866 until 1912, by which time she was known throughout the United States.

all except one daughter died in infancy. An exceptionally strong woman, she sometimes worked from 6 A.M. to 6 P.M., bent over washtubs and ironing boards, sweeping floors and making beds. She earned the typical wage of a black working woman—often only $6.00 a month, and she prayed continually while she labored. "[A] good deal of praying fills you up pretty well when you cannot get anything else," she later recalled.[9]

Although she had been converted as a child in the Methodist Episcopal Church, it was not until she was a middle-aged woman that she experienced a spiritual power that gradually took possession of her. She began to give testimony in a Methodist church in Philadelphia and discovered that she was no longer afraid of anyone, "not even white people."[10] She also stopped worrying about money. "God will provide" became an objective certainty for her because he always did.

Maggie Van Cott had been brought up to love beautiful things, and though she never wanted great wealth her early career as an evangelist did not provide an income adequate to keep her in a style appropriate to her station in life. An excellent businesswoman, she took over her dead husband's business, and for some years augmented her income with the sale of medicines like "Frog-in-the-throat" cough lozenges and "Enuff" cough syrup. Amanda Smith never owned anything but a few articles of clothing, and she required nothing but a roof over her head and an occasional meal. Though she never asked anything for herself, a pair of shoes or a winter coat or a dollar for dinner were always provided by someone moved by her words and songs.

The black woman's fame spread rapidly and invitations came from camp meetings and churches. Tall, well-proportioned, graceful, she alternately awed her listeners or moved them to tears. When she spoke, she once remarked, she saw the Spirit fall on people—"just like you would sprinkle hot coals on them. ... "[11] By 1878 she was invited to preach in the nation's most prestigious houses of worship, Henry Ward Beecher's Bethany and May Flower churches in Brooklyn, then a fashionable suburb of New York City. But in her expeditions into the South, she braved the hostile stares of whites, and in Washington, D.C., at a conference, she spent two days looking for a restaurant that would serve her.

During the next decade Amanda Smith journeyed to India, Egypt, Africa, Italy, Scotland and England. Isabella Thoburn met her on board a ship in the Suez Canal; her stay in Liberia where she led a temperance campaign was written about in letters by Mary Sharp; her visit to Sierra Leone was celebrated at the United Brethren mission. Everywhere she went she was provided for and fêted, and she returned to the United States as penniless as she was when she left it.

Amanda Smith
Methodist Episcopal Church

Influenced by the "Tuesday Meetings" held at Phoebe Palmer's house, Amanda Smith, an African-American woman, began preaching in colored churches of the New Jersey–New York area in 1869. Though she sometimes met with resistance from African Methodist Episcopal pastors who felt that it was not proper for a woman to preach or conduct services, there were enough who felt otherwise. In the summer of 1870, with the encouragement of a white employer, Amanda Smith attended one of the "holiness" camp meetings devoted to spreading the doctrine of Christian perfection. Though diffident at first about speaking before white audiences, she quickly won the respect at this and later camp meetings by her spiritual fervor. In the fall of 1870 she gave up domestic work to devote herself to evangelism. Amanda Smith inherited her parents' concern for Africa and its spiritual needs; and at the close of 1881, following a sojourn in England, she sailed to Monrovia, Liberia. She returned to the United States in 1890 with an "adopted" native Gredebo boy named Bob. She was a fervently religious person, desiring only to serve her God. Yet, as an ex-slave and a woman, she was conscious of the problems facing those who shared her race and sex. As an internationally famed evangelist, she helped expand the accepted role of women in both the African Methodist Episcopal and Methodist churches.

Amanda Smith's personal charisma as well as her race set her apart and contributed to the fascination she held for church people. And she made friends. James Thoburn reported of her in India:

> The penetrating power of discernment which she possessed in so large a degree impressed me more and more the longer I knew her. Indeed, through my association with her I learned many valuable lessons, more that has been of actual value to me as a preacher of Christian truth, than from any other person I ever met.[12]

Though revival meetings were widely applauded into the 20th century, their influence gradually waned after the Civil War, and women began to look for approval for their ministry from church bureaucracies. When Mary Clarke Nind read an article by a Methodist divine suggesting that she and Jennie Fowler Willing be licensed to preach, she was annoyed. But her irritation soon turned to thoughtfulness. She remembered playing "preacher" as a child and wondered "after all these years is God about to honor me to preach the gospel? Is it possible that my youthful aspirations are to be realized?"[13] Her activity for the Woman's Foreign Missionary Society provided the opening wedge. Visiting churches to proselytize for the organization, she so impressed one minister that he invited her to preach. Other invitations followed, but Mrs. Nind never sought or received official sanction: she was, as a friend commented, not ordained, but "fore-ordained."

Jennie Fowler Willing, married to a lawyer-turned-minister, enjoyed an unusual relationship with her husband: "You and I are partners," he told her, "with equal rights and ownership." As if to demonstrate the sincerity of this sentiment, he arranged a preacher's license for her and, as the presiding elder of an Illinois conference, he gave her all but nominal control over one congregation. But it was not so much Jennie Willing's preaching that disturbed church people; it was her vociferous advocacy of woman's rights. An article she wrote in the *Ladies Repository,* describing parsonage life as a "cross," outraged readers. The author was "strong and mannish" and her ideas "offensive to refined taste," the critics complained.[14]

Mrs. Willing was so independent in her moods and actions that she had difficulty working with other women, much less men. Nevertheless, she devoted most of her life to organizing for foreign and home missions and the WCTU, and later, after her husband's death, in training school and city settlement work. She had little time to pursue a ministerial career.

Amanda Way took a different course, beginning as a temperance and woman's rights organizer and ending as a minister. As early as 1851, she helped to form the Woman's Rights Society in Indiana, and at the same time she was a pioneering figure in the temperance movement in that state. After the Civil War she was named as a delegate to the founding convention of the Prohibition Party. When she was given a preacher's license in the Methodist Episcopal Church, Amanda Way combined the roles of lecturer and preacher. But in 1880 the General Conference declared an end to the licensing of women as preachers. Raised a Quaker, she returned to the Society of Friends rather than give up preaching, and for the remainder of her life she quietly devoted herself to the ministry.

In March of 1875 the *Ladies Repository* reported that,

> Ordinances, canons and disciplines wilt have to be modified in accordance with the spirit of the age; for the discussion no longer turns upon a woman's fitness, piety or ability—all these having long since been conceded—but simply on the question: Shall she be allowed to preach?[15]

Apparently, the Methodist Episcopal Church would not be responsible for officiating over woman's ascendance to the ministry. Quakers, Universalists and Unitarians might have their quota of women preachers, but the Methodists were not prepared to preside over the demise of "the lady."

The action of the General Conference that caused Amanda Way's break with Methodism was precipitated by the request for ordination of two women graduates of Boston University School of Theology, both licensed preachers: Anna Oliver and Anna Howard Shaw. Frances Willard and a companion were at the same Conference with the object of presenting a message from the WCTU inviting the gentlemen to send representatives to their next convention. The idea of a woman speaking on the floor of the Conference was greeted with delirium. "We have no precedent," the men told Miss Willard, and while she waited they studiously avoided her.

> Somehow, they were always busy, and never could be seen. Meantime the buzzing went on. Poor Anna Oliver, who was trying to gain recognition as a preacher, seemed hardly more of a black sheep than we two white ribbon women with our harmless little message.[16]

Frances Willard never spoke at the Conference. Under the circumstances, it was not surprising that the two women ministers were not given ordination, and, what's more, were stripped of their license to preach under a new church statute. "Poor Anna Oliver," the first Methodist woman to earn a divinity degree, went back to her preaching and continued to fight for recognition from her church. Estranged from her family because of her "unnatural" ambition, she had changed her name to save them from embarrassment (her real name was Snowden and Oliver was the name of a

Jennie Fowler Willing
Methodist Episcopal Church

I never preached at a place without having the satisfaction to learn that they desired me to return. I mention this only as a matter of encouragement to some of my sisters who feel that they have a call to the ministry. Do your whole duty, and look to God for help.

—Lydia Sexton as quoted in *The Autobiography of Lydia Sexton,* Dayton, OH: United Brethren Publishing House, 1882, 867

maiden aunt). Her first church was so badly in debt that it was put up for sale. To save it, and herself, she bought it. Later she was called to another poverty-stricken church in Passaic, New Jersey—probably because she would work for less salary than a man. Evidently she was popular there, and for a short time Amanda Smith joined her as an assistant. Reported a local newspaper: "Passaic is having a lively time; what with stirring up sinners and Christians on one hand, and on the other two women in the pulpit, and one black, the buzzing grows apace."[17] Anna Oliver died not long after this notoriety in 1893.

Anna Howard Shaw did not look for any change of heart from the Methodist Episcopal hierarchy; she took the same course as Amanda Way and left the church. A few months later she joined the Methodist Protestants and petitioned the New York Conference of that church for ordination. Though she met some bitter opposition, this time she was ordained. Not that it ended there—the act was afterwards declared unconstitutional. But the New York Conference reaffirmed its position, and the ordination of Mrs. F. St. John, a Kansas Woman's Foreign Missionary Society leader, by the General Conference of 1892 was further confirmation of its legality. At any rate, Anna Howard Shaw titled herself "Reverend" for the rest of her life.

Ministerial ambitions not only meant a rather unequal tug of war with officialdom and social repudiation, but penury as well. Anna Oliver evidently had an independent income, but Anna Howard Shaw could depend only on her own resources. While the young men at the theological school were given free accommodations and inexpensive board, she received just $2.00 a week for a room outside the school's environs and got nothing towards her meals. As a licensed preacher she sometimes found a week's employment, but just as often she subsisted on milk and crackers. One day an officer of the Woman's Foreign Missionary Society found her sitting on a flight of stairs, too weak to climb them. After that she received a weekly stipend that at least allowed her to eat.

Anna Howard Shaw went from theological school to a successful ministry on Cape Cod of 10 years duration. She was not unique—others did equally well. But women preachers remained a novelty in the ecclesiastical order of things. The attitude of the editor of the *Ladies Repository* was a typical one.

> The writer is a genuine Presbyterian in his opposition to woman preachers, as a rule; but he has always believed that there might be exceptions, as were Miriam and Deborah; and after hearing Mrs. Lathrop (a Michigan woman minister)

Anna Oliver
Methodist Episcopal Church

More than a century ago, a few women in the Methodist tradition served as evangelists; a few held a "local preacher's license," the first step toward ordination. But until Anna Oliver came along, no woman pressed the matter of ordination and full clergy rights among the Methodists. Following undergraduate studies and a master's degree with honors from a New York woman's college in 1862, Anna taught school in Connecticut and dabbled in temperance work. After the Civil War, she volunteered as a home missionary to teach black children in Mississippi. She resigned a year later when she discovered that the Mission Board was paying male teachers twice as much. Moving north to Cincinnati, she studied art and took up temperance work again. Here she felt called to the ministry and, despite major obstacles, earned the bachelor of divinity degree from a Methodist seminary (Boston, 1876), the first woman in America to attain that degree. Following graduation, Anna served pastorates in New Jersey and New York. Supported by her New York City parish, she brought the first test case on the ordination of women before the 1880 General Conference of the Methodist Episcopal Church. Although the Church refused to ordain women, Anna served as a powerful model for women of her generation. It would take 75 more years before full clergy rights were granted to women.

preach, and talking with her, he was convinced that she was truly called to preach as Deborah was to prophesy.[18]

The Methodists were at least more liberal than the Presbyterians. In 1877 a minister was brought to trial and convicted by his presbytery for allowing two women to preach in his church.

While the women in the missionary societies differed widely in their attitudes toward woman preachers, some of them were ready to press for clergy rights for women missionaries when they felt it would further the Christian cause. In 1885 three members of the Detroit Woman's Foreign Missionary Society prepared for the next General Conference a resolution arguing that woman missionaries could work more effectively if they were ordained with the right to baptize and officiate at communion. Despite the support of James Thoburn and Dr. William Butler, the petition was given short shrift. However, at least one missionary, Mary Sharp, took it upon herself to baptize on the strength of a local preacher's license granted her by a church in Pennsylvania.

Some woman missionaries in other denominations were ordained ministers. Sarah Dickey was voted full clergy rights by the United Brethren in 1894, and Dr. Mary Archer (one of those to die in the Sierra Leone massacre) received ordination in the following year. "Forceful, logical and intensely interesting," she had given up the ministry for a medical career before going to Africa.[19] After her death, a church elder remembered:

> Dr. Archer, with the simplicity of a child, in the first interview she ever had with anyone about foreign mission work for herself, related to me her heart struggles respecting the work of the ministry, and how, after having a license and preaching some, the public sentiment respecting woman's preaching confronted her and so impressed her as to turn her to the study and practice of medicine.[20]

Nevertheless, the United Brethren were relatively open to woman's ascendance in the ecclesiastical ranks. Though women and men sat on opposite sides of the altar in some churches as late as the 1850s, women were permitted to cast ballots in the councils of the denomination from its beginning. For the women in the Methodist Episcopal Church, both North and South, it took years of squabbles with men. It was 1887 when a number of women in Nebraska first began a movement to elect a woman as a delegate to the General Conference, and it was Angie F. Newman, a WCTU and home and foreign missions worker, who was asked to carry the standard of woman's rights to the all-male assembly. She consented, musing that if they desired someone as a subject of martyrdom she might serve as well as anyone else. The movement soon took hold in other parts of the church, and among the four women nominated were Frances Willard and Mary Clarke Nind. Arriving at the assembly hall, the women waited quietly for their case to be decided. Mary Nind noted in her journal that "Bishops' address and report on eligibility all against us, but if the Lord be for us, what matters?" Five days later, after a debate centering on obscure constitutional questions, she wrote: "Today we were ejected from our seats by a majority of 37 and two lay votes, and the great debate is over, to come up again in 1892. All is serene in my soul."[21]

Most of the controversy focused on the term "laymen." Obviously, the word was in the masculine gender and the ladies were not. Therefore, the permission to vote extended by the constitution to "laymen" could not apply to them. Many years later a southern Methodist woman, struck by the absurdity of the same argument, wrote,

> The question clearly resolved itself into this: Was she laity or was she not? The more she pondered this solemn theme, the deeper the darkness grew. If she wasn't laity, what was she? Nobody likes to be a what-is-it, and the writer was in genuine distress. One ray of hope she had, however—a faith in the General Conference, which was doomed to saddest blight. If she were laity, the

Mary Clarke Nind
Woman's Foreign
Missionary Society
Methodist Episcopal Church

Mary Clarke Nind became a member of the Central Methodist Church in Winona, Minnesota, in 1866, and in 1879 joined the Minneapolis Wesley Methodist Episcopal Church. Because of her deep passion for foreign missions, Mary held offices in the Woman's Foreign Missionary Society for thirty years, organized many Minnesota societies, traveled extensively, promoting the WFMS and visiting new mission fields. She helped establish the Mary C. Nind Home in Singapore, which was named in her honor, organized "flag festivals" to procure American flags for every mission station, and pioneered in promoting equal rights for women. In October 1887, she was elected the first lay woman delegate to General Conference by the Minnesota Conference, receiving the largest number of votes for any delegate even though she was not present at the election. However, the 1888 General Conference refused to seat her and four other women. Mary Nind was known as "the little bishop" for her missionary sermons and as "Mother Nind" to the missionaries. A book, *Mary Clarke Nind, A Memorial,* written by her children, was published in 1906.

—Excerpt from *They Went Out Not Knowing,* 1

Conference, of course, would give her the rights of laity; and the problem would be definitely solved; if she were not laity, surely the General Conference, in its wisdom and justice, would no longer allow her to dash wildly through the Church's established order like a tailless comet or an unknown bug, an anachronism without place or classification...[22]

Of course the real quarrel was not linguistic or constitutional, and many men were frank enough to admit it. Women held a subordinate position in the church, and it was understood that they were to *stay* there. The full weight of traditional and biblical authority was brought to bear. "It had never been otherwise; why should there be a change now?" was the common cry, accompanied by scriptural quotations from Genesis to Revelation. Eve's divinely decreed subjugation to Adam, and Paul's injunction to "keep silent" were special favorites. The debate was usually closed with funereal prophecies of the downfall of womanhood and extinction of the family, should women be permitted a vote in church or state governments.

It was 1904 before northern Methodist women were admitted to the General Conference. One of the new delegates was Lucy Rider Meyer. "If you can point to a man in the Conference who has done more for the church than has Mrs. Lucy Rider Meyer I will withdraw her name," announced the woman who nominated her.[23] No one came forward.

But the debate went grinding on, and in the South women were not to win laity rights until 1920, a year *after* the 19th amendment gave American women the vote in national elections!

Belle Bennett had quietly advocated woman's rights for years before the question came before the church. One of her intimate friends was Laura Clay, the best known of southern suffragettes. For the most part, the churchwomen around Miss Bennett only smiled indulgently when she brought up the subject. Mary Helm called it "just a notion of Belle's."[24] With her usual diplomacy, Belle Bennett waited for the moment to strike. She had an indomitable confidence that what seemed irremediable, but was nevertheless just, would come to pass. Perhaps another diplomatic woman, Frances Willard, expressed it best: "My shepherd collie, 'Prohibition' ('Hibbie' for short, and 'Hib' for shorter), is a perpetual gospel to me as he reaches out his shaggy paw with a wise look in his eyes that seems to say, 'Have patience with me and it shall grow to be a hand.'"[25]

When agitation for laity rights first began among southern Methodist women, Mary Helm was vehemently opposed to it. After 1906, and the General Conference threat to the independence of the women's societies, she quickly reversed her position and, as editor of the home missions periodical, began to campaign for women's right to vote in the church. And when women were denied a vote for or against union with the General Missionary Society, she resigned her editorship.

Mary Helm had held her church and its leaders in almost medieval reverence. She was bitterly shocked when those she thought could do no wrong, during one General Conference in 1910, refused women laity rights and took control of their hard-won missions programs. Belle Bennett was more realistic, and with characteristic forbearance, set about making the best of a bad situation and preparing for another day. In China, Dr. Margaret Polk, a woman's rights advocate and a missionary who had been doing the work of several men in her Shanghai hospital, stunned the mission societies by resigning her position and leaving the Methodist Episcopal Church, South, in disgust.

Bishop Hoss, in an article in the *Christian Advocate,* related the attitude of the large majority of southern gentlemen who cast a vote against women: ...It is alleged that sex is not an accident, God having made them male and female, that Christianity, though it assures men and women alike of a common standing-ground before God, does no more abolish differences of sex than it abolishes color, race or nationality; that all progress in civilization has meant an increasing differentiation in the spheres and the work of the sexes; and finally, that the headship of man is an apostolic doctrine, not to be got rid

Elizabeth Cady Stanton

As a child, Elizabeth was fascinated by her father's law office where she often overheard the pitiful stories of married women who came for help when deprived under the law of their property and their children. When her father, grieving over the death of his only son, said to Elizabeth, "Oh, my daughter, I wish you were a boy!" she resolved to prove to him that a daughter was as good and as valuable as a son. At the encouragement of her Presbyterian minister, Elizabeth studied Greek, first at home and later in Johnstown Academy, adding Latin and mathematics as well. She also learned to emulate her male schoolmates in riding horseback and became skillful at chess. She attended Troy Female Seminary, graduating in 1832. Involved in anti-slavery and temperance movements, Elizabeth teamed up with Quaker minister Lucretia Mott, and together they laid the foundation for the woman's rights convention that took place at Wesleyan Methodist Church in Seneca Falls, New York on July 19, 1848. Perhaps Mrs. Stanton's greatest contribution was her effort to emancipate women's minds. She was a torchbearer whose liberal thinking and courageous outlook were potent factors in freeing women from the psychological barriers that hedged them in, and in pointing the way to wider interests and activities.

of by sneering at Paul, as an old bachelor, nor by pointing out the obvious fact that many women have better brains and better characteristics than their husbands.[26]

Most of the women took exception to the Pauline "headship of man." They studiously listed the woman preachers of the New Testament and cited Paul again for the rallying cry of liberated churchwomen: "There is neither male nor female; for ye are all one in Jesus Christ." The biblical arguments were taken seriously on the national level since much of America subscribed to Christian belief. The prominent feminist Elizabeth Cady Stanton went so far as to produce a "Woman's Bible," commentaries that denied that there was divine inspiration in passages that denigrated women, and that interpreted other sections in a light favorable to independence and equality. The book created a furor, but the salty Mrs. Stanton had an answer for her critics:

> The criticisms on "The Woman's Bible" are as varied as they are unreasonable. ... One clergyman says: "It is the work of women and the devil." This is a grave mistake. His Satanic Majesty was not invited to join the Revising Committee, which consists of women alone. Moreover, he has been so busy of late years attending Synods, General Assemblies and Conferences, to prevent the recognition of women delegates, that he has had no time to study the languages and "higher criticism"... The Old Testament makes woman a

mere after-thought in creation; the author of evil; cursed in her maternity; a subject in marriage; and all female life, animal and human, unclean. ... Now, to my mind, the Revising Committee of "The Woman's Bible," in denying divine inspiration for such demoralizing ideas, shows a more worshipful reverence for the great Spirit of All Good than does the Church. We have made a fetich [sic] of the Bible long enough. The time has come to read it as we do all other books, accepting the good and rejecting the evil it teaches.[27]

Not long after its appearance, "The Woman's Bible" was formally repudiated by woman's rights organizations. Most women felt that there was ample biblical support for feminist positions, or at least as much as there was for their opponents. And they were not about to follow the anti-clerical Mrs. Stanton and alienate Bible-loving Americans. When the Rev. Anna Howard Shaw took over leadership of the National American Woman Suffrage Association from Susan B. Anthony, she established a Committee on Church Work to win ministers to the cause. Despite the churches' traditional contrariness towards female leadership in their domain, clergymen responded more affably to the woman's rights movement than men of other professions. Lucy Stone noted:

No class of men knows the scriptures so well, or is influenced by them so strongly, as the ministers; and we find there are six ministers ready to speak for woman suffrage at our meetings to one man of any other profession. It is because the ministers are especially interested in questions of practical righteousness, in which they know that the women's votes would help; and the solidity of the vicious elements against woman suffrage has gone far to solidify the ministers in its favor.[28]

In matters of "practical righteousness," it was still universally agreed that women were the superior sex. Whatever else had changed in the turbulence of a century of progress, the reputation of the lady remained. Most men no longer argued for her inferiority or her weakness. Yes, she was man's equal, *but in her own orb.* There resided in her an extra measure of compassion and patience, civility and humility—all of those qualities imagined to be special to her because they were a natural buttress to her role of homemaker. She loved beauty and was beautiful: when Minnesota women went to the polls for the first time they decorated the ballot boxes with flowers.

While anti-suffragists contended that the vote would place women outside the home and contribute to its destruction, woman's rights advocates turned the argument on its head and maintained that the vote would strengthen the home. Playing into the myth, they explained that women would vote temperance and other social legislation because the first area of their concern was the family—and because of their superior moral sense. No one did more to popularize this position than Frances Willard, and in its behalf the legislative victories influenced by the WCTU spoke so well that at least one powerful group of men took it seriously—the liquor interests, who fought the suffragettes vigorously!

Anna Howard Shaw and the other leaders of the woman's movement at the turn of the century progressively narrowed their campaign to one emphasis, that of political enfranchisement for women. And while they argued for it as simple justice, ironically their best weapon was the ostensibly superior and refined morality of "the lady." The individual women who had achieved so much in the professions once thought to be man's province were nearly forgotten, and the lady with her superior virtue was elevated to new heights. When suffrage was finally won, surprisingly enough it was "the lady" who won it.

PROGRAM GUIDE

WORSHIP CENTER

Prepare a simple worship table or designate a space for some candles and an opened Bible. You will need matches to light the candles at the appropriate time.

FOCUS STATEMENT

This is a story of Protestant Christian mission and women's involvement. It is the story of the struggle for women's rights in church and society. "If it can give [you] some sense of [your] own history (or herstory), some feeling for [your] beginnings, then it will have fulfilled its aim."[29] We are here to communicate the struggle of our foremothers in the Methodist tradition and to gain a new perspective on their life and work. As we read, study, discuss, reflect, pray and worship, may we come to appreciate the course they have charted for our future as women organized for mission and accept our role to continue the story and the journey toward women's full and equal participation as partners in God's mission.

OPENING WORSHIP

CALL TO COMMUNITY FOR STUDY AND REFLECTION:

As the leader reads the focus statement (see above), one member of the group lights the candles on the worship table. Another member then reads the scripture.

SCRIPTURE: Luke 4:14–21

Leader: O God, Creator, Redeemer and Sustainer, Pattern of mutual love, forgive us for failing to understand that being Church means loving well.

All: **Help us to create loving community.**

Leader: God of justice and integrity, forgive us for all the times we have not identified ourselves with the oppressed and deprived, and for the times we have put down others.

All:	**Help us to uphold each other.**
Leader:	God the Disturber, forgive us for the times we have taken the easy path in comfort rather than facing discomfort in spreading your good news.
All:	**Help us to be joyful announcers of the word.**
Leader:	God, maker of both men and women in your own image, forgive us for presenting a distorted understanding of what it means to be human or divine.
All:	**Help us to mirror the truth.**
Leader:	O Creator God, forgive us for not affirming the goodness of the bodies you have given us, and for forgetting the importance of Mary caressing Jesus' feet with her hair.
All:	**Help us to accept ourselves in our God-given wholeness.**
Leader:	O God, Friend and Lover, forgive us for our failing to understand our calling to friendship and honesty.
All:	**Help us to be creative and healing in our relationships.**
Leader:	O God, source of all insight, forgive us our shallow understanding of your presence, when we fail to recognize the meal taken together, the joy or sorrow shared, as a meeting with the divine. Strengthen our understanding so that our lives may become more Christlike and so draw others to you.
All:	**Help us to recognize where you are among us.**
Leader:	O Spirit that empowers the powerless,
All:	**Give us the strength to forge communities of loving friends to bring about the new life promised in the resurrection.**[30]
HYMN:	"God of the Sparrow, God of the Whale" (*The United Methodist Hymnal, #122*)

PRAYER OF INTERCESSION[31]

Leader: Holy God, as you have touched us, may we touch others with your love.

Reader 1: The oppressed and the persecuted, crying out for the liberating touch of justice.

All: Touch them with your justice in us.

Reader 2: The poor and the outcast, crying out for the life-giving touch of compassion.

All: Touch them with your compassion in us.

Reader 1: The battered victims of war and violence, crying out for the healing touch of peace.

All: Touch them with your peace in us.

Reader 2: The lost and the lonely, crying out for the welcoming touch of friendship.

All: Touch them with your friendship in us.

Reader 1: The prisoners of their own fear and cruelty, crying out for the generous touch of mercy.

All: Touch them with your mercy in us.

Reader 2: And those we love, crying out for the continuing touch of love.

All: Touch them with your love in us.

Leader: May our lives be the place where you touch us, and we touch others in your name, for you are the source of our life and love.

All: Amen.

QUESTIONS FOR DISCUSSION AND REFLECTION

Together, reflect on these questions. List examples from the sixth chapter of Conduct, *"Shall She Be Allowed to Preach?" and make any obvious connections with previous chapters.*

1. What were the main challenges and obstacles to women becoming preachers and ordained clergy? How did these challenges and obstacles continue to support and/or serve to refute the myth of the "lady" or "woman" and the conduct thought to be "becoming" of her?
2. How did the earliest female "preachers" deal with this "male" role in light of obvious conflicts with a woman's role and place in church and society?
3. What were the prevailing biblical views of women that were used to keep women from being ordained or recognized as valid spokespersons for God? *(See some of the passages listed in the program guide after chapter one, "What is the Sphere of Woman?") for some suggestions.*
4. How did women respond to these biblical references and their applications of them on those in pursuit of fulfilling God's call?
5. How did women's struggle for ordination and equality in church leadership benefit and/or suffer from the woman's rights movement?

VOICES FROM THE PAST

Share these quotes with the group and invite brief reflections.

"I have made almost every conceivable sacrifice to do what I believe [to be] God's will. Brought up in a conservative circle in New York City, that held it a disgrace for a woman to work. ... I gave up home, friends and support, ... worked for several years to constant exhaustion, and suffered cold, hunger, and loneliness. The things hardest for me to bear were laid upon me. For two months my own mother did not speak to me ... And through all this time and today, I could turn off to positions of comparative ease and profit. However, I take no credit to myself for enduring these trials, because at every step it was plain to me, that I had no alternative but to go forward or renounce my Lord."

—Anna Oliver, *"Test case on the ordination of women,"* 1880

[An] old man ... was at first a persecutor of preaching women. ... One day after the congregation was dismissed, he stood in the aisle until I came along by him, when he handed me twenty-five cents. That quarter was of great value to me, as I looked upon him as my persecutor. The brethren told me he had said that our work was a money-making scheme; and if the people would quit paying the preachers they would quit preaching. When he handed me the quarter he told me to pray for him. That was a good omen. That same man professed religion [and] joined the church."

—Lydia Sexton, *Autobiography of Lydia Sexton,* 1882

RISING TO THE CHALLENGE

For this portion of the session, you will invite each member of the group to select one woman from the list, review her story as it is presented in the chapter and retell her story to the rest of the group in first person, narrative form—as if the story were her own. Each group member will also create a "quilt" square of the woman she is representing to the group and add it to the "quilt."

- Anna Howard Shaw
- Lydia Sexton
- Phoebe Palmer
- Maggie Van Cott
- Amanda Smith
- Anna Oliver
- Elizabeth Cady Stanton

Leader: Our quilt is complete. Or, is it? We have named and remembered many of the dedicated women from our personal and collective histories and many from our predecessor organizations, yet there are many, many more women who remain unnamed. Take a moment to reflect on this quilt, on those named, on those forgotten, on the many women who have formed the pattern of women organized for mission. How has this pattern made an impact on your life? What pattern will your life form in this quilt? What patterns will future generations create?

CLOSING WORSHIP

SCRIPTURE: Numbers 27:1–7

Leader: Let us now praise noble women and our mothers who lived before us.

All:	**Through whom God's glory has been shown, in each successive generation.**
Reader 1:	Some ruled nations with authority and were renowned as queens.
Reader 2:	Others gave counsel by their wisdom and spoke with prophetic power.
Reader 3:	A few were leaders of the people because of their deep understanding; their custody of tradition.
Reader 4:	Some composed musical tunes and set forth verses in writing.
Reader 5:	Others were rich and respected, peacefully keeping their homes.
All:	**All these were honored in their lifetime and were a glory of their day.**
Leader:	Such women have left a name which is remembered so that their praises are still sung.
Reader 1:	But others have left no memory, have vanished as though they had never lived.
Reader 2:	These are the nameless women of the ages; the work of their hands is not remembered.
Reader 3:	These women planted, picked, preserved, baked, boiled and brewed; they washed, cooked, cleaned, fed, clothed and nursed the world.
Reader 4:	A few were barren but most bore children, children and more children to carry on the father's name so his posterity continues forever.
All:	**All these were different in their lives, different and yet the same.**
Reader 5:	And they died in different ways; in childbirth, sickness, fever,

	madness, ripe old age. All died.
Leader:	They are now as though they had never been and so too are their daughters who followed them.
Reader 1:	There are numerous men whose good works have not been forgotten,
Reader 2:	Whose descendants remember their names and recall their forefathers with pride, rejoicing in their heritage.
Reader 3:	Their bodies were buried with honor and their names live on so that their glory lasts forever.
Reader 4:	Few of our foremothers are so remembered: most lie forgotten in the graves,
Reader 5:	Until their daughters shall claim their inheritance, recollecting them with joy and pride.
Leader:	Now their glory is not blotted out as we declare their wisdom and proclaim their praise;
All:	**Noble women and nameless ones, our mothers who lived before us.**[32]
HYMN:	"Bring Many Names" *(Global Praise 1, #9)*

PREPARING FOR THE NEXT SESSION

Before the group is dismissed, the leader should highlight the following opportunities for study and reflection beyond the session. Remember to select a leader and make any assignments, as needed, in preparation for the next group session.

1. Continue to reflect on the questions from chapter six, "Shall She Be Allowed to Preach?" and make additional notes in your journal.
2. Read the next two chapters, "Epilogue" and "Afterword: Thirty Years

Later," in preparation for the next session.
3. Review the questions for discussion and reflection in the program guide that follows chapter eight, "Afterword: Thirty Years Later." Begin to make notes on your thoughts and feelings related to the material in this chapter.
4. Continue to explore your own history (herstory) by working on your personal timeline. See "Suggestions for Individual and Group Study" on page xi for details.
5. Continue to work on your "quilt" squares, if you choose, between the sessions.

SENDING FORTH

Leader: Serve your God with patience and passion. Be deliberate in enacting your faith. Be steadfast in celebrating the Spirit's power. And may peace be your way in the world.[33]

As the group disperses—sharing signs of God's peace, if desired—the leader extinguishes the candles.

EPILOGUE

In one (Eucharist) all of the masculine words and images were changed to be feminine. This was done partly to make the point of how ridiculous it is to establish sexual identity for God, but I heard many of the women say they felt really included and involved in the process and heard the words differently than they ever had before. I think maybe this was a by-product that wasn't even aimed for. Every time I saw one individual, she expressed this as the most profound experience in the last 10 years of her life.[1]

The 19th century churchwoman would be astounded and even shocked by this innovation—a worship service invoking God in the feminine gender. But the long and frustrating struggle of churchwomen to continue their efforts to achieve equal voice in the councils of the church and full effectiveness in mission proved that this kind of innovation was precisely what was needed. Without some more fundamental transformation of themselves and of the cultural and religious presuppositions that have traditionally defined them, all progress is so halting and slow as to be, at times, almost nonexistent.

When the 19th amendment became law in 1920, women swarmed to the polls. But to the dismay of the suffragists, very few women ran for public office, and the nation, in its fickle way, went on to other causes. In the church, women were admitted to General Conferences, and gradually—very gradually—assumed positions of authority, but only in token numbers and then usually with less status and at lower pay. The divines of the 20th century who hesitated to give women preacher's licenses for fear of their imminent ascension to the hallowed office of bishop could rest easy in their graves. When a woman received votes for bishop in 1964, many churchmen thought it was a joke. Women dragged themselves up the proverbial ladder of success at a pace snails would have no cause to envy.

By 1972, only a small minority of the positions of real power and responsibility in The United Methodist Church are held by women. Most of these were in the Women's Division (descendant of the woman's missionary societies) or filled by women who received training and experience in the

Theressa Hoover
Woman's Society of
Christian Service
United Methodist Women
The United Methodist Church

Theressa Hoover spent her entire professional life in the women's mission organizations of The United Methodist Church. Joining the Woman's Division of Christian Service as a field worker in 1948, she made her way to the Division's head position as its chief administrative officer (Deputy General Secretary) in 1968 and served in this capacity until her retirement in 1990. Theressa was instrumental in the merger of United Methodist Women and retaining the Women's Division as a part of the newly-formed United Methodist Church from 1968–1972. Theressa Hoover is a native of Fayetteville, Arkansas, and a graduate of Philander Smith College with a master's degree from New York University. Deeply committed to the role of women in the church and to the ecumenical movement, she served as a member of the World Council of Churches' Central Committee, a delegate to three Assemblies of the World Council, a member of the Executive Committee of the National Council of Churches and numerous other ecumenical institutions and associations as well as the National Council of Negro Women.

Division and in local women's societies. Though women comprised 54 percent of the membership of the church in 1972, this statistic was not mirrored in the membership of church boards and agencies, where only 21.9 percent were women.[2]

The situation was no better in the legislative bodies of the church: the higher the level of responsibility, the fewer the number of women. In annual conferences in 1970 women were 36.9 percent of all the *lay* delegates; in jurisdictional conferences—11.8 percent; at the 1970 General Conference 10 percent of the delegates were women.

By 1972, of course, women's liberation had become an important issue inside as well as outside the church. Nevertheless, women were only 13 percent of the 1972 General Conference, far less than the number at either national political party's convention of the same year. As has always been the case, women held almost no positions of power: no woman has ever served as secretary, treasurer or presiding officer of a General Conference. In the more than 30 years of history of The United Methodist Church, women have chaired legislative committees only three times before 1972; and they never chaired a committee at Evangelical United Brethren general conferences. But at last, in 1972, women actually chaired three out of 14 legislative committees. There was a "Women's Caucus" working for the passage of certain legislation, and "more women spoke out on the conference floor than ever before"—68 years *after* women were admitted as delegates to a Methodist General Conference, and nearly 100 years *after* four women dared to storm the gates of that all-male bastion of power.[3]

For example, Sunday school teachers are usually women. As a matter of fact, except for the minister, women are the most visible participants in nearly every *local* church activity. A survey conducted in 1971 showed, for example, that 64 percent of the chairpersons of Commissions on Education, 84 percent of the heads of Commissions on Missions, and 74 percent of the leaders of Commissions on Worship were women. On the other hand, they chaired only 13 percent of the Committees on Finance and only two percent of the Boards of Trustees of local churches. Woman's place in the church has been clearly marked out, and she is effective in its confines—she is the mainstay of most of the activities of the church. But men are almost invariably the final repository of power and authority. Usually they end up by being directors of religious education, teachers, or a matron in a home for aged male ministers."[4]

Always there have been those women who were unsatisfied by the slight progress made by women in the upper echelons of the church. Their efforts were reflected not only in the acquisition of full clergy rights in The Methodist Church, but also in the relative independence of the new Woman's Division of Christian Service established at the time of union in 1940 (when the boards of most women's mission organizations in other denominations had been absorbed into general, male-dominated boards). From all accounts, that independence, which was to last until 1964, was not easily won. Some idea of the kind of difficulty women have faced throughout the 20th century is provided in the following excerpt from a letter written by a prominent southern Methodist missionary leader to Mary Culler White in China in 1938:

> The Committee on Unification held its first meeting last week in Evanston, Illinois. Mrs. Perry is the only woman on the whole Committee; the other churches failed to appoint any, and our General Conference "forgot" to appoint one until some of us had the report amended, and Mrs. Perry substituted for one of the men.[5]

While the men "forgot," the women never did, though woman's rights usually remained in the background and other efforts took precedence. Their organizations grew; their interests expanded; and their understanding of the world, and Christian mission, deepened. They led the way in the ecumenical movement, meeting each other and planning across denominational lines

**Woman's Society of
Christian Service
Wesleyan Service Guild**
Methodist Church

The purpose of the Woman's Society of Christian Service shall be to unite all women of the church in Christian living and service; help develop and support Christian work among women and children around the world; develop the spiritual life; study the needs of the world; take part in such service activities as will strengthen the local church, improve civic, community, and world conditions. To this end this organization shall seek to enlist women, young people, and children in this Christian fellowship; secure funds for the activities in the local church and support of the work undertaken at home and abroad for the establishment of a world Christian community.

even before the turn of the 20th century. Many times they faced social issues before churchmen were even aware of them. Because they had grappled with problems of race, the Evangelical United Brethren Women's Society of World Service, for example, was prepared for the tumult of the 1960s in a way that the men of the church were not. Even today in The United Methodist Church, the Women's Division is envied by other segments of the Board of Global Ministries of the Church, both for its quickness to grasp significant social and moral issues before they become currency in the rest of the denomination, and—contrary to the rumors of woman's poor business sense—for its organizational and financial strength.

One moral and social issue that was also a woman's issue was the Equal Rights Amendment. Year after year it failed to come to a vote in the U.S. Congress, and year after year it was denounced in social policy resolutions handed down by the women's organizations. They would favor passage only with one very important qualification: that protective laws for women not be jettisoned by it. But by 1971 when the Equal Rights Amendment finally came to a vote, women's groups, including United Methodist Women, were adamantly opposed to any qualification to the Amendment; they no longer wanted "protection."

A 1970 study of United Methodist nursery school curriculum found that girls are actually taught "to be helpless, frightened, passive, waiting and weak."[6] They need protection. Women expect it for themselves; society expects it for them. It is difficult to think of women in positions of power—as executives, ministers or bishops. Even though everyone knows God has no gender, and words are only a poor human way of religious expression, it seems almost sacrilege to many to say "She" instead of "He." God is the ultimate authority figure, and women being weak are not respectable authority figures; the designation of God as "She" is outrageous.

What women have discovered is that though doors have been opened to them and some progress made, the image of "the lady" has only been modified in some particulars. Essentially the image is unchanged, and both men and women act as if it were a scientifically established fact of nature instead of a cultural myth. But it can be changed and women have set out to change it.

Simultaneously with the reawakening of the women's movement at the end of the 1960s, the General Conference appointed a Study Commission on the Participation of Women in The United Methodist Church. Typically, it took some time before the Commission was funded and could begin its work, but at the 1972 General Conference it reported the results of its investigation, recommended changes in the language of *The Book of Discipline* (e.g. the alteration of masculine pronouns where both sexes were meant), and the establishment of a permanent Commission on the Status and Role of Women. The Women's Caucus lobbied for the new Commission; the Women's Division supported it, and the legislation establishing and funding it was passed.

Though the Women's Division gave active moral support to churchwomen engaged in women's liberation projects before 1970, it was not until then that they organized the Ad Hoc Committee on Churchwomen's Liberation, and began to put money into the new movement. All over the country women in local churches, in annual conferences and at theological seminaries were talking to one another and making plans, changing themselves and the institutions around them. The Ad Hoc Committee recommended funding a wide variety of projects: groups to plan women's studies curricula in seminaries; women's centers to offer counseling, child care or other aids to women students; research groups; and teams working to transform theological understandings or whole bureaucracies that traditionally have been cast in masculine terms.

The Ad Hoc Committee itself was no typical bureaucratic entity. Like the women they sought to help, the members spent many of their sessions in

Women's Society of World Service
Evangelical United Brethren

The purpose of the society shall be to unite all women of The Evangelical United Brethren Church in a Christian fellowship to make Christ known throughout the world and to develop a personal responsibility for the whole task of the church.

The scope of work of the society shall be the needs and interests of women and the concerns and responsibilities of the church in today's world.

The society shall foster spiritual growth, missionary outreach, and Christian service.

"consciousness-raising," or trying to understand themselves as women in a male-dominated society and church. The group also made recommendations and reports to the Women's Division, cooperated in the development of a study packet on abortion and provided resources for the organization of conference task groups in churchwomen's liberation. In 1972 the Ad Hoc Committee was replaced with a permanent Committee on Women's Concerns.

The Women's Division and the Women's Caucus are not officially related, but their members share the same concerns. The caucus was first organized by women meeting in Evanston and Nashville to plan strategy for the 1972 General Conference, but because of its effectiveness it has become an ongoing organization. It was largely responsible for the nominations of women for bishop in three jurisdictional conferences. Each received a respectable number of votes—and no one laughed (at least out loud). Only one of the nominees was an ordained minister however, because women clergy are so few in number and so little known. Since then the case of lay bishops has been taken to the Judicial Council (which maintained that only ordained persons could ascend to the episcopacy), and the issue will probably be joined again and again in the future. As they did a century ago, women are changing the church—and this time the changes may be even more profound.

If any one group can be said to have

begun the movement of women into the larger world in the 19th century, it was churchwomen. They started it—moved by compassion and an ambition for a better world. And they proceeded as far as they were able with the schizophrenia born of the antagonism between "the lady" and her flesh and blood counterpart in the real world. Divided against themselves women have been nearly stymied. Just as contemporary missions have come to be interpreted more and more as a ministry to make people whole, so women's liberation, however chaotically at times, is a movement to heal the division in women, to make them whole. The beginning was made in the 19th century for women to cease repressing their potentialities with a myth whose basis is at best tenuous, and whose biblical basis is nearly nonexistent.

Anna Howard Shaw, when she was off the political hustings and speaking to the issue of woman's future, described the church's complicity in the preservation of the myth of "the lady":

> The great defect in the religious teaching to and accepted by women is the dogma that self-abnegation, self-effacement, and excessive humility were ideal feminine virtues. ... But we are learning from the teaching and example of Jesus that life itself is a religion, that nothing is more sacred than a human being, that the end of all right institutions, whether the home or the church or an educational establishment, or a government, is the development of the human soul.[7]

In 1972, it was said of a prominent churchman that "he would as soon vote for The Godfather as for a woman for bishop!" Perhaps there will always be those who will support and perpetuate the myth of the inferiority of women, who will insist that women's ambitions are a terrible notion that must lead, inevitably, to "conduct unbecoming to a lady." But women, with a vision of whole persons, whole church, whole Christians, will continue to face down prejudice to create a system of conduct *becoming* to a *woman!*

AFTERWORD: THIRTY YEARS LATER

"The new history always comes when people least believe in it. But, certainly, it comes only in the moment when the old becomes visible as old and tragic and dying, and when no way out is seen. We live in such a moment; such a moment is our situation."[1]

Thirty years ago when Elaine Magalis put the finishing touches on the manuscript of *Conduct Becoming to a Woman,* the Equal Rights Amendment to the Constitution of the United States had just been passed (March 22, 1972), but still today not every state in the Union has ratified the Amendment. In 1973, when *Conduct* was released, the Supreme Court upheld the decision of Roe v. Wade which essentially cancelled anti-abortion laws in 46 states. Since this landmark case, countless appeals have been waged to overturn the Supreme Court's decision. Hence, the ebb and flow of strides forward and backward continue to dominate the landscape for women in church and society.

For the women of the early 1970s, holding positions of real power was scarce at best, particularly in The United Methodist Church outside the confines of the Women's Division. Today, women are no longer absent from membership at the tables of general church agencies and boards. Within the General Board of Global Ministries, of which the Women's Division is a part, women comprise no less than 30 percent of the directors and are visible in positions of real power by mandate of *The Book of Discipline.* It would be nice to think that women have come by these positions of power of their own right without a mandate from General Conference as transcribed in the Church's official rule book. But until the day comes when "conduct becoming to a woman" equals conduct becoming any human being, we will settle for the rule book to help balance the scales, however tenuous that balancing act may be.

After 42 years of women having full clergy rights in The United

Marjorie Matthews
The United Methodist Church

Marjorie Matthews was born in Onawa, Michigan. In 1959 she decided to enter the ministry, and she was ordained an elder in 1965 at the age of forty-nine. Until she completed her undergraduate and seminary education, she served as pastor of a number of small churches in Michigan, New York and Florida.

As her experience grew after ordination, she was selected for the position of district superintendent—the second woman in the denomination to attain that role. Although she never intended to be a bishop, her election was confirmed on July 17, 1980. Marjorie Matthews was the first woman elected bishop of any mainline denomination. She served as bishop of the Wisconsin area for four years, retiring in 1984.

Methodist Church, we can claim some victories. In 1980, the first woman, Marjorie Matthews, was elected as a bishop of The United Methodist Church in the United States. Since then, ten more women have been elected to serve as bishops. Of all retired and active bishops in The United Methodist Church, 8 percent are women. Fifteen percent of the district superintendents are women. By 2001, women comprised 14 percent of elders in full connection and 18.5 percent of all women serving as ordained or licensed pastors in The United Methodist Church. However, only 2 percent of the clergy serving as lead pastors of churches of 1,000 members or more are women. Clergywomen with the same number of years' experience as men and with the same type of appointment make 9 percent less than their male counterparts. This discrepancy not only reduces clergywomen's current income, but it also reduces their pension and retirement income. In the 1996 and 2000 General Conferences, clergywomen (elders) made up 20 percent of clergy delegates and 36 percent of all delegates (lay and clergy).[2]

Women in the Master of Divinity (M.Div.) degree program at 13 United Methodist seminaries make up over 50 percent of all M.Div. degree students (the statistic has been more than 40 percent for over 12 years). Yet the number of ordained women is still very low (less than 18 percent). The major obstacles for clergywomen in acceptance and appointments continue to be institutional and systemic sexism.[3]

In 1997, *The United Methodist Clergywomen Retention Study,* conducted by the Anna Howard Shaw Center of the Boston University School of Theology and co-sponsored by the Division of Ordained Ministry of the General Board of Higher Education and Ministry found that clergywomen leave local church ministry at a 10 percent faster rate than clergymen, despite an overwhelming commitment to local church ministry. The data indicated four major reasons:

- Lack of support from the hierarchical system,
- Being unable to maintain one's integrity in the system,
- Rejection from congregations/parishioners, and
- Conflict of family and pastoral responsibilities.

The most common challenge to clergywomen is balancing work and family responsibilities given the expectations of congregations for 24-hour availability. *The United Methodist Clergywomen Retention Study* stated it well in saying: "The church must ask itself why the traditional values and the theology of family do not apply to clergywomen as clergy but are applied to them as women."[4]

The ebb and flow of women's advances and shortfalls in the ministry over the last thirty years seems to mirror women's advances and shortfalls in the public sector as well. In 1970, the top managers of major American corporations were 99 percent male. A young woman joining a corporation then had every right to believe that by the time she had achieved seniority, the percentage would have changed in her favor. It did. Twenty-five years later in 1995, only 95 percent of top managers of major corporations were men. At this rate, it will be the year 2270 before women and men are equally likely to be top managers of major corporations.[5]

In terms of the employment status of the civilian population (non-institutional), 43.3 percent of women were in the civilian labor force in 1970 compared to 60.2 percent of women employed in the civilian labor force in 2000. While the percentage of women in the civilian labor force increased over 25 percent in three decades, men's participation decreased by 3 percent from 79.7 percent in 1970 to 74.7 percent in 2000.[6] By the year 2000, women and men are nearly even in terms of the percentage holding jobs based upon educational attainment.[7]

Civilian Labor Force	Men (60.5 million)	Women (53.5 million)
Less Than High School Diploma	11.1%	8.4%
High School Graduate, no degree	31.8%	31.8%
Less Than Bachelor's Degree	26.1%	30.9%
College Graduate	30.9%	29.8%

However, and not surprisingly, in terms of compensation for the same job and with the same amount of educational attainment, women come up very short. On average, women today earn 76¢ for every dollar men earn. The greatest discrepancy is in the technical, sales and administrative support industry where women only earn 69¢ for every dollar men earn. Conversely, women fare better in the farming, forestry and fishing industries where they earn 85¢ for every dollar men earn.[8] Finally, 4.8 percent of women in today's civilian labor force work at or below the $5.15 minimum hourly wage compared to only 2.6 percent of men, and the median hourly wage for women workers is $9.03 compared to $10.85 for men.[9]

In the political arena, women have fared a little better in terms of advances in the past thirty years, as the following table[10] reveals:

Political Office	1977	1997
Member of Congress	3.7%	11.2%
House of Representatives	4.1%	11.7%
Senate	2.0%	9.0%
Statewide Executive	9.9%	25.1%
State Legislator	9.1%	21.5%
Mayor of City (30,000 or more)	6.2%	20.6%

For over 130 years, women in the Methodist tradition have been working hard to improve the status and role of women in church and society. The question of "woman" and her conduct has been the subject of heated debate among men inside and outside the church for at least as long, if not longer. In the middle of the 19th century, women had to answer their male counterparts' questions regarding their rights for education, activities outside the home and dress reform; and with the suffragettes' help, the spectrum was expanded to include the right to have personal freedom, to earn a living, to claim wages, to own property, to sue and be sued, to make contracts, to testify in court, to obtain a divorce for just cause, to possess her children, to claim a fair share of the accumulations during marriage and to vote.[11] All of these strides toward justice and equality for women were considered "conduct unbecoming to a woman." Today, thanks to the valiant women of the 19th and 20th centuries, women in the 21st century can enjoy all of these rights but not always on equal footing with men. And for the most part, these attainments are no longer viewed as "conduct unbecoming to a woman."

It is the story of women organized for mission since the mid-1800s that has rich implications for how women and men can continue to transform institutional sexism and strengthen women in the exercise of their gifts on behalf of the entire church and society, in fact the entire world and all of humankind. In general, our foremothers did not claim leadership on the basis of exceptional spiritual gifts, nor were they called to the preaching ministry. Instead, they were inspired to meet the combined evangelical, physical and social needs of marginal people—especially women and children—who could not be reached by male missionaries abroad and who were ignored by church and society at home. They did this primarily by establishing mission institutions staffed by women. The resilience of the women's organizations in the Methodist tradition is born of deep commitment to God's mission. Through determined, mature, loving, mutually supportive and corporately-minded strong women these nine predecessor organizations in six denominations have charted a course for the future that is now encompassed in the ministry and mission of United Methodist Women in The United Methodist Church.

Conduct Becoming to a Woman is the story of Protestant Christian mission and women's involvement. It is the story of the struggle for women's rights in church and society. That story has written many chapters in history toward women's full and equal participation as partners in God's mission and God's world. However, the story is not ended. There is still much more work to do. May the course our foremothers charted for our future inspire us to continue the journey as women organized for mission and to accept our role of living the story—until there is no longer a standard of "conduct" either becoming or unbecoming to a woman.

"The Women's Division shall be actively engaged in fulfilling the mission of Christ and the Church and shall interpret the PURPOSE of UNITED METHODIST WOMEN. With continuing awareness of the concerns and responsibilities of the Church in today's world, the Women's Division shall be an advocate for the oppressed and dispossessed, with special attention to the needs of women and children; shall work to build a supportive community among women; and shall engage in activities which foster growth in the Christian faith, mission education, and Christian social involvement throughout the organization."

—¶1317 of *The Book of Discipline* of The United Methodist Church, 2000

PROGRAM GUIDE

WORSHIP CENTER

Prepare a simple worship table or designate a space for some candles and an opened Bible. You will need matches to light the candles at the appropriate time.

FOCUS STATEMENT

This is a story of Protestant Christian mission and women's involvement. It is the story of the struggle for women's rights in church and society. "If it can give [you] some sense of [your] own history (or herstory), some feeling for [your] beginnings, then it will have fulfilled its aim."[12] We are here to communicate the struggle of our foremothers in the Methodist tradition and to gain a new perspective on their life and work. As we read, study, discuss, reflect, pray and worship, may we come to appreciate the course they have charted for our future as women organized for mission and accept our role to continue the story and the journey toward women's full and equal participation as partners in God's mission.

OPENING WORSHIP

CALL TO COMMUNITY FOR STUDY AND REFLECTION

As the leader reads the focus statement (see above), a member of the group lights the candles on the worship table.

Leader: We gather to worship God.

All: We are women of faith! We are women of courage! We are women of hope!

Leader: May we see new visions of what faithfulness in mission now requires of us. Let us focus on a future where Christ leads us to a new creation filled with justice, peace, unity and hope.

All: God, give us courage to accept the challenges of such a future.

HYMN: "Lord God, Your Love Has Called Us Here" *(The United Methodist Hymnal,* #579)

SCRIPTURE: Philippians 3:13-14

LITANY: "By Faith We Journey"[13]

Reader 1: We are surrounded by the Living God. We come from every race. We are called forth, and we claim our heritage. Along the river that flows then to now, hope streams from sea to sea.

All: **By faith we journey, moving toward God's city yet to be.**

Reader 2: Our hearts are full, our memories deep with those now gone before. They urge us to fresh faithfulness of heart and mind and soul. Our God we love and serve and praise, in all our future's length.

All: **By faith we journey, moving on in truth that gathers strength.**

Reader 3: The suffering world will not give ease to those baptized in Christ. For he underwent suffering to give us all new life. He bore the cross. Death's sting he knew to wake us from the lie.

All: **By faith we journey, moving on in love that does not die.**

Reader 4: The cross and empty tomb still stand as mystery and as power. With fear and trembling grace, we come to each new hour where human need still cries in anguished tears.

All: **By faith we journey, moving on in hope-transforming years.**

Reader 5: When at last God's love is known in every human heart, and justice flows a mighty stream through this world's meanest part, we will still be called to serve and praise God's gracious Word of life.

All: **By faith we journey, moving on from faith to glorious sight!**

PRAYER: *Read by the leader or another member of the group.* As women of God, called to love through mission and ministry, help us, O God, to jump to our feet and eagerly pursue the goal that is set before us. May we press on in your name, O God, our Creator, Jesus Christ, our Redeemer, and the Holy Spirit, our Sustainer. Amen.

QUESTIONS FOR DISCUSSION AND REFLECTION

While we cannot and should not eliminate all the male-oriented points of view in the Gospels and throughout the Bible, we can look for alternative interpretations and search for principles in Jesus' teaching that affirm women and give them a more prominent role in the teaching and ministry of Jesus. Consider these questions for group discussion and personal reflection. Bring to bear all that you have learned, discussed and experienced throughout this study of Conduct *as well as your personal reflections.*

1. How might using alternative interpretations of scripture and principles from Jesus' teachings help to shape and change the future role of women in the church and in society?
2. How have the structures of church and society been re-evaluated, rewritten or reshaped by listening to the stories of women who are reclaiming their biblical heritage?
3. How do you feel about participating in this reconstructing and revisioning of the traditional interpretations of women in the Bible?
4. What are the risks for you, for the church, for society and the world?
5. What are the possible transformations for you, for the church, for society and the world?
6. What leadership roles do women hold in your local church? In your annual conference? What leadership roles have you or do you hold in your local church, district, conference and community?

A VOICE FROM THE PAST

Share this quote with the group and invite brief reflections.

First they gave us a day, International Women's Day; then they gave us a year, 1875; then they gave us a U.N. Decade for Women, 1975–1985; and maybe if we behave, they may let us into the whole thing. Well, we haven't behaved, and that's why we're making progress."

—Bella Abzug, 1994, as quoted in *The American Woman 1999-2000,* p. 95

RISING TO THE CHALLENGE

Leader: Name ten women, living or dead, who have significantly influenced and shaped your life. There may be some important women who were less than positive influences and shapers for you, but through a negative relationship, you were empowered. Do not forget them. Develop a "ten most wanted" list. Beside each name on your list, record what you can remember about them? How did they help to encourage and empower you? What values did they hold that have become a part of you? How are you passing these values on to future generations? Choose one woman from the list of ten and briefly share her story, her witness, and the impact she has had on your life? *If your group is large, more than 8 people, consider doing this in smaller groups of 4 to 6 people.*

CLOSING WORSHIP

"Stones of Remembrance"

You will need a basket and enough stones to give one to each person.

SCRIPTURE: Joshua 4:1–7 and Psalm 78:5–7

Leader: In the Old Testament when God made a covenant with the people, it usually included some tangible sign or symbol to help them to remember their commitment. One such symbol is a stone. God told each of the twelve tribes of Judah to take a stone from the Jordan and carry it with them. This was to be a sign among them that in the days to come, when their children would come to them and ask, "What do these stones mean?" that they were to tell them how God has been their dwelling place in this generation. These stones were to be a memorial forever—a living heritage to all generations.

All: **God, you have been our dwelling place in all generations. And your favor has rested upon us. You have established the work of our hands. One generation playing its part and passing on; another generation playing its part and passing on.**

Leader:	*Holding the basket of stones and lifting a few up for everyone to see.* Such is the significance of these stones. Take one and carry it with you. *The leader takes a stone and passes the basket to the next person in the group, and so on until everyone has received a stone.* When someone asks what the stone means, tell them how God has been our dwelling place in this generation, a living heritage to all generations of United Methodist Women.
All:	**God, you have been our dwelling place in all generations. And your favor has rested upon us. You have established the work of our hands. One generation playing its part and passing on; another generation playing its part and passing on.**
Leader:	Others, by the grace of God, have laid the foundation, and now we build upon it. For no other foundation can anyone lay, than that which is laid—namely, Jesus Christ. Others, by the grace of God, have laid the foundation, and now we build upon it. But let each one take care how she builds.
All:	**God, you have been our dwelling place in all generations. And your favor has rested upon us. You have established the work of our hands. One generation playing its part and passing on; another generation playing its part and passing on.**
SONG:	"This Is a Day of New Beginnings" *(The United Methodist Hymnal, #383)*

Preparing for Your Next Steps

Before the group is dismissed, the leader should highlight the following opportunities for study and reflection beyond this group experience.

1. Consider how you will continue to learn and listen to the stories of women organized for mission since the mid-1800s. What resources will you use to further your understanding? *See the "Bibliography," "Resources" and "Appendix" sections for suggestions.*
2. How will you tell the story of women organized for mission for over 130 years? Consider creating a way to share the group's "quilt" with your local unit of United Methodist Women, congregation, conference and/or community as a way of continuing the journey and the story of women organized for mission.

3. What of your own story as a woman organized for mission? Will you share and how will you share it? What new commitments and challenges are you willing to accept to keep the legacy alive as women organized for mission through United Methodist Women?
4. What issues of injustice or inequality will you address and how will you take action?

SENDING FORTH

Leader: Before us it is blessed. Behind us it is blessed. Below us it is blessed. Above us it is blessed. Around us it is blessed as we set out with Christ. Our speech is blessed as we set out for God. With beauty before us, with beauty behind us, with beauty below us, with beauty above us, with beauty around us, we set out for a holy place indeed. Amen.[14]

As the group disperses—sharing signs of God's peace, if desired—the leader extinguishes the candles.

APPENDIX

That Handful of Women

A Melodrama of the Organizing of the Woman's Foreign Missionary Society of the Methodist Episcopal Church, 1869

Writer's Notes: This play is meant to be extremely melodramatic and over-emphasized, especially in actions. It will resemble a silent movie in some respects with the audience providing the sound effects while the cast of six pantomime the actions. The pace is very slow with some uncomfortable pauses between the speaking parts and the audience reaction. Those speaking should actually look to the audience in anticipation of their response. The skit makes use of audience participation by using an LCD projector, one or two screens and Microsoft PowerPoint to display the audience's part. The words displayed on the screen are for the audience to perform. Instructions are given for the left side (L) and the right side (R) of the auditorium. Each slide should be displayed for 10 seconds. If an LCD projector and Microsoft PowerPoint will not be used, assign the "audience" part to a small group of participants.

CAST: Six women dressed in 1869 period clothing.
Mrs. Edwin Parker
Mrs. William Butler

PROPS: eight umbrellas
eight matching teacups with saucers
a silver tea service
a silver serving tray

SCENE: Two chairs center stage separated by an end table. Three chairs together stage left and three chairs together stage right of the center chairs. A coffee table downstage center. Use 19th century furniture, if possible.

APPENDIX

Go to BLACK. The cast of six women, dressed in period clothing, with overcoats, hats and umbrellas, stand frozen in position, ready for action when the first light appears on stage.

SLIDE 1: L—RUB YOUR HANDS TOGETHER
R—SIT QUIETLY

SLIDE 2: L—SNAP YOUR FINGERS
R—RUB YOUR HANDS TOGETHER

SLIDE 3: L—PAT YOUR HANDS ON YOUR THIGHS
R—SNAP YOUR FINGERS

SLIDE 4: L—CLAP YOUR HANDS
R—PAT YOUR HANDS ON YOUR THIGHS

SLIDE 5: L—STOMP YOUR FEET
R—CLAP YOUR HANDS

SLIDE 6: L—SIT QUIETLY
R—STOMP YOUR FEET

SLIDE 7: —BLANK—

Additional sound and light effects—sound of thunder, flash of lightning, sound of rain falling.

NARRATOR: It was a dark and stormy night in Boston on March 23, 1869.

The lights come up to 1/4 on center stage as the cast of six begin to remove their coats, shake out their umbrellas, remove their hats, dry off with handkerchiefs and take their seats in the meeting room. They do not talk but pantomime talking to one another, greeting one another and making conversation. They help themselves to the tea on the coffee table, sipping, with pinky fingers extended and showing the utmost dignity and proper etiquette. They do not cross their legs when they sit, but can cross their ankles, and sit sideways in their chairs, their backs not touching the back of the chair, with absolutely correct posture.

SLIDE 8: L—CLAP YOUR HANDS
R—STOMP YOUR FEET

As the lights come up to 1/2, a dim follow spot picks up two women entering from the doors of the auditorium and walking down the center aisle. Both are carrying opened umbrellas, dressed in period clothing, and struggling against the imagined wind and rain as they make their way to the stage.

SLIDE 9: L—SNAP YOUR FINGERS.
R—MAKE THE SOUND OF WIND.

NARRATOR: Mrs. William Butler and Mrs. Edwin Parker, wives of missionary husbands to India, arrive at Tremont Street Methodist Episcopal Church. Six other women have already gathered to hear them speak.

As Mrs. Butler and Mrs. Parker reach the stage, the lights come up full. Both women remove their rain gear, dry off with handkerchiefs, and begin to greet the women, shaking hands every so daintily, each woman rising to return the greeting, teacup in hand, and curtsying. Mrs. Butler and Mrs. Parker help themselves to tea and then take their seats. They take the teacups in hand and sip, then place their cups on the side table.

MRS. BUTLER: *Clearing her throat.* Ladies, thank you for coming.

SLIDE 10: L—APPLAUSE
R—CHEER

MRS. PARKER: We know how treacherous the weather is tonight.

SLIDE 11: L—CLAP YOUR HANDS
R—STOMP YOUR FEET

MRS. BUTLER: We hope this will not cause you ill health.
Each of the six women either coughs gently into her handkerchief or sneezes delicately in a high pitch into her handkerchief.

SLIDE 12: "God bless you."

MRS. PARKER: Ladies, we have some very important news to tell you ...

MRS. BUTLER: About the plight of women and girls in India.
Each of the six women covers her mouth in horror, a few say "Oh, my."

SLIDE 13: GASP

MRS. PARKER: Please, ladies, hear us out.

SLIDE 14: "Shhh."

MRS. BUTLER: The girls are not being educated.

SLIDE 15: "Oh no!"

SLIDE 16: "This can't be!"

MRS. BUTLER: Please, ladies, we must do something.

MRS. PARKER: Yes, our help is greatly needed.

SLIDE 17: "What can we do?"

MRS. BUTLER: Oh, thank you for asking.

SLIDE 18: "You're welcome."

MRS. PARKER: We think we have a plan.

MRS. BUTLER: But it will require our being a bit unruly.

SLIDE 19: HISS

MRS. PARKER: Now, now, it's not all that bad.

MRS. BUTLER: After all, we are proper Christian women.

SLIDE 20:	"Amen."
MRS. PARKER:	We would not want to do anything to upset the men.
MRS. BUTLER:	Oh, goodness, no.
SLIDE 21:	"Why not?"
MRS. PARKER:	*Looking to Mrs. Butler for reassurance.* Well then, here is our plan.
MRS. BUTLER:	We are going to raise the money
MRS. PARKER:	To send a woman educator
MRS. BUTLER:	And a woman doctor
MRS. PARKER AND MRS. BUTLER:	*In unison.* To India.
SLIDE 22:	LAUGH
MRS. PARKER:	Oh dear, Mrs. Butler, I was afraid of this.
MRS. BUTLER:	Now Mrs. Parker, do not fret. This is not the time to lose courage.
SLIDE 23:	SNIFFLE
MRS. PARKER:	Ladies, please, we must work together.
MRS. BUTLER:	Yes, Mrs. Parker, that is correct, we must.
MRS. PARKER:	If we women do not band together for our sisters in India
MRS. BUTLER:	Who will?
MRS. PARKER:	The girls will be left uneducated,

MRS. BUTLER: And the women without medical care.

MRS. PARKER AND MRS. BUTLER: *In unison.*
They shall surely perish!

MRS. BUTLER: In God's name, we must do something.

SLIDE 24: "But how can we help?"

MRS. PARKER: Oh, I'm so glad you asked.

SLIDE 25: "You're welcome."

MRS. BUTLER: We can raise the money

MRS. PARKER: By wearing cheap calico robes,

MRS. BUTLER: Instead of buying these expensive fashions.

SLIDE 26: SCREAM

MRS. PARKER: Now, ladies, there's no need to over-react.

MRS. BUTLER: Please, do maintain your composure.

SLIDE 27: CLEAR YOUR THROAT

MRS. PARKER: Ladies, consider the sacrifices our Lord Jesus has made for us.

MRS. BUTLER: It is the least we can do in gratitude and service to Him.

MRS. PARKER: Are we not as much His disciples

MRS. BUTLER: Called to care for the poor, the widows, the orphans in every land?

SLIDE 28: "Absolutely."

MRS. PARKER:	We could raise the money in no time
MRS. BUTLER:	If we just deny ourselves some frills.
SLIDE 29:	"But calico?"
MRS. PARKER:	Yes, well, it is a bit coarse,
MRS. BUTLER:	But it is very durable,
MRS. PARKER:	And easy to care for.
MRS. BUTLER:	Who knows, we might even make a fashion statement.
SLIDE 30:	"Calico! Calico!"
MRS. PARKER:	Now, that is the spirit.
MRS. BUTLER:	Praise God, we are united.
SLIDE 31:	"Hallelujah!"
MRS. PARKER:	I know a woman educator named Isabella Thoburn.
MRS. BUTLER:	And I know a woman doctor named Clara Swain.
MRS. PARKER:	They have agreed to go to India
MRS. BUTLER:	As our first female missionaries.
SLIDE 32:	APPLAUSE
MRS. PARKER:	We will build a school to educate girls.
MRS. BUTLER:	And we will build a hospital to provide medical care for women.
SLIDE 33:	"Justice! Justice!"

MRS. PARKER: This is going to be the start of something big

MRS. BUTLER: Really big.

MRS. PARKER AND MRS. BUTLER: *In unison.*
And it all begins right here.

SLIDE 34: CHEERS

MRS. PARKER: Sisters, let us commend our plans to God's care,

MRS. BUTLER: Trusting that God will bring this to pass.

SLIDE 35: "Let us pray."

Lights begin to fade as the narrator speaks. The women bow their heads and fold their hands in prayer.

NARRATOR: So it was, on that stormy night in Boston on March 23, 1869, that the Woman's Foreign Missionary Society of the Methodist Episcopal Church was organized. It was the first of eight women's missionary societies founded by our predecessor organizations. Today, we continue the legacy of women organized for mission as United Methodist Women.

SLIDE 36: L—RUB YOUR HANDS TOGETHER
R—SIT QUIETLY

SLIDE 37: L—SNAP YOUR FINGERS
R—RUB YOUR HANDS TOGETHER

SLIDE 38: L—PAT YOUR HANDS ON YOUR THIGHS
R—SNAP YOUR FINGERS

SLIDE 39: L—CLAP YOUR HANDS
R—PAT YOUR HANDS ON YOUR THIGHS

SLIDE 40: L—STOMP YOUR FEET
R—CLAP YOUR HANDS

SLIDE 41:   L—SIT QUIETLY
                    R—STOMP YOUR FEET

SLIDE 42:   —BLANK—

Additional sound and light effects—sound of thunder, flash of lightning, sound of rain falling. A few begin to stand and embrace one another in congratulations. Some put their raincoats and hats on. All prepare to stand center stage, holding hands, on cue. Lights come up full as the cast forms one line, joins hands and takes their bows.

SLIDE 43:   THE END

Lights fade to black. CURTAIN.

"Conduct Becoming to a Member of United Methodist Women"

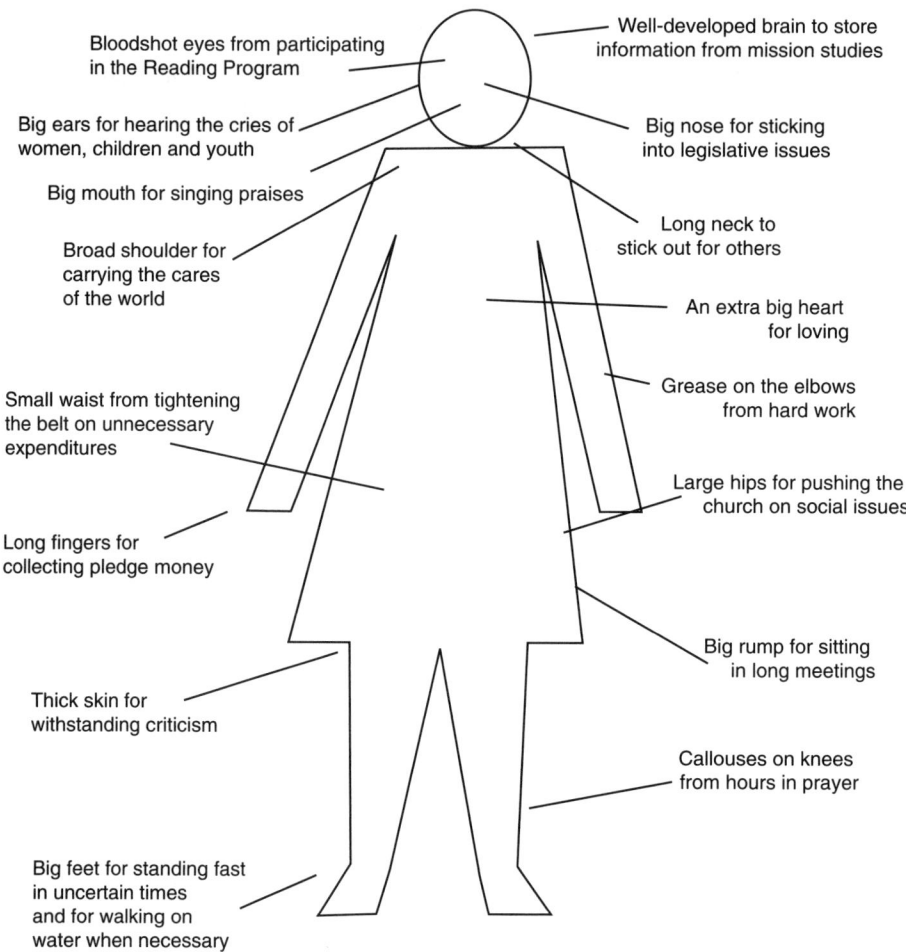

This caricature was created by Carol Potter & Molly Cummingham. It is not intended to be inclusive or exclusive of the role of United Methodist Women and its members.
Permission is granted for use within the organization of United Methodist Women.

Women's Organizations in The United Methodist Tradition

Methodist Episcopal Church, 1784–1939
Woman's Foreign Missionary Society, 1869-1939
Woman's Home Missionary Society, 1880–1939
Wesleyan Service Guild, 1921–1972

Methodist Episcopal Church, South, 1844–1939
Woman's Foreign Missionary Society, 1878–1910
Woman's Home Missionary Society, 1890–1910
Woman's Missionary Council, 1910–1939

Methodist Protestant Church, 1830–1939
Woman's Foreign Missionary Society, 1879–1928
Woman's Home Missionary Society, 1893–1928
Woman's Work of the Methodist Protestant Church, 1928–1939

The Methodist Church, 1939–1968
Woman's Society of Christian Service, 1939–1972
Wesleyan Service Guild, 1921–1972

United Brethren in Christ, 1800–1946
Woman's Missionary Association, 1875–1946
Young Women's Mission Band—Otterbein Guild, 1883–1946

Evangelical Association, 1803–1922
Woman's Missionary Society, 1884–1922

United Evangelical Church, 1894–1922
Woman's Home and Foreign Missionary Society, 1891–1922

Evangelical Church, 1922–1946
Woman's Missionary Society, 1922–1946
Christian Service Guild, 1944–1958

(continued on pg.196)

APPENDIX

The Journey to United Methodist Women

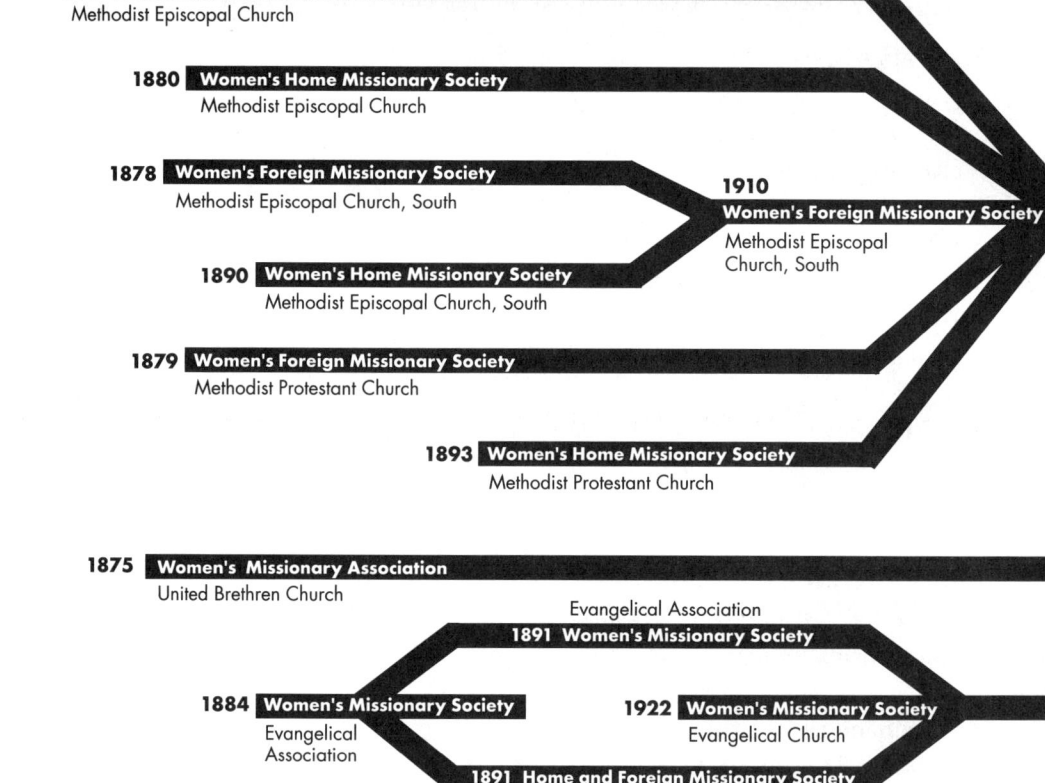

APPENDIX   195

1939 Women's Society of Christian Service
Wesleyan Service Guild
The Methodist Church

1968 Women's Society of Christian Service
Wesleyan Service Guild
The United Methodist Church

1972 United Methodist Women
The United Methodist Church

1946 Women's Society of World Service
Evangelical United Brethren

Evangelical United Brethren, 1946–1968
Women's Society of World Service, 1946–1972
Christian Service Guild, 1944–1958

The United Methodist Church (1968–Present)
Women's Society of Christian Service, 1968–1972
United Methodist Women, 1972–Present

Other Organizations of Interest

Ladies' Aid Societies (Date from the beginning of American Methodism; flourished at the local church level in the various predecessor denominations; formally recognized in 1904 by the Methodist Episcopal Church in their *Discipline* but never an official agency of any Methodist denomination.)

The Female Missionary Society of New York, 1819–1861 (Auxiliary to the Methodist Episcopal Missionary Society.)

Ladies' China Missionary Society, Methodist Episcopal Church, 1848–1871 (Reorganized in 1871 as the Baltimore Branch of the Woman's Foreign Missionary Society of the Methodist Episcopal Church.)

Ladies' and Pastors' Christian Union, 1868–1870s

World Federation of Methodist Women, 1939–Present (Currently known as the World Federation of Methodist and Uniting Church Women.)

Websites Related to the History of Women in Church and Society

The Women's Division, General Board of Global Ministries, The United Methodist Church
http://gbgm-umc.org/umw

Visit the website for United Methodist Women and the Women's Division to learn more about the history and present work of women organized for mission. This website is linked with the General Board of Global Ministries' site that includes extensive resources on mission work and mission projects throughout the United States and around the world, many of which are sponsored by the Women's Division and United Methodist Women.

The General Commission on the Status and Role of Women, The United Methodist Church
www.cosrow.org

United Methodist Women and the Women's Division were instrumental in pushing General Conference to create COSROW. The site has valuable information and resources related specifically to women in ordained ministry in The United Methodist Church.

The General Commission on Archives and History, The United Methodist Church
www.gcah.org

There are many helpful resources on this site to assist you in developing your own—or your church's—history as a part of the United Methodist tradition. The site has many resources, and you can request assistance for more in-depth research on specific people and topics.

National Women's History Project
www.nwhp.org

This site contains a wealth of information, facts and stories of women involved throughout history in all aspects of life. There are many resources, bibliographies and photographs to view and use. A main component of the National Women's History Project is to promote Women's History Month, and there are many resources available for celebrating women's history within your congregation or community.

National Women's Hall of Fame
www.greatwomen.org

Visit this website to learn about many great women in our history who have made significant contributions. You can search by name or topic.

Distinguished Women
www.distinguishedwomen.com

This site offers a search engine for locating any prominent (or not so prominent) woman in history up to the present day.

TIMELINE

Abbreviations

	EA	the Evangelical Association
	EC	the Evangelical Church
	EUB	the Evangelical United Brethren Church
	M	The Methodist Church
	ME	the Methodist Episcopal Church
	MES	the Methodist Episcopal Church, South
	MP	the Methodist Protestant Church
	UB	the United Brethren Church
	UE	the United Evangelical Church
	UM	The United Methodist Church

1766 **Barbara Heck** is instrumental in organizing the first Methodist congregation in America (New York City), which includes **Hetty,** her Black slave.

1800 Women's missionary societies begin to be formed for the purpose of raising funds for domestic and foreign missions.

1812 **Ann Judson** and **Harriet Newall,** with their husbands, go to Asia as the first U.S. foreign missionaries.

1817 **Jarena Lee,** a black evangelist, is allowed to exhort and to hold prayer meetings in her home but she is denied a preaching license.

1818 The Female Benevolent Society of Baltimore (ME) is organized to assist retired preachers and their widows, wives and children and to do missionary work. **Mary Hewitt** is president.

1819 The Missionary and Bible Society (ME) is founded. Shortly after the New York Female Society is organized as an auxiliary.

1824 A Wesleyan Female Society is organized in Jonesboro, Tennessee.

1827 **Harriet Livermore** preaches before Congress.

1828 A group leaves the Methodist Episcopal Church and forms the Methodist Protestant Church.

1830 Slavery north of the Mason-Dixon line is virtually abolished.

1834 The first Methodist single woman missionary, **Sophronia Farrington,** goes to Liberia. (NE)

1835 **Phoebe Palmer** institutes a weekly prayer meeting in her home. For 37 years, she is Methodism's most famous woman evangelist. (ME)

1836 **Ann Wilkins,** with the support of the New York Female Missionary Society (ME), goes to Liberia. She remains there, except for two health furloughs, until shortly before her death in 1857.

1839 Women at the Evangelical Church in Philadelphia are urged by their pastor to get together for reading, sewing and providing support to conference missionary projects. This group is the first known local society of the Evangelical Association.

— Local women of the Methodist Protestant Church begin to raise money through the Woman's Union Missionary Society of New York and support mission work in India and Japan.

— The Methodist Episcopal Church acquires Wesleyan Female College in Macon, Georgia. It is the oldest woman's college in the world (founded in 1836).

1843 **Ann Wilkins** establishes the Millsburg Female Academy in Liberia.

— **Sojourner Truth** begins traveling through the United States preaching and lecturing on abolition.

1848	The Ladies' China Missionary Society of Baltimore (MES) is organized. **Juliana Hayes** is the first president and **Anna L. Davidson** is secretary.
—	A convention in Seneca Falls, New York, launches the women's rights movement.
1849	United Brethren quarterly conference gives **Charity Opheral** a preacher's license.
—	**Harriet Tubman** escapes from slavery in Maryland and subsequently returns to the South 19 times, rescuing over 300 slaves.
1850	The New York Ladies' Home Missionary Society, (1918, ME) under the leadership of Phoebe Palmer, begins the Five Points Mission.
—	**Lucy Stanton** is the first black woman to complete a collegiate course of study (Oberlin College).
1851	**Lydia Sexton** is voted "recommendation" as a pulpit speaker by the United Brethren General Conference.
1852	**Sojourner Truth** delivers her famous "Ain't I a Woman?" speech at the Second National Women's Suffrage Convention in Akron, Ohio.
1858	The Ladies' China Missionary Society (MES) supports a girls' school and two teachers, **Sarah** and **Beulah Woolston**, in China.
—	**Clementina Rowe Butler** and her husband, Dr. William Butler, arrive as the first missionaries to India (ME).
—	The United Brethren General Conference passes a resolution that no women should be licensed to preach.
—	**Mrs. M. L. Kelley** organizes a fundraising effort for missionaries in China. This is the earliest effort on record by women of the Methodist Episcopal Church, South (MES) in support of foreign missions.

1861–1865   Civil War

1866   **Maggie Newton Van Cott,** known as the Widow Van Cott, begins a career of more than 30 years as a preacher and evangelist.

—   **Helenor M. Davison** is ordained a deacon by the Indiana Conference (MP), probably the first ordained woman in the Methodist tradition.

1869   The Woman's Foreign Missionary Society of the Methodist Episcopal Church is formed in Boston at the instigation of missionary wives **Clementina Butler** and **Lois Parker.** The newly formed Society sends **Isabella Thoburn** and **Clara Swain** as its first missionaries to India. The first issue of the magazine *The Heathen Woman's Friend,* is published.

—   **Anna L. Davidson** and other women from the Methodist Episcopal Church, South withdraw from the Ladies' China Missionary Society of Baltimore and form the Trinity Home Mission, later known as Trinity Bible Mission. **Juliana Hayes** is president. Money is given to a Bible woman in Baltimore and to the poor.

—   German-speaking women of the Ohio-German Conference of the United Brethren Church begin to meet to pray for missionaries.

—   **Maggie Newton Van Cott** is granted a local preacher's license (ME).

—   **Fanny Jackson Coppin** becomes head principal of the Institute for Colored Youth in Philadelphia. She spends 37 years at the Institute, now Cheyney State College.

—   **Lydia Sexton** (UB) is appointed chaplain of the Kansas State Prison at the age of seventy, the first woman in the United States to hold such a position.

—   **Susan B. Anthony** and **Elizabeth Cady Stanton** found the National Woman Suffrage Association.

—	**Emily Duncan Harwood** (ME) opens the first Protestant school in New Mexico Territory in a whitewashed, adobe former henhouse.
1870	**Isabella Thoburn** opens a girls' school in Lucknow, India.
1871	The Ladies' China Missionary Society of Baltimore (MES) decides to unite with the Woman's Home Missionary Society of the Methodist Episcopal Church and becomes the Baltimore Branch. Southern Methodist Episcopal Church African-American women join the Woman's Foreign Missionary Society and become the Atlanta Branch. This branch ceases to exist after only a few years.
1872	The Woman's Bible Mission at Home and Abroad of the Methodist Episcopal Church, South is formed in Baltimore. **Juliana Hayes** is president.
1873	**Sarah Dickey** begins Mt. Hermon School, known as the Mt. Holyoke of the South, in Mississippi and continues as its principal for more than 30 years.
—	Women of the Trinity Bible Mission (MES) send money to a Bible woman in China. The group becomes the first local society of what will later be the Woman's Home Missionary Society.
1874	The Woman's Christian Temperance Union is formed by a group of women at Chautauqua following a lecture by **Jennie Fowler Willing** (ME) who presides over the first meeting. **Annie Wittenmyer** (ME) is the first president. **Frances Willard** becomes corresponding secretary. Two years later she openly espouses woman's suffrage.
—	The Woman's Foreign Missionary Society (ME) opens the first hospital for women in Asia (Bareilly, India).
—	**Dora E. Schoonmaker** is sent to Japan as the Woman's Foreign Missionary Society (ME) begins mission work in that country.
1875	Women of the United Brethren Church organize the Woman's Missionary Association with **Mrs. T. N. Sowers** as president.

1876 **Jennie Hartzell** begins to organize mission work with black women in New Orleans who ask for help in obtaining missionaries and teachers for their daughters. Their work eventually gives impetus to the formation of the Woman's Home Missionary Society of the Methodist Episcopal Church.

— **Anna Oliver** is the first woman to receive the Bachelor of Divinity degree from an American theological seminary (Boston University School of Theology). Two years later, **Anna Howard Shaw** earns the same degree.

1877 A Presbyterian minister is brought to trial and convicted by his presbytery for allowing two women to preach in his church.

— **Emily Beekin** is sent to Sierra Leone as the first missionary of the United Brethren Woman's Missionary Association (UB).

1878 Women in the Methodist Episcopal Church, South organize the Woman's Foreign Missionary Society of the church and are given recognition by General Conference. **Lochie Rankin** goes to China as the organization's first missionary.

— **Amanda Smith,** black evangelist, preaches in two of the nation's most prestigious churches. Soon afterwards, she spends more than a decade preaching and singing in England, Scotland, Italy, Egypt, India and Africa.

1879 The women of the Methodist Protestant Church organize the Woman's Foreign Missionary Society in Pittsburgh with **Mrs. Dr. John Scott** as president. **Lizzie Guthrie** is appointed to go to Japan as their first missionary. She dies en route. **Harriet Brittan** goes in her place.

1880 The General Conference of the Methodist Episcopal Church refuses to ordain **Anna Howard Shaw** and **Anna Oliver,** and denies women the right to preachers' licenses. **Anna Howard Shaw** joins the Methodist Protestant Church and is ordained by its New York Annual Conference.

—	The Woman's Home Missionary Society of the Methodist Episcopal Church is organized and **Lucy Webb Hayes** is elected president. The meeting takes place at Trinity Church in Cincinnati, Ohio, the same place where the Freedman's Aid Society was formed.
—	**Minerva Strawman Spreng** begins some local women's mission societies which are a prelude to organization of the Woman's Missionary Society of the Evangelical Association.
1881	Women in the Texas and Texas West Conferences, two of twenty black conferences, organize as the Woman's Home Missionary Society of the Methodist Episcopal Church. Women in other black conferences quickly follow.
—	Methodist Protestant women of the Maryland Conference organize a conference Woman's Home Missionary Society before a national group exists.
1882	**Laura Askew Haygood** heads an extensive home missions effort in Atlanta.
1883	The Young Women's Mission Band (later Otterbein Guild) for girls over 15 years old is organized by the Woman's Missionary Association (UB).
—	Women of the Evangelical Association organize the Woman's Missionary Society.
1884	Women of the Evangelical Church organize a Woman's Foreign Missionary Society auxiliary to the church's General Society with **Mrs. Ella J. Yost-Preyer** as president.
—	The Methodist Protestant General Conference rules **Anna Shaw Howard's** ordination out of order (see 1880).
1885	**Lucy Rider Meyer** opens the Chicago Training School for women missionaries.
—	At the age of 52, **Mary Fletcher Scranton** becomes the first female

missionary of the Women's Foreign Missionary Society to Korea for the Methodist Episcopal Church.

— *Funjinkai* (women's organization) begins in the Japanese church.

1886 **Mary Fletcher Scranton** opens her home as the first school for girls in Seoul, Korea. She begins with one student. In November, nine months after construction started, the new school building, Ewha (which means "pear blossom") Girls High School is ready to open. This institution later gave birth to Ewha Woman's University. Despite financial difficulties, **Mary Fletcher Scranton** (ME) completes the building with an additional $3,000 from a **Mrs. M. E. Blackstone** of Oak Park, Illinois, and $700 from the New York branch of the Woman's Foreign Missionary Society. The house accommodates 35, and teachers and students move into the new school.

— The first issue of the magazine *Heinden Frauen Freund (The Heathen Woman's Friend)* is published for the German constituency of the Woman's Foreign Missionary Society of the Methodist Episcopal Church.

— **Miss Nannie B. Gaines,** a missionary for the Woman's Foreign Missionary Society (MES), arrives in Hiroshima, Japan and founds Hiroshima Jyo Gakuin women's school. The school celebrated its centennial in 1986.

1887 **Isabella Thoburn** begins the first Christian woman's college in Asia.

— **Emma Virginia Levi Brown,** a black woman, becomes a Woman's Home Missionary Society (ME) missionary and matron at Browning Home, Camden, South Carolina.

1888 **Frances E. Willard, Mary Clarke Nind, Amanda C. Rippey, Angie F. Newman,** and **Elizabeth D. Van Kirk** are elected delegates to the General Conference (ME) but are denied seating because they are women.

	The Chicago Preachers Meeting successfully petitions General Conference (ME) to recognize deaconess work as an official institution of the church. Deaconess work is placed under the control of annual conferences.
1889	**Ella Niswonger** becomes the first woman ordained in the United Brethren Church.
—	**Eugenia St. John** is ordained an elder by the Kansas Annual Conference of the Methodist Protestant Church.
—	The New England Deaconess Home and Training School is founded in Boston (ME).
1890	The Woman's Home Missionary Society of the Methodist Episcopal Church, South, under the leadership of **Lucinda Helm,** is recognized by the church's General Conference. **Elizabeth Reaves Riley** is the first president.
1891	The Woman's Missionary Association is reorganized after a denominational split (EA) with **Minerva Strawman Spreng** as president. The organizers take care that the needs of both English and German-speaking members are met.
—	The Woman's Home and Foreign Missionary Society is founded after the United Evangelical Church leaves the Evangelical Association. **Elizabeth Krecker** is the first president.
1892	Scarritt Bible and Training School, headed by **Maria Gibson,** is opened in Kansas City thanks to the efforts of **Belle Harris Bennett,** Woman's Home Missionary Society (MES).
—	Four women delegates—**Melissa M. Bonnett, Mrs. M. J. Morgan, Mrs. A. E. Murphy,** and **Eugenia St. John**—are seated at the General Conference (MP).
—	The General Conference (ME) passes legislation stating that educational work among Native Americans can no longer be done by the Woman's Home Missionary Society. The women give up this work,

with the exception of Alaska and the Jesse Lee Home.

1893　The Woman's Home Missionary Society (MP) is founded with **Miss S. A. Lipscomb** as president. It funds its first home mission project, the People's Church, in Kansas City in 1894.

1894　**Sarah Dickey** is ordained by the United Brethren Church.

1895　New York Evangelical Training School and Settlement House is founded by **Jennie Fowler Willing** (ME) to train deaconesses and serve Hell's Kitchen, an infamous New York slum.

1898　Missionaries of the Woman's Missionary Association (UB) and many of their African co-workers are massacred in Sierra Leone in an uprising touched off by a hut tax imposed by the British Government. Within two weeks after the event, the association decides to continue its work there.

—　**Hattie Carson** (MES) is transferred from Mexico to begin mission work in Cuba by opening a school for girls.

1900　The Woman's Missionary Association (UB) approves a Reading Course.

1901　The Woman's Home Missionary Society of the Methodist Episcopal Church, South begins its first work with black Americans at Paine Institute (founded in 1883) in Augusta, Georgia.

—　**Ella Niswonger** (UB) is elected the first woman clergy delegate to a General Conference.

1902　**Susan Collins** is the first black woman sent as a missionary by the Woman's Foreign Missionary Society (ME). She travels to Angola.

1904　Women are given laity rights and admitted to the Methodist Episcopal Church General Conference as delegates.

—　Twenty women of the Pacific Japanese Mission Conference (ME) form the Oakland Women's Society, *Funjinkai*, a ladies' aid type group.

—	The Woman's Missionary Society (EC) founds the Bible Woman's Training School in Japan.
—	Ladies' Aid Societies, as old as American Methodism, are officially recognized in the *Discipline* (ME) although there is never an official denominational agency.
—	**Anna Shaw Howard** becomes president of the National American Woman Suffrage Association, a position she holds until 1915.
—	**Mary McLeod Bethune** founds the Daytona Normal and Industrial School for Negro Girls in Daytona Beach, Florida.
1906	The independence of the Woman's Home and Foreign Missionary Societies of the Methodist Episcopal Church, South is threatened by General Conference.
—	**Martha Drummer,** a black deaconess of the New England Deaconess Training School (Boston) is sent to Angola by the Woman's Foreign Missionary Society (ME). **Anna Hall,** another black deaconess, goes to the mission field in Liberia.
1907	The Woman's Home Missionary Society (MP) revises its constitution and bylaws and changes its name to the Woman's Board of Home Missions. **Mrs. M. O. Everett** becomes the first missionary to work with mountain people in Kentucky.
—	**Miss Constante Field** is sent as a missionary (MP) to a Native American mission in Tolchaco, Arizona.
—	**Bessie Harrison** is named a field worker for the black conference by the Woman's Home Missionary Society (MES).
1909	The Woman's Missionary Association (UB) becomes part of the General Board of Missions. Women gain wider and more influential responsibilities as a result.
1910	The Woman's Societies and the Methodist Episcopal Church, South are joined under one Woman's Missionary Council and made part

of the general missionary organization of the church. **Belle Harris Bennett** is its first president.

— The General Conference (MES) denies women laity rights.

— One out of five wage earners is a woman. One out of four women over 14 is employed, as are one-quarter of children between 10 and 14.

1911 A disastrous fire at the Triangle Shirtwaist Company in New York kills 146 women, but leads to improvements in laws regulating factory working conditions.

1912 **Mellie Perkins** begins work as a United Brethren missionary in Velarde, New Mexico. Later she founds McCurdy School.

1913 The Alvan Drew School is opened in Pine Ridge, Kentucky by the Woman's Board of Home Missions (MP).

— The Woman's Missionary Society of China is organized in Foochow. Earlier there had been local auxiliaries affiliated with the Woman's Foreign Missionary Society (ME).

1914–1918 World War I

1914 Night shift work for women is internationally forbidden.

1915 **Margaret Sanger** is jailed for writing *Family Limitation,* first book on birth control.

1916 The Woman's Board of Home Missions (MP) opens the Pittsburgh Mission, an urban mission center for immigrants.

1917 **Mrs. Kane Yajima,** most famous of all of the Japanese Bible women (ME), begins work that will take her to Seattle, San Francisco, Honolulu and San Leandro.

1919 The 19th Amendment, giving American women the vote, is passed by Congress.

1920	Women in the Methodist Episcopal Church, South are given laity rights.
—	Methodist women in Cuba organize Woman's Missionary Societies.
—	**Carrie Johnson** is selected to head a standing committee of the Woman's Missionary Council (MES) to study the race question and develop ways for black and white women to work together, a task she continues until her death in 1929.
—	The local preacher's license, the first step to ordained ministry, is officially extended to women in the *Book of Discipline* (ME).
1921	The Wesleyan Service Guild (ME) for business and professional women is founded as an auxiliary to the Woman's Foreign and Home Missionary Societies through the efforts of **Marion Lela Norris** and others.
1922	The Woman's Missionary Society is reorganized after a merger of the Evangelical Association and the United Evangelical Church to form the Evangelical Church. **Minerva Strawman Spreng** is president.
—	Eighteen women are the first to be seated as delegates at General Conference (MES).
1923	**Helen Kim,** a Korean woman recently graduated from Ewha Woman's College in Seoul, Korea, speaks to the Executive Committee of the Woman's Foreign Missionary Society (ME) about her vision of a worldwide organization for women, later to become the World Federation of Methodist Women and known today as the World Federation of Methodist and Uniting Church Women.
—	The Japan Mission Council of the Woman's Home Missionary Society (MP) includes Japanese women as members of its policy-making body for the first time.
1924	Women in the Methodist Episcopal Church are given limited clergy rights.

1926	**Mrs. Takagi** becomes the first Japanese chairwoman of the Women's Japan Mission Council (MP).
1929	The Woman's Foreign Missionary Society and the Woman's Board of Home Mission merge to form the Woman's Missionary Convention (MP) and become a department under the Board of Missions. The first program book for women is published and a prayer calendar appears in *The Missionary Record*.
—	The women's missionary organization of the Ohio-German Conference merges with the Ohio Branch of the Woman's Missionary Association (UB).
1930	**Mrs. B. W. Lipscomb** of the Woman's Missionary Council (MES) organizes Spanish-speaking women in the Western Mexican Conference. **Mrs. Esther Hernandez** is the first president.
1933	The Woman's Missionary Association (UB) renames its business and professional evening circles of women Harford Circles in honor of **Mrs. L. R. Harford,** one of the founders of the association.
1939–1945	World War II
1939	The various women's home and foreign missionary societies, ladies' aid societies, etc. of the three uniting churches — Methodist Episcopal, Methodist Episcopal, South and Methodist Protestant — are joined and become the Woman's Society of Christian Service and the Wesleyan Service Guild. They come under the authority of the Board of Missions.
—	**Mrs. J. D. Bragg** is the first president of the Woman's Division of Christian Service (M).
—	The Central Jurisdiction is formed as part of a North-South compromise to create The Methodist Church (M). This jurisdiction is based on race and covers most of the African-American churches in the Southeastern and South Central states and the North. **Mary McLeod Bethune** opposes the organization of the Central Jurisdiction because it might increase segregation.

— The charter for the World Federation of Methodist Women is signed.

— Native American women who are part of an Indian Mission in Oklahoma have formed 42 local mission societies (MES).

— **Georgia Harkness** (ME) becomes professor of applied theology at Garrett Biblical Institute, the first woman at a major seminary to hold such a position.

1940 The women of Puerto Rico organize a conference organization of the Woman's Society of Christian Service (M). **Mrs. Antonio R. Pereles** is the first president.

— The Woman's Society of Christian Service of the Central Jurisdiction (M) has its charter meeting in Cincinnati, Ohio.

— **Ellen Barnette** and **Pearl Bellinger** are among the first African-American missionaries sent to a country not in Africa. They go to India as part of the mission work of the Woman's Society of Christian Service (M).

1941 The U.S. enters World War II. During the war, over six million women enter the American workforce for the first time, mostly in defense plants. The majority of these workers are married.

1942 The first Assembly of the Woman's Society of Christian Service and the Wesleyan Service Guild (M) is held in Columbus, Ohio, which has one hotel that does not practice segregation. The event had been planned for Kansas City but was moved because the city had no "open" hotels.

— The Woman's Division of Christian Service (M) holds its first National Seminar, an educational program inherited from the Woman's Missionary Council (MES). The interracial event is held at Garrett Theological Seminary in Evanston, Illinois.

1943 The first Spanish translation of the program book for the Woman's Society of Christian Service (M) is made by **Mrs. Elida G. Falcón.**

1944	The Christian Service Guild (EC) is formed for employed women.
—	The Woman's Division of the Board of Missions of the Methodist Church forms a Committee on the Status of Women.
1946	The Women's Society of World Service and its auxiliary, the Christian Service Guild (for business and professional women), are formed after a merger of the Evangelical and United Brethren churches to form the Evangelical United Brethren (EUB) church. **Justina Showers** is the first president.
—	The first reports from women's societies in the Latin American Provisional Conference appear in the Woman's Division (M) report.
—	**Irene Haumersen** and **Mrs. Edward Stukenberg**, the first women delegates, attend the General Conference (EC) and the joint General Conference (EUB).
—	Women are denied ordination in the United Brethren Church (UB).
1949	The first reports from women's societies in the Cuba Provisional Conference appear in the Woman's Division (M) report.
1950	Japanese women of the Oakland Women's Society, *Fujinkai*, become part of the Woman's Society of Christian Service (M).
—	Asian women (Chinese, Filipina, and Korean) of the Oriental Provisional Conference organize a conference for the Woman's Society of Christian Service (M) and **Helen Marquez** becomes the first president.
1951	A new facility built to house the Literature Headquarters for the Woman's Society of Christian Service (M) is opened.
1952	The first Charter of Racial Policies is adopted by the Woman's Division of Christian Service (M).
1954	Japanese women in Oakland form a Wesleyan Service Guild (M).

1956	Women in The Methodist Church win full clergy rights. **Maud Keister Jensen** is the first woman to be granted such rights.
1958	The Christian Service Guild (EUB) ceases to exist.
1960	A joint United Nations Office is opened in New York City by the Department of Social Relations of the Woman's Division of Christian Service (M) and the Division of Peace and World Order of the Board of Christian Social Concerns (M).
1962	The second Charter of Racial Policies is adopted by the Woman's Division of Christian Service (M).
1963	The Church Center for the United Nations is dedicated.
1968	The Women's Society of Christian Service is formed and the Wesleyan Service Guild is continued after the merger of the Methodist and Evangelical United Brethren Churches to form The United Methodist Church. **Eunice Harrington** is the first president of the Women's Division.
—	**Theressa Hoover** becomes the first associate general secretary of the Women's Division. She is the first African-American woman to become the top staff person of any of the national women's mission organizations in the history of The United Methodist Church and its predecessor denominations.
1972	Women in The United Methodist Church adopt a new name: United Methodist Women. The Wesleyan Service Guild and the Women's Society of Christian Service together with women who are members of neither are urged to come together in the new organization. In the revision of church structure, women make new gains. The General Commission on the Status and Role of Women is established and funded by the General Church.
—	Title IX of the Education Amendments requires that "no person in the United States shall, on the basis of sex, be excluded from participation in, be denied the benefits of, or be subjected to discrimination under any education program or activity receiving federal financial assistance."

— After languishing since 1923, the Equal Rights Amendment is passed by Congress on March 22 and sent to the states for ratification. Hawaii approves it within the hour. By the end of the week, so have Delaware, Nebraska, New Hampshire, Idaho and Iowa.

— **Sally Priesand** becomes the first U.S. woman ordained as a rabbi in Reform Judaism.

1973 In *Roe v. Wade,* the Supreme Court establishes a woman's right to abortion, effectively canceling the anti-abortion laws of 46 states.

1974 Alliance of Displaced Homemakers is founded by **Tish Sommers** and **Laurie Shields** to address issues of divorced and widowed homemakers seeking employment.

— Little League agrees to include girls "in deference to a change in social climate," but creates a softball branch specifically for girls to draw them from baseball.

— The Women's Educational Equity Act, drafted by **Arlene Horowitz** and introduced by **Rep. Patsy Mink** (D-HI), funds the development of nonsexist teaching materials and model programs that encourage full educational opportunities for girls and women.

— The Coalition for Labor Union Women is founded, uniting blue-collar women across occupational lines.

1976 The Organization of Pan Asian American Women is founded to impact public policy.

— Title IX goes into effect, opening the way for women's increased participation in athletics programs and professional schools. Enrollments leap in both categories. Title IX withstands repeated court challenges over time (see 1997 entry).

— U.S. military academies open admissions to women.

— A *New York Times* survey shows that women's enrollment in theological seminaries has risen from 3% to 35% of all students within the previous decade.

— The Episcopal Church votes to allow the ordination of women as bishops and priests, and recognizes the earlier "irregular" ordination of **Jacqueline Means** and ten other women.

1978 The third charter addressing racism, the Charter for Racial Justice Policies, is written and adopted by the Women's Division (UM). The division urges ratification of the charter by each jurisdiction and conference organization and implementation of the principles and goals of the charter within each jurisdiction, conference and local unit.

— **Mai H. Gray** is elected the first African-American president of the Women's Division (UM).

— The Older Women's League is founded to address age and gender discrimination issues including health insurance and retirement benefits.

— For the first time in history, more women than men enter college.

— The Pregnancy Discrimination Act amends the 1964 Civil Rights Act to ban employment discrimination against pregnant women.

1979 **Owanah Anderson** founds and directs the Ohoyo Resource Center to advance the status of American Indian and Alaska Native women.

— The National Association for Black Women Entrepreneurs is formed by **Marilyn French-Hubbard** to offer advice, training and networking for black businesswomen.

1980 At the Women's Division recommendation, the Charter for Racial Justice Policies is adopted by the General Conference for implementation by The United Methodist Church.

— **Marjorie Matthews** is the first woman to be elected bishop of The United Methodist Church. She is the nation's first woman to sit on the governing body of a major religious denomination.

1981	At the request of women's organizations, President Carter proclaims the first "National Women's History Week," incorporating March 8, International Women's Day.
—	**Sandra Day O'Connor** is the first woman ever appointed to the U.S. Supreme Court. In 1993, she is joined by **Ruth Bader Ginsberg.**
1982	The Equal Rights Amendment is defeated, three states short of ratification.
1983	**Marjorie Suchoki** (an Episcopalian) is selected as the first woman Dean of a United Methodist seminary (Wesley Theological Seminary).
1984	Sex discrimination in the admission policies of organizations such as the Jaycees is forbidden by the Supreme Court in *Roberts v. United States Jaycees,* opening many previously all-male organizations to women.
—	**Geraldine Ferraro** is the first woman vice-presidential candidate of a major political party (Democratic Party).
—	**Judith Craig** and **Leontine Kelly** become the second and third woman bishops of The United Methodist Church. **Kelly** is the first black woman bishop of the church.
1985	**Wilma Mankiller** becomes the first woman installed as principal chief of a major Native American tribe, the Cherokee in Oklahoma.
—	First Hispanic women's consultation in The United Methodist Church takes place.
1986	**Amy Eilberg** is the first woman ordained as a rabbi by the Conservative Rabbinical Assembly.
1988	**Rev. Barbara Harris,** an African-American, becomes the first female bishop of the Episcopal Church.

	Susan Morrison and **Sharon Brown Christopher** become United Methodist bishops.
1990	Fifty women serve The United Methodist Church as district superintendents.
1992	Women are now paid 71¢ for every dollar paid to men. The range is from 64¢ for working-class women to 77¢ for professional women with doctorates. Black women earned 65¢, Latinas 54¢.
—	Women win all five of the gold medals won by Americans during the Winter Olympics.
1993	*Take Our Daughters to Work Day* debuts, designed to build girls' self-esteem and open their eyes to a variety of career possibilities for women.
1994	Congress adopts the Gender Equity in Education Act to train teachers, promote math and science learning by girls, counsel pregnant teens and prevent sexual harassment.
—	*The Violence Against Women Act* funds services for victims of rape and domestic violence, allows women to seek civil rights remedies for gender-related crimes, provides training to increase police and court officials' sensitivity and a national 24-hour hotline for battered women.
1996	Total number of female bishops, priests, ministers and rabbis: Baptist: 2,313 ministers; Episcopal: 6 bishops, 1,452 priests; Evangelical Lutheran: 1,838 pastors; Judaic, Reform: 259 rabbis; Judaic, Conservative: 72 rabbis; Judaic, Orthodox: 0 rabbis; Latter-Day Saints: 0 priests; Presbyterian: 3,026 ministers; Roman Catholic: 0 priests; Seventh-Day Adventists: 0 priests; Unitarian Universalist Association: 4,443 ministers; United Church of Christ, Congregationalist: 2,080 ministers: United Methodists: 10 bishops, 4,995 ministers.
—	The Women's Division (UM) launches a six-year membership campaign which includes emphasis on actively involving teen women

(ages 12-17), college/university women (ages 18-25), young women (ages 18-39), newly retired women, and women of various ethnic and language groups. Through the provision to organize as a district unit, groups can form in the workplace, on campuses, in prisons or retirement homes, as well as other locations outside the local church.

1997   Elaborating on Title IX, the Supreme Court rules that college athletics programs must actively involve roughly equal numbers of men and women to qualify for federal support.

2002   Of the 51 active bishops of The United Methodist Church, 11 are women. A total of 14 women have been elected bishop since 1980 when **Marjorie Matthews** became the first.

RESOURCES

A Journey in Song: Lenten Reflections on Hymns by Women (#2831, $4.95). A Lenten devotional booklet consisting of scripture references, songs written by women, questions for reflection and sentence prayers. Explore how God is revealed through scripture, hymns and songs of both contemporary and historical women of faith.

Concepts of Mission (#2820, $6.00). Intended as an understanding of mission for beginners, this clarifies selected major missional concepts. A good introduction for those interested in mission.

Count me in, too! What Young Women are Saying about United Methodist Women (#2743, $5.00). This 10-minute video with program guide offers vignettes of candid discussions with teens and college/university women about United Methodist Women. With honesty, love, and hope, these young women share how they are involved in the organization and how the organization can be more inviting to them. Designed for use by local units, districts and conferences to explore the implications of working effectively with teens and college/university women.

Empowering Young Women (#2742, $5.00). A comprehensive guide to inviting and involving teens and college/university women in United Methodist Women.

Global Praise 1 (#2572, $6.95). Songs from around the world and many regions of Methodism, from diverse cultures and languages that everyone can sing.

Global Praise 2: Songs for Worship and Witness (#2918, $8.95). Includes 127 faith songs from over 30 nations and traditions. All original languages are accompanied by singable English translations.

Invitation to Membership (#5365). A free brochure that introduces new members to United Methodist Women.

Let's Get Together (#2910, $5.00). A comprehensive packet with steps for organizing district units, circles and subgroups of teens and college/university women in United Methodist Women.

Make Plain the Vision: Songs of Women (CD #2747, $12.95 or Cassette

#2748, $8.95). Songs by women authors and composers performed at the 1998 Women's Assembly. Women's vision of God's family, peace, justice, redemption, mission, and ministry as expressed in the words and music of Hildegard of Bingen, Fanny Crosby, and contemporary hymn writers such as Shirley Erena Murray, Jane Marshall and Mahalia Jackson.

Material Resources for Mission Catalog (#2579, $3.50). A listing of opportunities for giving material resources that will be distributed to projects and for emergency relief.

Membership Joys and Responsibilities (#5513). A free brochure includes the PURPOSE of United Methodist Women, a membership card, a pledge to mission card and a subscription form for *Response* magazine.

Ministries with Women and Ministries with Children and Youth: A Gift for the Whole Church (#1892, 30¢). A policy statement of the Women's Division, with study guide, that reviews the position of women, children and youth in our society to discern our ongoing mission.

Mission: Responding to God's Grace, A Policy Statement on Giving of the Women's Division (#2581, 50¢). A policy statement that stresses the biblical and theological reasons for giving. This booklet includes a study guide.

Mission Volunteers (#5487). A free brochure describing a wide variety of opportunities for individuals and groups interested in becoming mission volunteers.

New Member Packet (#4099, 75¢). A choice assortment of resources to introduce a new member to United Methodist Women.

New World Outlook ($19.95/year subscription). As the mission magazine of The United Methodist Church, it reports on the work of the General Board of Global Ministries and the ecumenical mission of the church. Order with *Response* for $28/year.

One Million Plus—United Methodist Women (#5091). A free, colorful leaflet that describes United Methodist Women as a community that is unique, faithful, purposeful, supportive and global.

On PURPOSE. A newsletter for teens and college/university women in United Methodist Women that focuses on information and opportunities for full participation in the organization. To subscribe FREE, send your name, address, city, state and zip code to Executive Secretary for Young Women, 475 Riverside Drive, Room 1501, New York, NY 10115 or e-mail to youngumw@gbgm-umc.org.

Prayer Calendar ($7.50). A daily guide to prayer for mission workers and mission projects in the United States and around the world. Includes names, addresses, birthdays, special prayers, daily scripture readings, maps and pages of special interest.

Program Book for United Methodist Women ($3.75). A collection of program suggestions for United Methodist Women on a variety of mission topics, including a Quiet Day Service, a Pledge Service, and a World Thank Offering Service.

Reading Program. (#5584) A free booklet published annually that describes the Reading Program plans and books. Books are listed under each of the four mission emphases.

Response ($15/year subscription). The official voice of United Methodist Women in mission. It is essential for every leader and member. Regular reading of this magazine increases your understanding of the current program and concerns of the Women's Division and United Methodist Women in global mission. The focus is on women, children and youth. In addition, there are organizational and program aids. Order with *New World Outlook* for $28/year.

Report of the Women's Division ($3.75). This annual report of the Women's Division updates the ways in which United Methodist Women continue their heritage of mission work with women, children and youth. It is a good resource for programming and for understanding how funds are distributed within the organization.

Ten Best Books on the History of United Methodist Women (#2829, $40.00). This CD-ROM contains the complete manuscripts of ten books on the history of United Methodist Women and its predecessor organizations.

Theressa Hoover: A Woman with PURPOSE (#3004, $15.00). An 11-minute video of Theressa Hoover, one of the first black women to work for the Women's Division.

Twenty Questions (#5436). A free brochure answering basic questions about United Methodist Women.

United Methodist Women in Mission (#2139, 25¢). This is a resource for new members, pastors and all United Methodist Women. Designed with brilliant sunburst colors, it expands on *One Million Plus–United Methodist Women,* and includes the biblical basis for our long heritage of mission.

Upfront with Youth: Great Mission Ideas for Youth and Their Leaders (#2752, $5.00). A manual designed to help youth and their leaders understand the mission program of The United Methodist Church. It includes ideas for education, fundraising and service.

What's the PURPOSE? (#2913, $3.50). This foundational program resource is an essential part of developing understanding among teens and college/university women about the PURPOSE of United Methodist Women. In six sessions, with reproducible handouts, activities, worship and ideas for expanded sessions and a retreat format, this resource gives young women the tools they need to become active members and partners in mission.

Why Have a Charter for Racial Justice Policies? (#5297). A free brochure containing the Charter for Racial Justice Policies for United Methodist Women, which has also been adopted as a resolution of The United Methodist Church.

You Belong Here! Poster 'N Facts (#2685, $2.00). This colorful, two-sided poster with mailing envelope is designed to excite and inform teens and college/university women about United Methodist Women. Consider sending one to each teen or college/university woman with a personal note to let her know about your local unit and opportunities for her involvement. At $2.00 each, it's as inexpensive as a greeting card, but with a lot more information and pictures.

NOTE: In some cases, the resources in this listing are also available in Spanish and Korean. Refer to the Service Center Catalog or inquire when placing an order. See inside back cover for order information.

ENDNOTES

Foreword

[1] Introductory comments by Peter J. Gomes to the second edition of *The Courage to Be* by Paul Tillich, p. xxvii, New Haven: Yale University Press, 2000.

Chapter 1

[1] Wise, the Rev. Daniel, *The Sphere, the Duties and Dangers of Young Women,* Swormstedt and Poe for the Methodist Episcopal Church, Cincinnati, 1855, pp. 91-92.
[2] Shaw, Anna Howard, *The Story of a Pioneer,* Harper & Bros., New York, 1915, pp. 25-26.
[3] Montgomery, Helen Barrett, *Western Women in Eastern Lands,* Macmillan Company, New York, 1910, p. 5.
[4] Chestnut, Mary, *Diary from Dixie,* Boston: Houghton Mifflin ed., 1951. Passage dated January 24, 1862.
[5] Letter of Caroline Merrick "to my dear friend," May 23, 1857, Dept. of Archives and Manuscripts, Louisiana State University, Baton Rouge.
[6] Hooper, the Rev. William, "Address on Female Education before the Sedgwick Female Seminary," Feb. 27, 1847, pamphlet in Duke University Library.
[7] Diary of Fanny Moore Webb Bumpas, March 5, 1842, Southern Historical Collection, University of North Carolina.
[8] Diary of Charlotte Beatty, 1843, Southern Historical Collection, University of North Carolina.
[9] Sarah Wadley Journal, Feb. 4, 1863, Southern Historical Collection, University of North Carolina.
[10] Lucilla McCorkel Diary, May 1846, Southern Historical Collection, University of North Carolina.
[11] Annie to Lollie, Dec. 14, 1859, Lucy Cole Burwell Papers, Manuscript Dept., Duke University.
[12] *An Account of the Rise, Progress, and Present State of the Boston Female Asylum, together with the Act of Incorporation, etc.* (Boston: pr. by Russell and Carter, 1810); Jedediah Morse, *Reminiscences of the Boston Female Asylum* (Boston: pr. by Eastburn's Press, 1844).
[13] Panoplist, VIII, pp. 12 (1816), pp. 256-260.

[14]Montgomery, *op. cit.*, p. 30.

[15]Elaine Magalis, *Conduct Becoming to a Woman,* p. v.

[16]The Ceremony of Lights was conducted by the President and Keeper of Lights of the Wesleyan Service Guild unit. It has been adapted slightly to incorporate the use of inclusive language and the PURPOSE of United Methodist Women.

[17]Alan Paton, South Africa, 20th century. "For Courage to Do Justice," *The United Methodist Hymnal,* p. 456. Copyright © 1968, 1982 Seabury Press, Inc.

[18]Adapted from Helen Bruch Pearson, *Do What You Have the Power to Do,* pp. 28-29.

Chapter 2

[1]Montgomery, Helen Barrett, *Western Women in Eastern Lands,* Macmillan Company, New York, 1910, p. 215.

[2]Tracy, Joseph, a 19th-century historian. Quoted in Beaver, R. Pierce, *All Loves Excelling,* William B. Eerdmans Publishing Co., Grand Rapids, Michigan, 1968, p. 55.

[3]Howell, Mabel K., *Women and the Kingdom, Fifty Years of Kingdom Building by Women of the Methodist Episcopal Church South,* 1878-1928, Cokesbury, Nashville, 1928, pp. 24-25. Used with permission.

[4]*Ibid.*

[5]Barclay, Wade C., *History of Methodist Missions, Early American Methodism,* 1769-1844, Part 1, Vol. 1, Board of Missions of The Methodist Church, 1919, p. 334.

[6]*Ibid.,* p. 338.

[7]North, Louise McCoy, *The Story of the New York Branch,* New York Branch, Woman's Foreign Missionary Society of the Methodist Episcopal Church, 1926, p. 10.

[8]Letter from Mary Mason to Ann Wilkins, Oct. 26, 1845. Quoted in North, pp. 19-20.

[9]Letter from Ann Wilkins to Mary Mason, Aug. 10, 1839. Quoted in North, p. 21.

[10]A reminiscence of Mrs. A. L. Davidson in a letter to Mrs. Juliana Hayes, first president of the Woman's Foreign Missionary Society in the South. Quoted in Butler, Mrs. F. A., *History of the Woman's Foreign Missionary Society, Methodist Episcopal Church, South,* Methodist Episcopal Church, South, 1912, pp. 24-25.

[11]Howell, *op. cit.,* pp. 38-42. Used with permission.

[12]From an 1841 report of the Lynchburg, Virginia, Female Missionary Society. Quoted in Howell, p. 27.

[13]Butler, Clementina, Mrs. William Butler, *Two Empires and the Kingdom,* The Methodist Book Concern, 1929, p. 45.

[14]*Ibid.,* p. 84.

[15]Isham, Mary, V*alorous Ventures,* Woman's Foreign Missionary Society, Methodist Episcopal Church, Boston, 1936, p. 14.

[16]*Ibid.,* pp. 15-16.

[17]*Ibid.,* p. 16.

[18]*Ibid.,* p. 17.

[19]*Ibid.,* p. 18.

²⁰Magalis, *op. cit.*, p. v.

²¹Adapted from Jane McKay Lanning, "Three Candles" in the *Annual Report of the Woman's Foreign Missionary Society of the Methodist Episcopal Church* (November 1928).

²²Words written by Minerva Strawman Spreng to the women of the Woman's Missionary Society of the Evangelical Association just prior to her death, as quoted in *Along the Journey,* p. 6.

²³Adapted from Hannah Ward, Jennifer Wild and Janet Morley, editors. *Celebrating Women* (Harrisburg, PA: Morehouse Publishing, 1995), p. 109.

Chapter 3

¹Miller, Mrs. M. A., *A History of the Woman's Foreign Missionary Society of the Methodist Protestant Church,* Pittsburgh: the Society, 1896, pp. 36-37.

²Butler, Mrs. F. A., *History of the Woman's Foreign Missionary Society, Methodist Episcopal Church, South,* Methodist Episcopal Church, South, 1912, p. 42.

³Eller, Paul Himmel, *History of Evangelical Missions,* The Evangel Press, Harrisburg, Pennsylvania, 1942, p. 23.

⁴Day, Emeline, a letter in the *Religious Telescope,* October 13, 1875.

⁵*Ibid.*, November 24, 1875.

⁶Hoke, Brother J., letters to the *Religious Telescope,* December 1, 1875 and January 7, 1876.

⁷Rike, Salome Kumler, letter to the *Religious Telescope,* February 2, 1876.

⁸A reminiscence of Mrs. Mary A. Miller, quoted by Chandler, Mrs. E. C., *History of the Woman's Foreign Missionary Society of the Methodist Protestant Church,* Pierpont, Seviter & Co., Pittsburgh, 1920, p. 55.

⁹A comment of Mrs. F. A. Brown, quoted by Chandler, *ibid.,* p. 55.

¹⁰Agnew, Theodore L., "Reflections on the Woman's Foreign Missionary Movement in Late 19th-Century American Methodism", *Methodist History,* January, 1968, p. 13.

¹¹Quoted from an editorial in the *Christian Advocate,* September 15, 1904, by North, Louise McCoy, *The Story of the New York Branch,* New York Branch, Woman's Foreign Missionary Society of the Methodist Episcopal Church, 1926, p. 144.

¹²North, pp. 104-105.

¹³Butler, Mrs. F. A., *Mrs. Juliana Hayes: Life, Reminiscences and Journal,* Publishing House, Methodist Episcopal Church, South, (no date), p. 15.

¹⁴*Ibid.*, pp. 16-17.

¹⁵Howell, Mabel K., *Women and the Kingdom, Fifty Years of Kingdom Building by Women of the Methodist Episcopal Church, South, 1878-1928,* Cokesbury, Nashville, 1928, p. 64. Used with permission.

¹⁶Reminiscence of Mrs. J. E. D. Easter, quoted in North, pp. 188-189.

¹⁷Miller, *op.cit.*, pp. 17-18.

¹⁸White, Mary Culler, *The Life Story of Alice Culler Cobb,* Fleming H. Revell Co.,

1925, pp. 92-93. Used with permission.

[19]Howell, *op.cit.,* pp. 61-62. Used with permission.

[20]Goodson, Mrs. E. F., *Fifty Golden Years of Kingdom Building by the Woman's Missionary Society of the Louisville Conference, Methodist Episcopal Church, South, 1878-1928,* Methodist Episcopal Church, South, 1929, p. 35.

[21]North, *op.cit.,* p. 151.

[22]Keen, Mrs. S. L., unpublished essay dated 1889 in Commission on Archives and History library, The United Methodist Church, Lake Junaluska, North Carolina.

[23]North, *op.cit.,* p. 168.

[24]*Ibid.*

[25]*Ibid.,* p. 169.

[26]*Ibid.,* p. 185.

[27]White, *op. cit.,* p. 100. Used with permission.

[28]Schauffler, Julia B., "Concerning the Woman's Foreign Missionary Society," *The Gospel in All Lands,* January 1892, p. 24.

[29]Goodson, *op. cit.,* p. 59.

[30]Magalis, *op. cit.,* p. v.

[31]Adapted from a "Litany on the PURPOSE of United Methodist Women" by Nell Chance, Alabama-West Florida Conference.

[32]Morley, Janet, *All Desires Known: Inclusive Prayers for Worship and Meditation,* Morehouse Publishing: Harrisburg, PA, 1992, p. 82.

[33]Adapted from *Prayers and Poems, Songs and Stories* by United Church of Christ Women written for the Ecumenical Decade 1988-1998 Churches in Solidarity with Women.

[34]Shelly, Patricia J., *Let All Within Us Praise! Dramatic Resources for Worship,* Faith & Life Press, 1996, p. 152. Used by permission.

Chapter 4

[1]Butler, Clementina, *Mrs. William Butler, Two Empires and the Kingdom,* The Methodist Book Concern, 1929, p. 35.

[2]Cowen, Mrs. B.R., *History of the Cincinnati Branch of the Woman's Foreign Missionary Society of the Methodist Episcopal Church, 1869-1894,* published by the Society, Cincinnati, 1895, p. 70.

[3]Baker, Frances J., *Historical Sketches of the Northwestern Branch of the Woman's Foreign Missionary Society of the Methodist Episcopal Church,* Jameson and Morse Co., Chicago, 1887, p. 91.

[4]Comment of James Thoburn in Oldham, William F., *Isabella Thoburn,* Jennings and Pyle, Chicago, 1902, pp. 20-21.

[5]North, Louise McCoy, *The Story of the New York Branch,* New York Branch, Woman's Foreign Missionary Society of the Methodist Episcopal Church, 1926, pp. 74-75.

[6]Letter of Mary Sharp to Bishop Gilbert Haven, December 10, 1878, in the correspondence files of the United Mission Library, Methodist-Presbyterian, New York City.

⁷Baker, *op. cit.,* p. 34.

⁸North, *op. cit.,* pp. 83-84.

⁹*Woman's Evangel* (Journal of United Brethren Woman's Missionary Association), September 1898, p. 149.

¹⁰*Woman's Evangel,* July 1898. The issue was devoted to the martyred missionaries.

¹¹A letter from Lochie Rankin in *In Memoriam* (book of letters, etc. Dora Rankin, Elizabeth Davis Fielder), Publishing House, Methodist Episcopal Church, South, Nashville, 1906 (cc 1899), p. 65.

¹²Brother Deputie, a Liberian Methodist leader, in a letter dated April 1, 1881, in the correspondence files of the United Mission Library.

¹³Baker, *op. cit.,* p. 100.

¹⁴Her insanity was probably not widely known. The only reference to it that I discovered was in the unpublished 1889 essay of Mrs. S.L. Keen referred to above.

¹⁵Letters from Harriet Woolston published in *The Heathen Woman's Friend,* February and April of 1879.

¹⁶North, *op. cit.,* pp. 91-92. A phrase occurring regularly in the second paragraph of Mrs. Skidmore's annual reports from the New York Branch.

¹⁷Thoburn, James, *Life of Isabella Thoburn,* Jennings and Pyle, Cincinnati, Eaton & Mains, New York, 1903, pp. 141-142.

¹⁸A popular saying coined by one of the first missionaries to China. Quoted by Montgomery, Helen Barrett, *Western Women in Eastern Lands,* Macmillan Company, New York, 1910, p. 89.

¹⁹Letter from Mary Sharp, September 25, 1893, in the correspondence files of the United Mission Library.

²⁰*Ibid.,* September 17, 1886.

²¹Glenn, Layona (with Charlotte Hale Smith), *I Remember, I Remember,* Fleming H. Revell Co., Old Tappan, New Jersey, 1969, p. 84.

²²Tuttle, A.H., *Mary Porter Gamewell,* Eaton & Mains, New York, 1907, p. 183.

²³*Ibid.,* p. 175.

²⁴*Ibid.,* p. 32.

²⁵*Ibid.,* p. 39.

²⁶*Ibid.,* p. 44.

²⁷*Ibid.,* p. 91.

²⁸*Ibid.,* p. 95.

²⁹*Ibid.,* pp. 296-297.

³⁰Rankin, *In Memoriam,* pg. 18. (letter from Dora, August 1880).

³¹*Ibid.,* pp. 46-47. (letter from Lochie, November 5, 1884).

³²*Ibid.,* pp. 30-31. (letter from Dora, October 9, 1881).

³³*Ibid.,* p. 24. (letter from Dora, June 18, 1881).

³⁴*Ibid.,* p. 40. (letter from Lochie, August 7, 1884).

³⁵*Ibid.,* p. 89. (letter from Lochie sometime after December 10, 1886).

³⁶*Ibid.,* p. 84. (letter from Laura Haygood, December 1886).

³⁷Brown, Oswald Eugene and Anna Muse, *Life and Letters of Laura Askew Haygood,* Methodist Episcopal Church, South, Nashville, Dallas, 1904, p. 272 (letter October 1891).

³⁸*Ibid.*, p. 139. (letter February 1886).
³⁹*Ibid.*, p. 231. (letter July 22, 1889).
⁴⁰*Ibid.*, p. 237. (letter November. 12, 1889).
⁴¹*Ibid.*, p. 242. (letter June 13, 1890).
⁴²*Ibid.*, pp. 272-273. (letter 1891).
⁴³*Ibid.*, p. 456. (letter 1899).
⁴⁴Browne, Eva C., *Life of Dr. Martha A. Sheldon, Missionary to Bhot, India,* Woman's Foreign Missionary Society, Methodist Episcopal Church, 1917, p. 14.
⁴⁵*Ibid.*, p. 35.
⁴⁶Price, Willard D., "At Rest after Thirty-Five Years in Liberia" (a eulogy for Mary Sharp written for the Publicity Dept., Board of Foreign Missions, Methodist Episcopal Church, August 18, 1914, and published in several church periodicals).
⁴⁷Letter of Mary Sharp to Bishop Gilbert Haven referred to above, footnote 19.
⁴⁸Letter of Mary Sharp, December 1891, in the correspondence files, United Mission Library.
⁴⁹King, Willis J. (Bishop), *History of the Methodist Church in Liberia,* unpublished mimeographed manuscript, no date but probably 1950s, p. 55. In the Liberia file of the United Mission Library.
⁵⁰Miller, Mrs. M.A., *A History of the Woman's Foreign Missionary Society of the Methodist Protestant Church,* Pittsburgh, the Society, 1896, p. 109.
⁵¹Rankin, *op. cit.*, p. 42.
⁵²Reminiscence of Lilivati Singh quoted in Thoburn, *op. cit.*, p. 368.
⁵³Often repeated quote of Dr. Duff, well known missionary educator, in a speech of Isabella Thoburn in 1900, quoted by Thoburn, James, p. 325.
⁵⁴*Ibid.*, p. 90.
⁵⁵*Ibid.*, p. 173. (speech of Isabella Thoburn before Decennial Missionary Conference in Calcutta, 1882-1883)
⁵⁶*Ibid.*, pp. 190-191. (from an article by Isabella Thoburn, *The Heathen Woman's Friend,* July 1888)
⁵⁷Cook, Mrs. David, ed., *In Loving Memory of Lilivati Singh,* Northwestern Branch, Woman's Foreign Missionary Society, Methodist Episcopal Church, p. 10.
⁵⁸Thoburn, *op. cit.*, p. 113.
⁵⁹Reminiscence of Lilivati Singh in Thoburn, p. 360.
⁶⁰Montgomery, *op. cit.*, pp. 105-106.
⁶¹*Ibid.*, p. 133.
⁶²Baker, *op. cit.*, pp. 88-89.
⁶³Montgomery, *op. cit.*, pp. 100-101.
⁶⁴*Ibid.*, p. 112.
⁶⁵Thoburn, *op. cit.*, p. 361.
⁶⁶Reminiscence of Lilivati Singh in Oldham, *op. cit.*, p. 39.
⁶⁷Reminiscence of Elizabeth Hughes in White, Mary Culler, *Just Jennie,* Foote and Davies, Inc., Atlanta, 1955, p. 13.
⁶⁸*Ibid.*, p. 7.
⁶⁹*Ibid.*, p. 12.
⁷⁰A letter from Mary Culler White, date unclear but in 1930s in microfilm files in

Central Records, World Division, Board of Global Ministries, The United Methodist Church, New York.

[71]White, Mary Culler, *The Life Story of Alice Culler Cobb,* Fleming H. Revell Co., 1925, p. 49. Used with permission.

[72]White, Mary Culler, *I was there when it happened in China,* Abingdon-Cokesbury Press, New York, Nashville, 1947, p. 13.

[73]Magalis, *op. cit.*, p. v.

[74]Aikman, Z. Susanne, from Eastern Cherokee prayer tradition, 1992, as reprinted in *Voices: Native American Hymns and Worship Resources,* Nashville, TN: Discipleship Resources, 1992, p. 67.

[75]Morley, Janet, *All Desires Known: Inclusive Prayers for Worship and Meditation,* Morehouse Publishing: Harrisburg, PA, 1992, p. 64.

Chapter 5

[1]Meeker, Ruth Esther, *Six Decades of Service, 1880-1940,* Continuing Corporation of the Woman's Home Missionary Society of the Methodist Episcopal Church, cc 1969, p. 2.

[2]Noted at the end of the minutes of the 1901 annual meeting of the Methodist Protestant Woman's Foreign Missionary Society, the *Record,* May 1901.

[3]Dunn, Mary Noreen, *Women and Home Missions,* Cokesbury, Nashville, 1936. p. 10.

[4]Howell, Mabel K., *Women and the Kingdom, Fifty Years of Kingdom Building by Women of the Methodist Episcopal Church, South, 1878-1928,* Cokesbury, Nashville, 1928, p. 40. Used with permission.

[5]Tomkinson, Mrs. T. L., *Twenty Years' History of the Woman's Home Missionary Society of the Methodist Episcopal Church, 1880-1900,* p. 7.

[6]Meeker, *op. cit.*, p. 7.

[7]Sanborn, Kate, "Frances E. Willard," *Our Famous Women (Comprising the Lives and Deeds of American Women),* A. D. Worthington and Co., Hartford, Conn., 1883, p. 711.

[8]Brown, Oswald Eugene and Anna Muse, *Life and Letters of Laura Askew Haygood,* Methodist Episcopal Church, South, Nashville, Dallas, 1904, pp. 72-73.

[9]*Ibid.*

[10]*Ibid.*, p. 86.

[11]Perkins, Mellie, "Reminiscences of a Missionary," *Our Work in New Mexico,* The United Brethren Home Missionary Society, Dayton, 1916, p. 12.

[12]*Ibid.*, p. 13.

[13]Campbell, Richard C., "Los Conquistadores, The Story of Santa Cruz Church," *The Rio Grande Sun,* 1965, p. 5.

[14]From an August 1972 letter from Lillian Kendig Cole to author.

[15]Campbell, *op. cit.*, p. 8.

[16]*Ibid.*, p. 9.

[17]August 1972 letter from Lillian Kendig Cole to author.

¹⁸Dunn, *op. cit.*, p. 32. Used with permission.

¹⁹Keeler, Ellen Coughlin, *The Balance Wheel, A Condensed History of the Woman's Home Missionary Society of the Methodist Episcopal Church, 1880-1920,* Woman's Home Missionary Society, Methodist Episcopal Church, 1920, p. 159.

²⁰MacDonell, Mrs. R. W., *Belle Harris Bennett,* Board of Missions, Methodist Episcopal Church, South, Nashville, 1928, p. 31.

²¹Testimonial of Dr. Henry Allen Lane, Madison County Agent of Cooperative Extension Work in Agriculture and Home Economics, Kentucky, in MacDonell, p. 137.

²²Account of Mrs. J. D. Hammond in MacDonell, p. 121.

²³MacDonell, p. 55.

²⁴*Ibid.*, p. 65.

²⁵Norton, Isabelle, *High Adventure, Life of Lucy Rider Meyer,* The Methodist Book Concern, New York, Cincinnati, 1928, pp. 86-87.

²⁶*Ibid.*, p. 109.

²⁷Gibson, Maria Layng, *Memoirs of Scarritt,* (ed. and compiled by Sara Estelle Haskin) Cokesbury Press, Nashville, 1928, p. 57.

²⁸*Ibid.*, p. 130.

²⁹Glenn, Layona (with Charlotte Hale Smith), *I Remember, I Remember,* Fleming H. Revell Co., Old Tappan, New Jersey, 1969, p. 65.

³⁰Norton, *op. cit.*, p. 145.

³¹*Ibid.*, p. 187.

³²*Ibid.*, p. 321.

³³Gibson, *op. cit.*, pp. 134-135.

³⁴Magalis, *op. cit.*, p. v.

³⁵Adapted from "Memory" by Evelyn Hunt as it appeared in *Women Psalms* compiled by Julia Ahlers, et. al.

³⁶Morley, Janet, *All Desires Known: Inclusive Prayers for Worship and Meditation,* Morehouse Publishing: Harrisburg, PA, 1992, pp. 66-67.

³⁷Adapted from the PURPOSE of United Methodist Women and "Reflections on Bread" by Ruth Kulas as it appeared in *Women Psalms.*

Chapter 6

¹Hoxie, Elizabeth, "Harriet Livermore," *Notable American Women, 1607-1950,* Vol. II, The Belknap Press of Harvard University Press, Cambridge, 1971, pp. 409-410.

²Helm, Mary, "Laity Rights for Women," *Our Homes*, May 1910, p. 7.

³Sexton, Lydia, *Autobiography,* United Brethren Publishing House, Dayton, Ohio, 1882, p. 396.

⁴*Ibid.*, p. 20.

⁵*Ibid.*, p. 149.

⁶Drury, A.W., *History of the Church of the United Brethren in Christ,* Otterbein Press, Dayton, 3rd Printing, rev. ed., 1953, p. 426.

⁷McLoughlin, William, "Margaret Ann Newton Van Cott," *Notable American*

Women, 1607-1950, Vol. III, p. 507.

[8]*Windham Journal,* June 17, 1869. (a weekly newspaper, Windham, New York).

[9]Smith, Amanda, *The Lord's Dealings with Mrs. Amanda Smith,* quoted in Deen, Edith, "Amanda Smith—Negro Woman Evangelist," *Great Women of the Christian Faith,* Harper and Brothers Publishers, New York, 1959, p. 255.

[10]*Ibid.,* p. 254.

[11]*Ibid.,* p. 256.

[12]Cadbury, M.H., *The Life of Amanda Smith,* Cornish Brothers Ltd., Birmingham, 1916, p. 67.

[13]*Mary Clarke Nind and Her Work,* by her children, published for the Woman's Foreign Missionary Society by J. Newton Nind, Chicago, 1906, p. 31.

[14]Agnew, Theodore, "Jennie Fowler Willing," *Notable American Women, 1607-1950,* Vol. III, p. 623.

[15]"Women's Record at Home," *Ladies Repository,* March 1875, p. 267.

[16]Willard, Frances, *Glimpses of Fifty Years,* Woman's Temperance Association Publication, Chicago, 1889, p. 616.

[17]Culver, Elsie Thomas, *Women in the World of Religion,* Doubleday and Company, Garden City, New York, 1967, p. 215.

[18]Women's Record at Home," *Ladies Repository,* July 1876, p. 79.

[19]Field, Mrs. L., in reminiscence in the *Woman's Evangel,* July 1898, p. 125.

[20]Hott, J.W., in reminiscence in the *Woman's Evangel,* July 1898, p. 124.

[21]*Mary Clarke Nind and Her Work, op. cit.,* p. 47.

[22]"The Rights of the Laity, A Wail from the Editor Pro Tem," *Our Homes,* July 1910, p. 8.

[23]Horton, Isabelle, *High Adventure, Life of Lucy Rider Meyer,* The Methodist Book Concern, New York, Cincinnati, 1928, pp. 228-229.

[24]Hammond, L.M., *Memories of Mary Helm,* Woman's Missionary Council, Methodist Episcopal Church, South, Nashville, no date, p. 41.

[25]Willard, *op. cit.,* p. 615.

[26]Hoss, Bishop E. E., "The Southern Methodists," *Christian Advocate,* May 1910.

[27]Stanton, Elizabeth Cady, *Woman's Bible,* Part II, pp. 7-8 (no date, probably 1980s).

[28]Stone, Lucy, in *Woman's Journal* (Boston), October 26, 1895.

[29]Magalis, *op. cit.,* p. v.

[30]Bryden-Brook, Simon, *Take, Bless, Break, Share: Agapes, Table Blessings and Liturgies,* The Canterbury Press, Norwich, 1998, pp. 24-25.

[31]Morley, Janet, *All Desires Known: Inclusive Prayers for Worship and Meditation,* Morehouse Publishing: Harrisburg, PA, 1992, pp. 79-80.

[32]*Ibid.,* pp. 64-66.

[33]Rainsley, Glen E. as it appeared in *The United Methodist Book of Worship,* Nashville, TN: Abingdon Press, 1992, p. 559.

Epilogue

¹Ellen Kirby in "Process and Style at Grailville, Some Evaluations," pg. 8. In the packet *Women Exploring Theology at Grailville,* Loveland, Ohio, June 18-25, 1972, compiled by Church Women United.

²All statistics in this chapter are from "The Status and Role of Women in Program and Policy Making Channels of The United Methodist Church," Report of the Study Commission to the 1972 General Conference and Actions of the General Conference on the Participation of Women in Program and Policy Making Channels of The United Methodist Church, July 1972.

³Stevens, Thelma, "The United Methodist Women's Caucus: From Evanston to Atlanta," *The Yellow Ribbon* (second issue, undated), newsletter of the Women's Caucus.

⁴Fletcher, Grace Nies, "Woman's Status in Protestant Churches, 'Is She to be Forever a Sort of Holy Cook?'" *Zion's Herald,* December 11, 1941, p. 1206.

⁵Letter, Louise Robinson to Mary Culler White, July 8, 1938. In the microfilm files of Central Records, World Division, Board of Global Ministries, The United Methodist Church, New York.

⁶Grist, Miriam and Norberg, Tilda, "Sex Stereotyping in the United Methodist Nursery Curriculum," report prepared for the New York Conference Task Force on the Status of Women in the Church, cc 1970.

⁷Shaw, Anna Howard, "The Women Who Publish the Tidings are a Great Host," a speech, found in Linkugel, "The Speeches of Anna Howard Shaw" (Ph.D. dissertation), University of Wisconsin, 1960, II, 83-84; copy of original is in folder No. 82—Anna Howard Shaw papers, Dillon Collection, Radcliffe Women's Archives.

Afterword: Thirty Years Later

¹Quoted from *The Essential Paul Tillich: An Anthology of the Writing of Paul Tillich,* ed. F. Forrester Church, New York: Macmillian, 1987, p. 279.

²The General Commission on the Status and Role of Women, 2000.

³*Ibid.*

⁴*Ibid.*

⁵Pamela McCorduck and Nancy Ramsey, *The Futures of Women: Scenarios for the 21st Century,* p. 9.

⁶U.S. Census Bureau, Statistical Abstract of the United States: 2001, No. 569 "Employment Status of the Civilian Population: 1970 to 2000," p. 368.

⁷*Ibid.* No. 571 "Civilian Labor Force and Participation Rates by Educational Attainment, Sex, Race and Hispanic Origin: 1992 to 2000," p. 369.

⁸*Ibid.* No. 621 "Full-Time Wage and Salary Workers—Number and Earnings: 1985 to 2000," p. 403.

⁹*Ibid.* No. 625 "Workers Paid Hourly Rates by Selected Characteristics: 2000," p. 405.

¹⁰*The American Woman 1999-2000.*

[11] Carol Marie Herb, *The Light Along the Way: A Living History Through United Methodist Women's Magazines,* pp. 38-39.

[12] Magalis, *op. cit.*, p. v.

[13] Adapted from *By Faith We Journey,* the hymn for Assembly 1986, by Don E. Saliers.

[14] Traditional Navaho Prayer.

BIBLIOGRAPHY

The Abiding Past: or, Fifty Years with the Woman's Missionary Society of the Evangelical Church, 1884-1934. Cleveland: W.M.S., Evangelical Church, 1936.

Along the Journey: Vignettes of Predecessor Women's Mission Organizations. New York: Women's Division, General Board of Global Ministries of The United Methodist Church, 1980.

Baker, Frances J. *The Story of the Woman's Foreign Missionary Society of the Methodist Episcopal Church,* 1869-1895. Revised edition. Cincinnati: Curts and Jennings, 1898.

Behney and Eller. *History of the Evangelical United Brethren Church.* Nashville: Parthenon Press, 1979.

Bennett, Mrs. H. *Her Story: History of the Woman's Missionary Society of the Evangelical Assocation (1884-?).* Cleveland: Mattill and Lamb, 1903.

Billings, Peggy. *Speaking Out in the Public Space: An Account of the Section of Christian Social Relations.* New York: Women's Division, General Board of Global Ministries of The United Methodist Church, 1995.

Born, Ethel W. *By My Spirit: The Story of Methodist Protestant Women in Mission 1879-1939.* New York: Women's Division, General Board of Global Ministries of The United Methodist Church, 1990.

Brummit, Stella Wyatt. *Looking Backward, Thinking Forward: Jubilee History of the Woman's Home Missionary Society of the Methodist Episcopal Church (1880-1930).* Cincinnati: 1930.

Butler, Sarah Frances Stringfield. *History of the Woman's Foreign Missionary Society, Methodist Episcopal Church, South (1878-1904).* Nashville: Publishing House of the M.E. Church, South, 1904.

Campbell, Barbara E. *In the Middle of Tomorrow.* New York: Women's Division, General Board of Global Ministries of The United Methodist Church, 1975.

Chandler, (Mrs. E.C.) Rosalie Porter. *History of the Woman's Foreign Missionary Society of the Methodist Protestant Church, 1879-1919.* Pittsburgh: Pierpont, Seviter and Company, 1920.

Costello, Cynthia B., Shari Miles and Anne J. Stone, eds. *The American Woman 1999-2000: A Century of Change.* New York: W.W. Norton and Company, 1998.

Davis, Angela Y. *Women, Race and Class.* New York: First Vintage Books Edition, 1983.

Dharmaraj, Glory E., Ph.D. *Concepts of Mission.* New York: General Board of Global Ministries, 1999.

Dunn, Mary Noreen. *Women and Home Missions (1885-1935).* Nashville: Cokesbury Press, 1936.

Fagan, Ann. *This Is Our Song: Employed Women in the United Methodist Tradition.* New York: Women's Division, General Board of Global Ministries of The United Methodist Church, 1986.

Fiorenza, Elizabeth Schussler. *In Memory of Her: A Feminist Theological Reconstruction of Christian Origins.* New York: The Crossroad Publishing Co., 1994.

Gordon, Jane and Hammer, Mrs. W.C. *History of the Woman's Home Missionary Society of the Methodist Protestant Church (1893-1919).* Thirteen-page booklet, 1920.

Gorrell, Donald K., ed. *Woman's Rightful Place: Women in United Methodist History.* Dayton: United Theological Seminary, 1980.

Gracey, Annie Ryder. *Twenty Years of the Woman's Foreign Missionary Society (1869-1889).* Boston: Heathen Woman's Friend, 1889.

Harford, Lillian Ressler and Alice E. Bell. *History of the Women's Missionary Society of the United Brethren in Christ (1875-1921).* Dayton: W.M.A., United Brethren in Christ, 1921.

Haskin, Sara Estelle. *Women and Missions in the Methodist Episcopal Church, South (1858-1920).* Nashville: Publishing House of the M.E. Church, South, 1921.

Helm, Mary. *Why—How: A Descriptive Narrative of the Work of the Woman's Home Mission Society of the Methodist Episcopal Church, South (1885-1912).* Nashville: Woman's Missionary Council, M.E. Church, South, 1912.

Herb, Carol Marie. *The Light Along the Way: A Living History Through United Methodist Women's Magazines.* New York: Women's Division, General Board of Global Ministries of The United Methodist Church, 1994.

Hill, Patricia R. *The World Their Household: The American Woman's Foreign Mission Movement and Cultural Transformation, 1870-1920.* Ann Arbor: University of Michigan Press, 1985.

History of the Woman's Missionary Association of the United Brethren in Christ (1875-1910). Dayton: United Brethren Publishing House, 1910.

Hoover, Theressa. *With Unveiled Face: Centennial Reflections on Women and Men in the Community of the Church*. New York: Women's Division, General Board of Global Ministries of The United Methodist Church, 1983.

Hough, Mary R. *Faith that Achieved: A History of the Women's Missionary Association of the Church of the United Brethren in Christ (1872-1946)*. Dayton: Women's Society of World Service of the Evangelical United Brethren Church, 1958.

Howell, Mabel Katherine. *Women and the Kingdom: Fifty Years of Kingdom Building by the Women of the Methodist Episcopal Church, South, 1878-1928*. Nashville: Cokesbury Press, 1928.

Isham, Mary. *Valorous Ventures: A Record of Sixty and Six Years of the Woman's Foreign Missionary Society of the Methodist Episcopal Church (1869-1935)*. Boston: W.F.M.S., 1936.

—Isham, Mary. *First Supplement (1935-1939)*.

—Lee, Elizabeth. *Second Supplement (1939-1940)*.

McCorduck, Pamela and Nancy Ramsey. *The Futures of Women: Scenarios for the 21st Century*. New York: Warner Books Edition, 1996.

Meeker, Ruth Esther. *Six Decades of Service, 1880-1940: A History of the Woman's Home Missionary Society of the Methodist Episcopal Church*. Cincinnati: Woman's Home Missionary Society, 1969.

Newsome, Carol A. and Sharon H. Ringe, eds. *The Women's Bible Commentary*. Louisville: Westminster John Knox Press, 1992.

North, Louise Josephine McCoy. *The Story of the New York Branch of the Woman's Foreign Missionary Society of the Methodist Episcopal Church (1819-1926)*. New York: NY Branch, W.F.M.S., M.E.C., 1926.

Reber, Audrie E. *Women United for Mission: A History of the Women's Society of World Service of the Evangelical United Brethren Church, 1946-1968*. Dayton: The Otterbein Press, 1969.

Robert, Dana L. *American Women in Mission: A Social History of Their Thought and Practice*. Macon, Georgia: Mercer University Press, 1997.

Schmidt, Jean Miller. *Grace Sufficient: A History of American Methodism 1760-1936*. Nashville: Abingdon Press, 1999.

Scott, Anne Firor. *The Southern Lady from Pedestal to Politics 1830-1930*. Chicago: University of Chicago Press, 1970.

Smith, Roy E. *The Woman's Foreign and Home Missionary Manual*. New York: Eaton & Mains, 1912.

—*The Ladies Aid Manual*. Cincinnati: Jennings and Graham, 1911.

Stamm, Mrs. John S. *Twelve More Years of the Abiding Past, 1934-1946*. Cleveland: Publishing House of the Evangelical Church, 1946.

Steinmetz, Estella Hartzler. *Reminiscences, Being a Record of Five and Twenty Years' Progress in the Woman's Home and Foreign Missionary Society of the United Evangelical Church (1891-1916)*. Harrisburg: United Evangelical Publishing House, 1910.

Stevens, Thelma. *Legacy for the Future: History of Christian Social Relations in the Woman's Division of Christian Service, 1940-1968*. Cincinnati: Women's Division, General Board of Global Ministries of The United Methodist Church, 1978.

Tatum, Noreen Dunn. *A Crown of Service: A Story of Woman's Work in the Methodist Episcopal Church, South 1878-1940*. Nashville: Parthenon Press, 1960.

They Went Out Not Knowing: An Encyclopedia of 100 Women in Mission. New York: Women's Division, General Board of Global Ministries of The United Methodist Church, 1986.

Thomas, Hilah F., Rosemary Skinner Keller and Louise L. Queen, eds. *Women in New Worlds: Historical Perspectives on the Wesleyan Tradition. Volumes 1 and 2*. Nashville: Abingdon Press, 1981-1982.

To a Higher Glory: The Growth and Development of Black Women Organized for Mission in The United Methodist Church, 1940-1968. New York: Women's Division, General Board of Global Ministries of The United Methodist Church.

Tomkinson, Mrs. T.L. *Twenty Years History of the Woman's Home Missionary Society of the Methodist Episcopal Church, 1880-1900*. Cincinnati: W.H.M.S., 1903.

Wheeler, Mary Sparks. *First Decade of the Woman's Foreign Missionary Society of the Methodist Episcopal Church, with Sketches of Its Missionaries (1869-1879)*. New York: Phillips and Hunt, 1881.

Wilson, Lois Miriam. *Stories Seldom Told*. Canada: Northstone Publishing, Inc., 1997.

Woolever, Elsie A. *Declaring His Glory (1940-1955)*. Cincinnati: W.D.C.S., Board of Missions, The Methodist Church, 1955.

THE AUTHORS

Elaine Magalis was born in Colorado and raised there and in California. She is a graduate of San Francisco State College with a Bachelor of Arts degree in Philosophy. Elaine continued her education at the University of Pennsylvania, where she has completed all the requirements for a doctorate in philosophy of religion except for the dissertation. She has held a wide variety of jobs, including waitressing, teaching and two years with the Audiovisual Department of the United Methodist Board of Missions. Currently she lives in Vermont.

Cheryl A. Hemmerle is a native of Pennsylvania. She earned the Bachelor of Arts degree in Religion and Psychology from LaGrange College in LaGrange, GA and the Master of Divinity degree from Candler School of Theology at Emory University in Atlanta, GA. Cheryl is a former executive staff member of the Women's Division where she assumed responsibility for the Division's work with teens, college/university and young women for six and a half years. She has worked as a director of Christian education and youth ministry in United Methodist churches in Georgia, South Carolina and New York. Cheryl is currently writing full-time and developing the fine art of pottery and bookmaking. She enjoys reading, music, cooking, gardening, tennis and hiking.

Please mail order with check payable to:

SERVICE CENTER
7820 READING RD CALLER NO 1800
CINCINNATI OH 45222-1800

Costs for shipping and handling:

sale items:
$25 or less, add $4.65
$25.01-$60, add $5.75
$60.01-$100, add $7.00
Over $100, add 6.5%

free items:
50 copies or less, add $3.50
51-400, add $4.50
Over 400, add $1.50 per 100

For billed and credit card orders:
CALL TOLL FREE: 1-800-305-9857
FAX ORDERS: 1-513-761-3722
E-MAIL: SCorders@gbgm-umc.org
If billing is requested, a $1.50 billing fee will be added.

$8.95   chlorine free   Stock #3209